was that really me?

was THAT really Me?

HOW EVERYDAY STRESS BRINGS OUT
OUR HIDDEN PERSONALITY

naomi L. Quenk

Davies-Black Publishing

mountain view, California

Published by Davies-Black Publishing, a division of CPP, Inc., 1055 Joaquin Road, 2nd Floor, Mountain View, CA 94043; 800-624-1765.

Special discounts on bulk quantities of Davies-Black books are available to corporations, professional associations, and other organizations. For details, contact the Director of Marketing and Sales at Davies-Black Publishing: 650-691-9123; fax 650-623-9271.

The following publishers have generously given permission to use extended quotations from copyrighted works: From *The Inferior Function,* by Marie-Louise Von Franz. © by Marie-Louise Von Franz. Reprinted by arrangement with Shambhala Publications, Inc., 300 Massachusetts Ave., Boston, MA 02115. From Jung, C. G., *Collected Works,* Volumes 6, 8, 9i, 11, 16, 18, and the *Vision Seminars.* Copyright 1976, 1960, 1959, 1969, 1954, 1976, 1976 by Princeton University Press. Reprinted by permission of Princeton University Press.

Visit the Davies-Black Publishing Web site at www.daviesblack.com.

Cover photograph: © Tomek Kikora/Getty Images/The Image Bank

Printed in the United States of America.
11 10 09 08 07   10 9 8 7 6 5

Library of Congress Cataloging-in-Publication Data
Quenk, Naomi L.
  Was that really me? : how everyday stress brings out our hidden personality / Naomi L. Quenk.— 1st ed.
    p. cm.
  Includes bibliographical references and index.
  ISBN 978-0-89106-170-0 (pbk.)
  1. Typology (Psychology). 2. Stress (Psychology). 3. Myers-Briggs Type Indicator.
  4. Jung, C. G. (Carl Gustav), 1875–1961. I. Title.

  BF698.3.Q47 2002
  155.2´64—dc21

                                                                          2002023413

FIRST EDITION
First printing 2002

TO ALEX

Contents

Foreword

I HAVE A VIVID RECOLLECTION OF NAOMI QUENK at the podium before a gathering of *Myers-Briggs Type Indicator®* (MBTI®) practitioners at a conference in Philadelphia in October 1982. She was presenting for the first time her understanding of our "hidden personality," which causes those unsettling moments when we are "not ourselves." Naomi described the different patterns of uncharacteristic behavior that express each of the eight inferior functions—the eight Jungian mental processes when they are used in a primitive and undeveloped manner. Members of the audience were intrigued as they recognized themselves in her type-related examples of these bewildering episodes. There was rueful laughter as we remembered behavior we had pushed aside in denial, shame, or guilt, or that we had readily blamed on others. It was heartening to be told that these experiences were part of being human; that if we recognized and faced them, they could serve as invaluable learning experiences for our personal growth. Naomi gave us specific steps through which we could integrate these moments and arrive at a more complete experience of our own positive selves.

Little did we realize at the time that this presentation was the beginning of a major and invaluable extension of the understanding and application of psychological type. Over the years, Naomi has led this exploration by gathering examples of inferior function experiences from workshops, psychotherapy clients, fellow practitioners, questionnaire data, and personal observations in everyday life. She used this information as the basis for *Beside Ourselves: Our Hidden Personality in Everyday Life,* published in 1993, which was followed in 1996 by a shorter work, *In the Grip: Our Hidden Personality* (revised in 2000 as *In the Grip: Understanding Type, Stress, and the Inferior Function*). And now, in 2002, we have this revision of the original book, which encompasses a wealth of new information and fresh insights into the depth and breadth of this aspect of Jungian psychology. As a result of these works, it is now customary for knowledgeable practitioners to include an introduction to the "hidden personality" in their workshops and consulting practices. Being "in the grip," or "beside oneself," has become common terminology among the many individuals who know their preference type.

Isabel Myers created the MBTI personality inventory to give individuals the benefits of knowing their Jungian preference type. Her focus was on each individual's potential for positive growth through type development. Over the years, knowledgeable type practitioners have introduced millions of people in diverse cultures to the MBTI instrument. Naomi Quenk has provided the next giant step in applying Jung's model of development in healthy personalities. That step is to understand, accept, and learn to handle our hidden personality responsibly. Naomi has given us a way to understand this part of ourselves as well as a practical guide for turning what appears to be negative into a positive awareness that enhances our growth and effectiveness. People typically find this to be a surprisingly freeing experience.

Isabel and Naomi shared a passionate belief that personality type and Jung's model of lifelong development provide a psychology that really works. Both focused their application of Jungian ideas on development in the healthy personality and worked hard to make these ideas meaningful and helpful in people's lives. In the period of reflection preceding my writing of this foreword, I became even more aware that it is Katharine Briggs, Isabel Myers, and Naomi Quenk who have been the major forces in bringing Jung's ideas out into the wide, wide world—what I have called the democratization of Jungian ideas. Katharine studied Jung's work and saw its potential; Isabel took the core piece (what I think of as the doorway to the entire theory) and developed the MBTI instrument, which gave individuals the entry key to the entire theory. Naomi has completed the circle by pointing out the necessity of integrating the light and the dark that are intrinsic in Jung's theory. Valuable as the initial understanding of typology has been, it is this last addition that is essential if we are ever to break the cycle of violence that threatens to overwhelm our world today.

Katharine Downing Myers
Kennett Square, Pennsylvania
July 2002

Preface

IN THE NEARLY TEN YEARS SINCE *Beside Ourselves,* the first edition of this book, was published, I have learned a great deal more about how and when our hidden personality emerges in daily life. I now have a much greater appreciation of out-of-character episodes as essential to our general well-being as well as to our continuing growth and development. I continue to be awed by the overwhelming evidence that we are born with everything we need to become effective and complete human beings.

In this new edition, the notion of stress is central. Stress is broadly defined as any external or internal event that lessens or depletes the energy we typically have available to conduct our daily lives. I use this expanded definition of stress to explain and illustrate the ways in which stress is a necessary and sufficient stimulus for bringing out our hidden personality. My goal is to help readers arrive at an enlightening and helpful answer to the question "Was that really me?"

I have often been asked just how and why I became interested in individual differences in healthy personalities. As with many of my colleagues, my earliest interest in psychology was in psychopathology. However, psychological problems—difficult childhood experiences, trauma, deprivation, and so on—seemed pretty easy to explain. Accounting for psychological *health* seemed a much more challenging enterprise. It was therefore fortunate that I was introduced to psychological type in 1960 on my first day of graduate school in the psychology department at the University of California at Berkeley. I took the *Myers-Briggs Type Indicator* (MBTI) personality inventory along with a number of other personality tests. At the time, the MBTI inventory was a little-known personality instrument used only by a few researchers. Later, when I received my test results, I was surprised that the description of my type, INFP, was so positive. Despite my interest in health rather than pathology, I had expected results that pointed out the negative and pathological.

Over the next several years I learned more about the MBTI inventory through the creativity studies at Berkeley's Institute for Personality Assessment and Research (IPAR). I used the instrument in my dissertation research, although it was not my central focus. I was impressed with its potential as a vehicle for exploring normal, healthy human behavior, which continues to be my focus as a researcher, psychotherapist, teacher, and participant in all other aspects of life.

A major influence that eventually led me to write *Beside Ourselves* was my reading of C. G. Jung's book *Psychological Types*. Over the course of several years I read most of Jung's writings, and my depth and breadth of understanding vastly increased as I came to understand the overall Jungian context within which typology exists. I have included a discussion of the inferior function, or hidden personality, in most of the introductory MBTI workshops I have taught and have developed workshops that focus specifically on this puzzling, yet readily understood, aspect of our everyday personality.

Since the publication of *Beside Ourselves* in 1993, a great many people have become familiar with their own and others' inferior function experiences through reading either the book itself or a booklet-length version called *In the Grip* (1996, 2000). Hundreds of people have attended workshops and shared their experiences and insights, which has formed the basis for this revision.

This revised edition has a simpler explanation of type dynamics, type differentiation, and type development than the previous edition and includes a discussion of what each type finds particularly energizing in the workplace. It focuses in part on expressions of the inferior function that persist over time. Using our broadened definition of stress, this may be the result of daily stresses, fatigue, illness, or other disruptions to our available energy. Work stress is used as an example of the kind of long-term, persistent stress that may keep a person chronically in the grip, and a new section describes what each type finds particularly stressful at work. In addition, the large amount of new information from individuals and groups permitted expanded discussion of the influence of the tertiary and auxiliary functions on different aspects of the inferior function experience. Gender differences are included where sufficient information was available.

New "stories" about people in the grip of their inferior function have replaced some of those from the first edition. Each of the eight inferior function chapters contains at least one story that describes the effects of persistent stress and the chronic grip expressions that occurred. The new stories, as well as the new quotations from different types that are sprinkled throughout the book, were obtained from the responses of hundreds of workshop participants, psychotherapy clients, and others who answered questionnaires or volunteered to contribute stories for the book. I was fortunate to have questionnaires provided by a sample of several hundred men and women in their early twenties whose training program included learning about psychological type and verifying their MBTI type. In addition, research data dealing with stress, coping with stress, and health and illness behavior were available from studies conducted for the revised *MBTI Manual* that was published in 1998. Readers who would like detailed information that covers both research results and anecdotal data on the inferior function will find it in summary form in the second edition of *In the Grip*.

The information in both the first and second editions of this book is rooted in Jung's many insights, especially his notion that people are naturally oriented toward becoming their individual selves as completely as possible. Such an effort on the part of individuals requires understanding and accepting the seemingly "negative" parts of ourselves as necessary, healthy, and productive. I hope that reading this book will encourage people to appreciate their innate and omnipresent capacity for self-knowledge and growth as individuals, in relationships, and as members of society.

Acknowledgments

PEOPLE OF ALL SIXTEEN TYPES HAVE CONTRIBUTED to both the first and second editions of this book by sharing their experiences, by distributing and/or responding to the questionnaires that provided much of the information about each type's experiences, or by reviewing the chapters about their respective types. I am most grateful to these individuals for confirming and enhancing my understanding of the eight inferior functions and the subtleties of the auxiliary and tertiary functions. Among them are Scott Anchors, MaryAnn Andrews, Joan Grobb Augustino, Mary Buller, Sally Carr, Lelys Ceballos, Gene Dickman, John DiTiberio, Karen Dorris, Carolyn Earnest, Catherine Fitzgerald, Diane Ganze, Sandra Hirsh, Judith Inge, Ruth Johnson, Barbara Johnston, Betsy Kendall, Jean Kummerow, Kay Kummerow, Al Lopez, Pam Lorenz, Rhonda McIntire, Tim McIntire, Rochelle Michaud, Jan Mitchell, Wayne Mitchell, Jim Newman, Connie Otis, Gerald Otis, Chuck Pratt, Kaleb Quenk, Karin Quenk, Roberta Rice, Eric Rounds, Betsy Schmidt-Nowara, Audrey Schuurmann, Julie Sparks, Kim Spencer, Jeanne Street, SueLynn, Derek Updegraff, and Sandra Van Sant.

Nancy Barger, Sue Clancy, Linda Kirby, Wayne Mitchell, and Alex Quenk read drafts of the manuscript of the first edition. Their excellent suggestions greatly enhanced the work and provided the standard for the second edition.

Rachel Quenk's preliminary editing of the first edition before it was submitted for publication provided excellent editorial and content suggestions. Karin Quenk contributed original artwork. Kathy Simon's superb developmental editing stimulated my thinking and allowed me to effectively explain some of the more subtle aspects of the topic. Lee Langhammer Law, Divisional Director of Davies-Black, made excellent editorial suggestions and encouraged me throughout the revision process. Laura Simonds added insight into the mysteries of publicizing the book, Jill Anderson-Wilson skillfully oversaw the final editing of the copy. Karen Stough thoughtfully and thoroughly proofread the pages. And Michael Ferreira masterfully created a readily navigable index.

Finally, I am indebted to the hundreds of unnamed people—colleagues, clients, workshops participants, respondents to questionnaires, and friends—who over the years have freely shared their knowledge of themselves. Their statements, which are quoted throughout the book, as well as the lengthier stories people contributed show that being beside oneself is a truly healthy and enhancing part of being human.

About the Author

NAOMI L. QUENK, PH.D., is a licensed clinical psychologist in independent practice. She received her master's degree from Brooklyn College and her doctoral degree from the University of California at Berkeley, both in psychology. For the past twenty years her psychotherapeutic focus has been on individual and couples therapy. Her enduring interest is in individual differences in normal personality functioning.

Quenk has written numerous research and theoretical articles exploring individual differences in personality, as well as several technical works relating to personality assessment. She is author of *Beside Ourselves: Our Hidden Personality in Everyday Life*; *In the Grip: Understanding Type, Stress, and the Inferior Function*; and *Essentials of the Myers-Briggs Type Indicator Assessment*. She is coauthor of *Dream Thinking: The Logic, Magic, and Meaning of Your Dreams*; *True Loves: Finding the Soul in Love Relationships*; *MBTI Manual: A Guide to the Development and Use of the Myers-Briggs Type Indicator*; and *MBTI Step II Manual: Exploring the Next Level of Type with the Myers-Briggs Type Indicator Form Q*. She has conducted workshops on the MBTI instrument for many years.

Jungian Psychology
and Hidden Personality

"I don't know what's gotten into him. He's always been so sensible, and here he is imagining the most bizarre possibilities!"

"It was weird, my obsession with a brain tumor. All I had was an ordinary headache. I tried to talk myself out of it, but it was overpowering."

"To our amazement, she suddenly stood up, burst into tears, and stormed out of the meeting!"

"I never knew he had it in him! He was quite the life of the party, dancing with every woman, telling ribald stories . . . not at all the straitlaced, conservative guy I'd known him to be."

"Here I was, an acknowledged expert in my field, and all I could think about was how stupid I sounded, how people must be bored and irritated with my lecture, and how foolish I was to put myself in such a humiliating position."

"I hardly ever speak out in public, but, with more than two hundred people in the room, I stood up and called the mayor a lying scoundrel! Was that really me?"

WE ALL HAVE TIMES when we are "out of character," feel outside and beside ourselves, and behave in unexpected ways. And we've all observed such aberrations in others. Sometimes we are intrigued or even amused by this atypical behavior; more often, however, we are puzzled, distressed, put off, or embarrassed by it. As a rule, we rely on our past experiences to guide our expectations of others. We expect people to be consistent and predictable from one day to the next. If this were not the case, our relationships with the people we know would be just as unpredictable as our encounters with strangers.

Yet, despite this general consistency in behavior, people sometimes act in unexpected, seemingly capricious ways. To explain such deviations from "normal," we usually assume that there is something "wrong" with them. When the out-of-character behavior is extremely odd and unusual, we may attribute it to irrationality, instability, or downright craziness.

We Are All Personality Theorists

Each of us operates from some system for understanding people, whether we use a formal theory or just an implicit set of general guidelines. Most of us use our daily observations of other people and our reactions to what we observe as a basis for generalizing, explaining, and predicting our own and others' behavior.

Whether formal or informal, personality theories attempt to organize observations of people by providing a framework for classifying and describing behavior. Formal personality theories, such as those put forth by psychologists, tend to use concepts and language that are not easily understood by most people. As a result, most of us devise our own system for making sense of people's attitudes, motives, and behaviors.

Occasionally, the concepts in a formal personality theory are also meaningful and useful to people who are not specifically trained to understand psychological complexities. When that happens, we benefit from both the conceptual power of a carefully developed system and the utility of a straightforward and practical way of understanding our own personality and the personalities of others. Jung's theory of psychological type is an example of such a theory.

A Formal Theory That Confirms Common Sense

Psychological type theory lends itself to an everyday understanding of personality consistency because it was formulated to describe and explain normal behavioral variations among healthy people. Although the style and language Jung used to describe his system can be confusing, other people, such as Katharine Briggs and Isabel Briggs Myers, have provided easily understandable clarifications and interpretations of Jung's work. Briggs' and, most notably, Myers' development and expansion of Jung's theory is formalized in the *Myers-Briggs Type Indicator®* (MBTI®) personal-

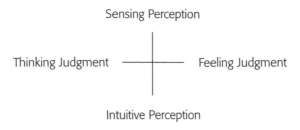

Figure 1 • Opposite Jungian Functions

ity inventory. Because our present understanding of type theory inter-weaves the work of Jung, Myers, and Briggs, we refer to it in this work as the Jung-Myers theory.

The Jung-Myers system focuses on how people go about gathering information about the world (perception), how they reach conclusions about what they have perceived (judgment), and what their sources of energy are (attitude or orientation). On the basis of many years of keen observation, Jung hypothesized two opposite ways of perceiving, *sensation* (or sensing) versus *intuition,* and two opposite ways of judging, *thinking* versus *feeling.* Figure 1 shows these opposite functions.

In addition to these opposite mental functions, Jung described two opposite attitudes or orientations of energy, *extraversion* versus *introversion.* A person habitually uses each of the four functions in one of these two attitudes. Thus, one person might habitually use sensing perception in the outer world of people and things and thus focus on staying open to the broadest range of sensory information that occurs in the outer environ-ment, while another person might habitually use sensing in the inner world of ideas and inner experiences, focusing on accumulating and cate-gorizing a broad range of facts, details, and internal sensory information. Myers added a fourth pair of opposites to those Jung proposed, a *judging* versus *perceiving* orientation toward the outer world. Combining the four individual preferences yields distinct **types**[1] of personality. The complex variations that result from combinations of these functions and attitudes are described in depth in Chapter 3.

Jung and Myers assumed that people are born with a preference for one of each pair of opposites—that is, they are more likely to use Sensing (S) or Intuition (N), Thinking (T) or Feeling (F), Extraversion (E) or Introversion (I), and a Judging (J) or Perceiving (P) attitude. These innate

ISTJ	ISFJ	INFJ	INTJ
ISTP	ISFP	INFP	INTP
ESTP	ESFP	ENFP	ENTP
ESTJ	ESFJ	ENFJ	ENTJ

Figure 2 • The Sixteen Types Identified by the MBTI Instrument

tendencies develop and reach their fullest potential over the course of a person's lifetime.

Understanding that people have opposite preferences, as defined by type theory, takes many of our characteristics out of the realm of the puzzling and peculiar by describing them as orderly, rational, and predictable. We can readily recognize the sixteen personality types that emerge when we combine the four preferences (see Figure 2) because they appear in our daily lives.[2] People appreciate and use information that helps them understand personality characteristics and that explains and predicts people's similarities and differences. The growing popularity of the typological approach attests to its usefulness in elucidating the consistencies found among individuals of the same type. In fact, in a study that asked people to evaluate a number of personality instruments (Druckman & Bjork, 1991), the majority identified the MBTI personality inventory as providing the most insights and as having the greatest impact on their behavior and decisions. The MBTI instrument, which is the best-researched and most reliable and valid way of accessing personality type available today, is the most widely used instrument for identifying healthy personality characteristics. It is used in a variety of settings in addition to the counseling and psychotherapy arena that was Jung's initial focus. These include such areas of application as education, career advisement, management, leadership, team building, and coaching.

Though it may not be readily apparent to people familiar with psychological type theory and the MBTI personality inventory, Jung's approach addresses not only the consistency and predictability of our personalities but also our inconsistencies. The theory includes a rationale for our modes of being when we are out of character, not acting normally, or otherwise "beside ourselves." For Jung, even our inconsistencies are consistent, predictable, logical, and valuable.[3]

Our out-of-character predictability is a critical aspect of the dynamic nature of psychological type theory. As a hidden part of personality, it is embodied in Jung's concept of the unconscious inferior function, especially in the often dramatic experience of "being in the grip of one's inferior function." When, how, and why this phenomenon occurs is the subject of this book.

Some Basic Concepts

During the early part of his career, Jung was a disciple of Sigmund Freud, whose insights into the nature of the human psyche, particularly the unconscious, have dramatically altered the way we think about ourselves. Later, Jung's thinking diverged significantly from Freudian psychology in ways that are directly relevant to the concept of the inferior function.

Jung viewed human personality from a broad perspective, so his system for understanding individual differences and similarities is quite detailed and complex. You won't need a comprehensive knowledge of Jung's theory to understand the subject of this book, but some background that places typology and the inferior function in the context of Jung's total system will be helpful.

The Psyche Can Balance Itself

Jung saw the human psyche as containing everything necessary to grow, adapt, and heal itself. He believed that people were capable of directing their own personality development and of recognizing and benefiting from both positive and negative life experiences. Clearly, not everyone successfully heals his or her psychological wounds or develops his or her personality maximally. But Jung focused primarily on the potential for growth and development of both individuals and humanity as a whole.

The Effects of a One-Sided Approach to Life

Jung's clinical work with people demonstrated to him that extreme one-sidedness was maladaptive. When a person devotes excessive energy to one thing, she ignores, rejects, or devalues its opposite. Jung and Myers were very clear that *all* the attitudes and functions embodied in type theory—not just the four a person prefers—are necessary for adaptation. If one of the preferred attitudes or functions is overemphasized, the opposite attitude or function will be neglected. When this happens, a person may risk having inappropriate perceptions or making poor judgments, or ignoring either the outer or inner world, since only one aspect of a situation is allowed into awareness. A person who uses only Intuition may imagine the beautiful rooms he is going to add to his house while ignoring the leaking roof that is damaging his computer! Similarly, a person who ignores her Feeling judgment in making a career decision may choose a career that is quite logical, but that she greatly dislikes.

As a general rule, when we overemphasize one function or attitude to the exclusion of its opposite, our use of it tends to become rigid, automatic, and stereotypical. Its exaggerated form appears as a caricature of a normal, effective mental process or attitude. Table 1 shows some of the typical adaptive qualities of type attitudes and functions and provides a comparison of how they appear in an exaggerated, one-sided form.[4]

The Principle of Compensation

Psychological opposites are a central feature of Jung's overall comprehensive personality theory, just as they are for his type theory. This opposition provides a way for our psyches to correct our natural tendency toward one-sidedness. Jung called the mechanism for correcting one-sidedness **compensation.**

In proposing compensation as a way to regulate and balance our functioning, Jung borrowed Newton's third law of motion: Every action force has a reaction force equal in magnitude and opposite in direction. Jung (1976a) concluded that

> whenever life proceeds one-sidedly in any given direction, the self-regulation of the organism produces in the unconscious an accumulation of all those factors which play too small a part in the individual's conscious existence. For this reason I have put forward the compensation theory of the unconscious as a complement to the repression theory. (p. 419)

Jung did not see compensation as necessarily disruptive. Rather, he viewed such seeming aberrations as having a complementary and not an oppositional role. Thus, while out-of-character inferior function experiences may be jarring, they play a critical role in encouraging and restoring the psyche's equilibrium by tempering a one-sided devotion to one or another

Table 1 Adaptive Versus One-Sided Type Preferences

Preference	Adaptive Form	One-Sided Form
Exraverted Attitude	Charming Enthusiastic Sociable	Boastful Intrusive Loud
Introverted Attitude	Deep Discreet Tranquil	Aloof Inhibited Withdrawn
Sensing Perception	Pragmatic Precise Detailed	Dull Fuzzy Obsessive
Intuitive Perception	Imaginative Ingenious Insightful	Eccentric Erratic Unrealistic
Thinking Judgment	Lucid Objective Succinct	Argumentative Intolerant Coarse
Feeling Judgment	Appreciative Considerate Tactful	Evasive Hypersensitive Vague
Judging Attitude	Efficient Planful Responsible	Compulsive Impatient Rigid
Perceiving Attitude	Adaptable Easygoing Flexible	Procrastinating Unreliable Scattered

typological function or attitude. Many examples of the compensatory nature of the psyche are included in Chapters 6 through 13.

The 40-year-old daughter of an army general held her father in high esteem. She admired his competence, self-confidence, and calmness in the face of crises. She could consistently rely on him for support during difficult times. She was therefore surprised and disturbed when, while visiting him, she dreamed that she saw him walking down a dingy street in a poor part of town. His usually immaculate uniform was torn and disheveled, his hair unkempt, his skin pasty, and his posture slouching.

This dream scene revealed her father as so out of character, so deviant from her conscious perception of him, that the woman was forced to explore its meaning. In doing so, she came to see that her 73-year-old father was getting old, frail, and tired, and that by exaggerating his strengths, she was denying his more vulnerable side and his ultimate mortality. She was thus forced to develop a more realistic perception of him, which led to a healthier, more adult relationship.

The Concept of Projection

Unconscious contents are charged with energy that must be discharged in order for a person to function comfortably and with minimal tension and distress. One of the most powerful and universal ways human beings deal with unacknowledged, unconscious thoughts and feelings is through **projection.** Because the inferior function is appropriately understood as an unconscious process that is subject to the mechanism of projection, an understanding of this concept is essential.

Simply stated, projection involves attributing to others an unacknowledged, unconscious part of ourselves—something that lies outside our conscious awareness. What we project onto others can be negative, repugnant, and undesirable—or positive, admirable, and wholesome. In either case, the projector unconsciously identifies someone who possesses at least *some* of the unacknowledged quality in question and then exaggerates the degree to which that quality is actually present. The "added amount" of the quality comes from the projector's unconscious. The recipient of this projection is then seen as more hostile, lazy, talented, or admirable, for instance, than is actually the case.

For the most part, projection is a normal psychological process that enables people to relate to each other by recognizing areas of similarity and mutually shared interests and values. We feel secure and comfortable when we see aspects of ourselves in others; similarly, we may be suspicious, fearful, and distrustful when we meet people who are very different from us. "Finding" ourselves in others thus serves as a connecting link to our shared humanity and prevents the isolation and loneliness we would experience if we were completely unique and disconnected from other people. If we withdrew all our projections, we would become so completely detached and unaffected by the world that we could no longer function as members of human society.

In Jung's psychology, projection often accounts for our initial attraction to or rejection of others. A person may be a ready "host" for one or more aspects of our own unconscious. And, like compensation, projection is one of the ways the psyche regulates itself. Equilibrium is maintained when people eliminate their contradictory ideas or feelings. Thus, a person who presents herself as exceedingly honest, strangely ignoring some of her more shady activities, may frequently and loudly complain about political corruption. Unable or unwilling to recognize her own immorality, she projects it on an easy target. Politicians provide a ready hook on which she can hang her own unacknowledged morally questionable behavior.

The Growth Instinct

Jung suggested that we all have an instinct that pushes us to grow toward completion, to become the best possible version of ourselves. He referred to this goal as **individuation,** a state of self-awareness or self-actualization we strive toward but rarely, if ever, achieve. Therefore, he saw the lifelong process of individuation as more important than a hypothetical, generally unattainable end point. Jung's psychology is therefore **prospective,** purposive, or goal oriented—the goal being individuation.[5]

Jung looked at all behavior, including neurotic symptoms, as ways of stimulating an individual's growth toward completion. He was interested in personality development as it occurred over the life span and saw it as an ongoing process that continued during adulthood and midlife and on into advanced age.

The way we move toward completion, or individuation, is by expanding our knowledge and awareness of ourselves, which increases our ability to control and direct our lives. We are continually discovering our actualities and potentialities through living, working, relating to others, and contemplating our lives. But for psychologists like Jung and Freud, the major repository of valuable new growth-enhancing information was the unconscious realm of our personalities.

The Character of the Unconscious

Jung and Freud agreed that the unconscious contains repressed memories, experiences, and ideas. But in Jung's view, the unconscious also includes neutral contents, such as latent or dormant potentials that are yet to be realized.

Jung also described a second, deeper, nonpersonal layer of the unconscious, which he called the **collective unconscious.** This part of the psyche makes us larger than our individual selves. It contains images related to common **archetypes**—human experiences and patterns such as birth, death, marriage, mother, father, hero, child, wise woman, and so on. These themes link us to other people and to our ancestors, providing the vital connection to our past, present, and future as individuals and as a species. Jung believed that the incorporation of such images into our awareness was vital to our completion through the individuation process.

The Inferior Function and Individuation

How does one gain access to the unconscious information required for human development? For Freud (1933), "the interpretation of dreams is the royal road to a knowledge of the unconscious activities of the mind" (p. 608). For Jung, the route to the unconscious is through the inferior function. In Jung's system, the inferior function is the undeveloped component of an individual's basic character or type. As we will see, of the four functions of type, three are capable of varying degrees of consciousness, while the fourth, the inferior function, remains largely unconscious. The inferior function therefore provides the first and most direct entry into information in the personal layer of the unconscious. This entry is the important first step toward acquiring the personal and archetypal information that encourages individuation. Figure 3 shows a map of the psyche, including selected features specified by Jung and the location of the inferior function within that structure.

Both Jung and Freud saw dreams as important sources of unconscious information, and both devoted much attention to the skillful interpretation of their patients' dreams. Although even uninterpreted dreams may aid psychological awareness, incorporating a dream's meaning into one's waking life is a much more potent way of expanding one's **consciousness.** Interpretation enables the new knowledge dreams provide to be consciously integrated and used.

In much the same way, inferior function experiences may aid our personality development, even when we don't understand and interpret them. Their very strangeness can force us to have a new awareness. Our other "off" experiences are likely to be passing idiosyncrasies, temporary fads, and momentary passions that do not startle us with their excessive-

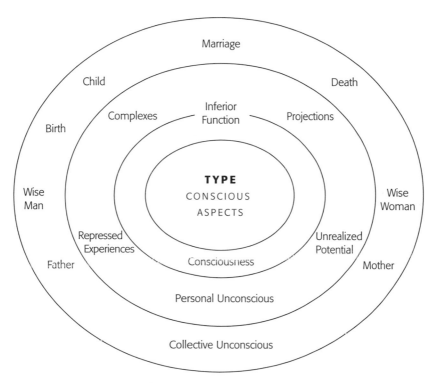

Figure 3 • Map of the Psyche

ness or jar us into a new perspective. Inferior function episodes, in contrast, often alarm us with their "Jekyll and Hyde" nature, forcing us to examine the essence of our character and personality. These experiences can therefore be understood as our psyche's attempt to move us in the direction of completion and individuation. In fact, when people describe being "beside themselves," "not themselves," or "taken over by something," they often spontaneously mention the valuable insights, new information, or change of perspective that resulted from the experience. Such reported beneficial effects of inferior function experiences demonstrate the natural ability of the psyche to restore its own equilibrium.

Access to Information from the Inferior Function

The inferior function phenomenon is a normal, adaptive way of promoting personality development. It can be observed in everyday life and occurs in mild and mundane, extreme and debilitating, and brief and lengthy manifestations. Because it is a natural part of personality, we can all benefit from the insights that can be gained from encounters with our inferior function. No special expertise is required. What is essential to understanding, however, is recognizing the characteristics of one's own and others' inferior functions and their adaptive place in our lives.

Just as most people readily recognize their own and others' personality types when they are first introduced to type theory, most people instantly recognize their own and others' expressions of the inferior function. In fact, the majority of examples and stories that appear in Part 2 were contributed by people who were entirely ignorant about the inferior function and its characteristics at the time the episodes occurred. Their recognition came "after the fact," sometimes many years later when they heard a lecture or attended a workshop addressing type and the inferior function.

But intellectual knowledge about one's inferior function by no means guarantees awareness of what is happening while one is "in the grip." *When we are under the influence of something that is unconscious, we are, for the most part, unconscious of it.* We may have a dim suspicion that the inferior function is involved in the episode, but we may also have insufficient conscious energy and perspective to be altogether sure. This is as true for me as it is for the other "aware" people whose stories are in this book. All we may know is that something is wrong, that we are feeling and appearing out of character and unbalanced while wondering whether this experience of ourselves is the "real" us, and our former selves the aberration.

Early writing on the inferior function tended to emphasize its pathological appearance. Prior to the publication of the first edition of this book (*Beside Ourselves,* N. L. Quenk, 1993a) Jung's work and that of Von Franz (1971) were the most complete resources on the subject available. Von Franz gives an insightful and informative exposition, although there is less focus on integration of the inferior function as an expected consequence of normal development than is true of my own approach. Angelo Spoto (1989) focuses on the negative and destructive potential of the inferior function for individuals and society. With the increased awareness of the inferior function that occurred after the publication of *Beside Ourselves* and the booklet *In the Grip* (1996; 2nd edition, 2000), a number of people who write about psychological type have incorporated the concept of the inferior function into their work.[6]

If we come equipped with a psyche designed to maintain its balance and move toward completion, intervention is only a helpful (if sometimes necessary) method of achieving what we are by nature "designed" to achieve. Our psyche operates regardless of whether we "know the rules." Dreams can compensate for a one-sided attitude, even if they are not fully interpreted and understood. Inferior function experiences can also compensate for one-sidedness or give us a much-needed alternative perspective and thus add richness to our lives.

But just as we can learn a great deal more from a well-interpreted dream, so can an understanding of the character of our inferior function increase its power to expand our self-knowledge. And just as there are "big" dreams that feel—and are—more significant than everyday dreams, so there are more important inferior function episodes and less notable ones. We tend to remember striking dreams in great detail and for long periods of time. The same is true for powerful inferior function experiences.

The Positive Focus of Myers and Briggs

Jung's writings on typology describe the effects of extreme and one-sided use of preferences, and the examples he gives often point out the more negative aspects of a particular attitude-function combination. It was indeed a tour de force for Isabel Briggs Myers to extract and fully describe mature and adaptive functioning for each type. Her careful consideration and further development of the concept of type dynamics was critical to this achievement.

Jung may have overemphasized the negative and maladaptive aspects of the inferior function. And, in adopting his pathology-centered approach, many Jungians miss the importance of the phenomenon for normal, everyday **adaptation.** Myers' primary focus on healthy adaptation perhaps led her to appropriately understate the more negative expressions of the unconscious inferior function. In doing so, she missed out on a very rich and fruitful aspect of normal functioning.

My goal is to bridge these two approaches by exploring the range of territories in which the inferior function appears. In this way, we can best understand this phenomenon as a natural response of healthy people making their way through the stresses and strains of their complex inner and outer worlds. I therefore present the inferior function

- As it is demonstrated in our everyday behavior—in characteristic sensitivities and typical projections onto others
- As it is revealed in what stresses us in our daily lives, especially in our work lives
- As it is revealed in our interests, hobbies, and ways of relaxing
- In the typical ways it is triggered or provoked
- In the forms it takes when it erupts, both as a brief episode and as a chronic state
- In the experiences people report while they are "in the grip" of their inferior function.
- In how the psyche returns to equilibrium using approaches that are most effective for each type
- As it appears during midlife and beyond
- In the kind of knowledge and awareness that are typically gained from inferior function experiences

The Organization of This Book

This book describes the character and form of the eight inferior functions. Each function is described in sufficient detail for readers to identify experiences of their own inferior function. There are ample examples of inferior function experiences, how they came about, and the benefits derived from them.

My goal in presenting the inferior function as a normal, adaptive aspect of personality is to provide readers with a new and useful approach to some of their own and others' puzzling behavior. Such enhanced understanding should encourage people to explore new and exciting parts of themselves. Ultimately, this kind of expanded knowledge will increase the scope of our life choices and the freedom with which we pursue our goals. Inevitably, such increased freedom of choice will have a positive impact on our effectiveness within ourselves as well as in our relationships with others.

The remainder of the book is divided into two parts. Part 1, "The Hidden Personality in Context," provides the information needed for understanding the dynamic character of typology in general. It begins with Chapter 2, which describes the most important aspect of the Jung-Myers theory, *type dynamics:* the interactions among the functions of Sensing, Intuition, Thinking, and Feeling, along with their Extraverted or Introverted attitudes. Chapter 3 offers the method for determining the dynamics of any one of the sixteen types and shows how different dynamic relationships affect attitudes and behaviors. These two chapters provide the background for understanding the specific dynamics of the inferior function, which is the topic of Chapter 4. Chapter 5 outlines the structure for approaching the inferior function of the sixteen types described in Part 2, "The Hidden Personality in Action." It provides a detailed introduction to the contents of Chapters 6 through 13, each of which is devoted to one of the eight inferior functions—beginning with Extraverted Thinking types and ending with Extraverted Intuitive types. Chapter 14 discusses the effects of the inferior function on relationships, and, finally, Chapter 15 offers some concluding remarks and intriguing issues concerning the inferior function.

There are two Appendices to this book. Appendix A contains an early version (1987) of Myers' descriptions of the sixteen personality types, and Appendix B contains selected quotations from Jung's *Collected Works.* Included are statements about the inferior function and important comments about typology that are of general interest.

Finally, a glossary provides definitions for the terms used in this book.

A Caution to Readers

Most books about personality discuss what is wrong with people, how they became that way, and what they can do about it. People are depicted as having too much or too little of this or that important characteristic, as being afflicted by this or that dysfunctional environment, and as being defined by membership in one or another pathological group. We are told what should be different and why, who treated us badly or how we are treating others badly, and what kinds of corrective measures are required to change us or those close to us into well-adjusted, functioning people.

People are so accustomed to being told what is wrong with them and how to change it that readers of this book may expect it to be about getting rid of some bad, pathological part of their personalities. If that is your expectation, you will be greatly disappointed!

- This book will *not* tell you what is wrong with your (or someone else's) personality.

- It *will* help you understand and appreciate yourself the way you are and help you identify other adaptive aspects of your personality and how they operate.

- It will *not* show you how to make the hidden and unconscious parts of your personality entirely conscious and under your total control.

- It *will* explain the importance of some unconscious aspects of your personality type and why they neither can nor should be made conscious.

- It will *not* teach you ways to become equally proficient with or to have equal access to all the personality elements defined by psychological type theory.

- It *will* explain the critical difference between developing skills in using all aspects of your personality type and having all those parts equally developed.

This book is not about abnormality and pathology. It explores a part of our personalities that often looks and feels abnormal and pathological but is in fact natural, adaptive, and healthy. You are unlikely to discover that something you believe to be a "good" part of you is really insidiously destructive. Rather, you are likely to recognize that some of the characteristics you find puzzling or distressing are adaptive, helpful, and essential to both your present well-being and your growth and development throughout your life.

THE HIDDEN

PERSONALITY

IN CONTEXT

The Dynamics
of Jungian Typology

THE DYNAMIC CHARACTER of type theory is commonly overlooked by people new to typology and the MBTI personality inventory. This leads to an often simplistic, categorical approach to the sixteen types. Similarly, psychologists familiar with trait approaches to personality often assume that the type system describes four personality dimensions whose effects are merely additive. Typical of this point of view is the work of McCrea & Costa (1989). In ignoring the dynamic interactions critical to the Jung-Myers theory, both laypeople and professionals miss out on the theory's greatest contribution to the explanation and prediction of healthy personality.

Opposites in Jungian Psychology

We saw earlier that Jung conceived of the psyche as active, vital, and energetic—as a dynamic system. This system draws vitality from sets of opposite mental processes whose interaction provides the system's energy. Jung's typological theory focuses on three pairs of opposites: opposite functions of perception, Sensing and Intuition; opposite judging functions, Thinking and Feeling; and opposite attitudes or orientations in which perception and judgment are used, Extraversion and Introversion. Myers and Briggs found a fourth pair of opposites implicit in Jung's type theory, Judging and Perceiving attitudes toward the outer world.

The Character of Opposites

When we practice something over a long period, we tend to become aware of subtleties, nuances, and fine distinctions among the various aspects of that activity. For example, when first learning to play a musical instrument, we focus on the notes and their sequence. As time goes on, we add tempo, volume, tonal shadings. Later, we become aware of nuances of emotional expression that further refine our rendition of the music. And so on. This is known as **differentiation.** According to both Jung and Myers, adequate differentiation of the opposite functions and attitudes is necessary for effective functioning and good **type development.** The Jung–Myers theory describes two different kinds or levels of differentiation—differentiation *between* the opposites in a pair and differentiation *within* a function or attitude.

Differentiation Between Opposites in a Pair The first level of differentiation enables us to distinguish between two opposites, for example, Sensing and Intuition. If a person has these two opposite ways of perceiving "fused together," neither can be used in a conscious, directed manner as a way of gathering information. Instead, facts and possibilities seem to be one and the same, and past, present, and future are indistinguishable. For a person operating in this fashion, something that *might occur* may be equivalent to something that *is actually occurring* and an *imagined* conversation may be accepted as having *actually occurred.*

Once a person is able to distinguish between the opposite functions and attitudes, the next requirement for good type development is that one of each pair become more conscious, accessible, practiced, and reliable than the other. This occurs when a person habitually devotes a larger amount of psychic energy to one of each pair of opposites, using it more, enjoying it more, becoming more and more confident and comfortable with it. This process of habitually favoring one of a pair of opposites over the other results in a psychological **preference.** If a person does not develop a preference, that is, if equal energy is devoted to both poles of a function, neither operates with sufficient psychic energy to be automatically available in situations that require that function or attitude.

This was the case for a nurse who appeared to be equally pulled toward Sensing and Intuition. While in nursing school, this woman had prided herself on the level of accuracy she demonstrated with the many details required in her work, and she enjoyed tasks involving details. She had also received positive evaluations of her ability to establish rapport with patients and anticipate their needs and concerns. However, in her first job, in a hospital pediatric unit, these two areas seemed to conflict. She would be preparing a medication for one of her young patients, carefully and systematically following the prescribed dosages, when suddenly she would find herself thinking about an impending meeting with the parents of another patient, imagining what she would say to them and how they might respond. Returning to her task of preparing the medication, she would find that she had lost track. She would begin again, only to find herself imagining what would happen if she gave a patient the wrong dose of medication. Once again, she would begin her task, only to be side-tracked by yet another intrusive thought about an anticipated future task. As time went on, she found herself habitually unable to focus on either the present or the future or on the concrete or the abstract long enough to successfully perform her work. She was unable to gather adequate data (perception) on which to base decisions regarding what needed to be accomplished and when. The distress, anxiety, and confusion she experienced finally led her to give up her career.

Differentiation Within a Function or Attitude The same process occurs when we become increasingly differentiated within a preferred function or attitude. Ideally, if one prefers Feeling over Thinking as a way of drawing conclusions, one's use of Feeling will be complex, encompassing several different expressions of Feeling—for example, attending to one's own values and well-being as well as those of others, and simultaneously empathizing with people who have quite different values and needs. In contrast, undifferentiated Feeling (often characterizing someone whose Thinking is differentiated) has a more black-and-white, all-or-none character with no shades of gray, perhaps focusing on one's own values exclusively, empathizing with no regard for differences in people and situations.

A Hierarchy of Energy in the Dynamic System A clear distinction between the preferences in each pair of opposites and differentiation of one preference over its opposite are desirable qualities for each of the four pairs of opposites in the Jung-Myers system. In addition, a vital aspect of type dynamics is the notion of different levels of consciousness characterizing the functions, with one of the four functions—Sensing, Intuition, Thinking, or Feeling—largely conscious and one largely unconscious. The two remaining functions fall somewhere in between these two extremes.

For Myers (1980/1995), the dynamic nature of these mental processes provided a model for the development of individual differences over the life span, causing her to conclude the following:

> Good type development, therefore, demands two conditions: first, adequate but by no means equal development of a judging process and a perceptive process, one of which predominates, and, second, adequate but by no means equal facility in using both the extraverted and introverted attitudes, with one predominating.
>
> When both conditions are met, the person's type development is well balanced. In type theory, balance does not refer to equality of two processes or of two attitudes; instead, it means superior skill in one, supplemented by a helpful but not competitive skill in the other.
>
> The need for such supplementing is obvious. Perception without judgment is spineless; judgment with no perception is blind. Introversion lacking any extraversion is impractical; extraversion with no introversion is superficial.
>
> Less obvious is the principle that for every person one skill must be subordinate to the other and that significant skill in any direction will not be developed until a choice between opposites is made. (p. 182)

Some people object to this aspect of type theory because it proposes a hierarchy of differentiation or development, and thus possibly different levels of capability in using four very important mental processes. Some see it as placing limits on human potential, even as contradicting our democratic notion of equal opportunity. "Why can't I be equally good at everything?" is a question frequently asked. A common misunderstanding of type theory is that equal development of all four functions is an appropriate and desirable goal. People who favor such a view may hope that reading a book about the inferior function will show them how to develop it fully and therefore control it.

As we will see, even if equal development were possible, it would diminish our capacity for positive growth and our ability to relate effectively to our environment. The dynamic character of our personalities would be eliminated, and with it the critical role of the inferior function as a link to that vital source of growth and renewal, our unconscious. Jung's rationale for the hierarchy of differentiation that characterizes our mental processes is discussed below.

A Model for Type Dynamics

The dynamic character of psychological type theory is consistent with Jung's overall approach to psychic functioning. The following discussion highlights key features of Jung's approach that are useful for understanding the dynamics of his typological system.

Primitive Unconsciousness

Civilization's advancement has been marked by increasing specialization in the knowledge and skills required for human survival and progress. Primitive people responded largely instinctually to their environment, having relatively little ability to control and direct it. Yet, given these limitations, each person in a primitive civilization possessed much of what was necessary for basic survival.

The ability of primitive civilizations to control and change the world, however, was severely limited because the skills needed for survival pretty much required an equal share of attention. Because the available time and energy were evenly divided among so many arenas, the development of a special skill in any one area was unlikely. Without devoting a fair amount of energy to something, people do not become adept at it. Without being better at some things than others, one person is largely indistinguishable from another, is likely to act and react in automatic, instinctual ways, and, as a result, is likely to lack what we recognize as individuality.

This describes the state of unconsciousness Jung ascribed to primitive people, in that their psychological functions were still operating in their unconscious and were not differentiated. A primitive person might therefore have been unable to differentiate between an intuition and an actual event. What occurred inside a primitive person's head and outside his or her body would have been indistinguishable. A tribe member might have said, "A spirit came to me and told me the tribe must move to the other side of the valley in order to survive." The tribe members might very well have trusted the importance of the spirit's message and thus followed a leader's "instinct" for survival.

In contrast, people in modern civilizations are ill equipped to exist on their own in an increasingly complex world. As individuals, we have become highly specialized or differentiated in our knowledge and skills and therefore require a large and complex society to meet our survival needs. But our increasing differentiation as individuals has led to our ability to significantly affect our environment (with both good and bad results) and thus to shape our individual and collective lives. If a person in a modern civilization were to say, "My intuition is that the company should invest in electronics stocks," the company's board of directors would evaluate this insight from a number of perspectives, accepting the intuition as one piece of data worth considering. It would not typically act on the advice unquestioningly.

Modern Consciousness

For Jung, the increased specialization associated with civilization parallels the development of human consciousness.[7] Having control and influence over the environment requires differentiation between such things as verifiable external events and inner psychic events like dreams and visions. The largely unconscious primitive psyche did not make these kinds of critical discriminations, without which neither causal connections nor effective control over the environment can occur. For primitive people, a dream message was just as real and valid as a concrete event.

Jung saw the differentiation of opposites as critical to consciousness. The ability to distinguish male from female, darkness from light, good from evil, outer from inner, real from imagined, and cause from effect is necessary for people to govern their lives. Similarly, the sets of opposites described by psychological type theory require differentiation in order for people to function effectively. The modern person's intuition about the company's stock investment is clearly identified as just that—an intuition—and not as a message from the gods.

Consciousness increases as we successfully differentiate opposites: The more-developed preference in a pair of functions or attitudes receives the greater quantity of energy. **Differentiated functions** and attitudes focus a person's intentions and direction. Psychological type theory assumes a hierarchy of consciousness among the functions, with a superior, most differentiated (dominant) function at the top of the ladder and a largely unconscious (inferior) function at the bottom. In between are a function somewhat less differentiated than the dominant function (the auxiliary function) and a function somewhat more differentiated than the inferior function (the tertiary function). As Jung (1959) put it:

Conscious Psychic Energy

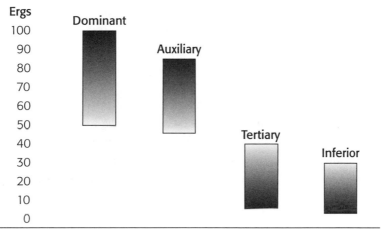

Figure 4 • Hierarchical Structure of the Jungian Functions
in Relation to Available Conscious Energy

Only one function becomes more or less successfully differentiated, which on that account is known as the superior or main function, and together with extraversion or introversion constitutes the type of conscious attitude. This function has associated with it one or two partially differentiated auxiliary functions which hardly ever attain the same degree of differentiation as the main function. . . . The fourth, inferior function proves . . . to be inaccessible to our will. (p. 238)

Within typology's system of opposites, it is the flow of psychic energy between and among the functions that provides its dynamic character. Figure 4 depicts the hierarchical structure of the Jungian functions in relation to available psychic energy, described as ergs, a unit of energy defined in the field of physics. Note that the energy available to each function is shown as varying within a hypothetical lower and upper limit. Such variation might be a function of an individual's stage of life development or particular current life situation.

Because type theory describes each personality type as healthy, adapted, and of equal inherent value, type descriptions emphasize the positive attributes of each type.[8] In fact, a significant asset of this approach as compared to pathology-focused systems is its validating and affirming nature.

Adaptive Access to All Mental Processes

It is important to remember that all four processes and all four attitudes identified by psychological type theory can be used effectively by everyone. Thus, even though a person's dominant function may be Feeling, for instance, that person can and will follow rules of logical analysis (Thinking) when it is necessary or advantageous to do so. Suppose that person is a writer. The act of writing requires the application of logical rules of grammar and language. The person can use his Thinking abilities comfortably and willingly because they can help him organize and communicate his ideas (Intuition) about something that is very important to him (his dominant Feeling function). This is an example of what is referred to as using a less-preferred function or attitude in the service of a preferred one.

Thus, a manager whose dominant function is Intuition may develop skill in devising and implementing detailed plans and structures that require him to use his inferior function, Sensing, because the increased efficiency will help him develop future strategies that engage his dominant Intuition. A manager whose dominant function is Sensing might lend her support to a brainstorming session for her many Intuitive employees, knowing that ultimately many practical plans might emerge from the process that will satisfy her preference for Sensing.

The dynamic approach of Jung and Myers permits the fullest opportunities for individual development of personality and personal effectiveness. Taking this idea a step further, psychological typology may constitute the basic structure of personality, serving as a template that guides and colors other aspects of our lives. If this is true, both genetic endowments and environmental influences affect and are affected by our underlying typological character structure.

The Effects of Type Dynamics

FOR THE MOST PART, Jung's writings on type dynamics are powerful but sketchy, insightful but unsystematic. It is therefore difficult to fully under stand the complex interactions of functions and attitudes implicit in the theory. Myers and Briggs faced this problem when they developed the MBTI personality inventory as a self-report questionnaire designed to elicit an individual's preferences regarding pairs of equally valuable mental processes and attitudes. The construction of the instrument allows a person to indicate his or her preference for Extraversion or Introversion, Sensing or Intuition, Thinking or Feeling, and Judging or Perceiving. A critical additional requirement for the MBTI personality inventory, however, was a method for determining the dynamic relationships among those preferences, as specified by Jung's theory.

Myers and Briggs' careful reading and interpretation of Jung's theory enabled them to devise a clever and accessible method for identifying dynamics based on an individual's responses to the instrument. Their method is reflected in the content and order of each four-letter type. As with any attempt to identify something as complex as a human personality, the MBTI personality inventory may not accurately identify a particular person's type and associated dynamics. Within such limits, however, it seems to provide the best available indicator of a person's dynamic personality type. And people whose MBTI results don't seem to fit them are given the opportunity to identify for themselves a "best-fit" type.

Many people take the MBTI personality inventory in situations that provide limited information about the dynamic character of the theory underlying the instrument. As a result, they may know the four letters of their type but not appreciate the depth of information type can provide. The first section of this chapter is designed with such people in mind. It describes the rationale and method for identifying the dynamics of any four-letter MBTI type. Those already familiar with the theory and method for identifying dominant, auxiliary, tertiary, and inferior functions may choose to skip to the following section, "Differing Dynamics and Their Effects," beginning on page 34. This section describes the effects of type dynamics on the character and behavior of different types and provides examples that demonstrate these dynamic differences. (Note: If you decide to skip the first section, you may want to read the endnote for this chapter, which discusses alternative hypotheses about the attitude of the tertiary function.)

Identifying Type Dynamics

To understand the dynamic relationships within each of the sixteen four-letter MBTI types, you must first examine the sequence of the letters.

The first letter, which is either E for Extraversion or I for Introversion, designates a person's preferred attitude or orientation of energy. People who prefer Extraversion tend to use their energies in the outer world of people, things, and activity and are in turn energized when they interact with their outer environment. People who prefer Introversion tend to orient their energies to the inner world of concepts, ideas, and reflection and are in turn energized when they interact with their inner environment.

The second letter, which is either S for Sensing or N for Intuition, identifies how a person typically gathers information, his or her preferred perceiving function. People who prefer Sensing tend to trust and use information acquired through their five senses, focusing on the individual facts and details in a present situation. People who prefer Intuition tend to trust and use information acquired through a "sixth sense," which focuses on patterns and possibilities that imply a future situation.

The third letter, which is either T for Thinking or F for Feeling, identifies a person's preferred judging function. People who prefer Thinking tend to make decisions or reach conclusions by focusing on nonpersonal logical analysis and include only information that seems directly and logically relevant to the problem at hand. They are most interested in arriving at the objective truth and the logical consequences of a decision. People who prefer to make their decisions through Feeling tend to focus on people-centered values relevant to the problem at hand and include in the decision-making process factors that may not be logically relevant to the problem. They are most interested in the Feeling, or value, consequences of a decision. Remember that Feeling in Jung's system refers not to emotions but rather to the application of rational Feeling values when making a decision. However, people with a preference for Feeling are more likely than those who prefer Thinking to include their own and others' emotional reactions in the decision-making process.

The fourth letter in a person's type, which is either J for Judging or P for Perceiving, identifies whether he or she takes a Judging or Perceiving attitude toward the outer world. People who prefer a Judging attitude when they are extraverting enjoy making decisions and reaching closure when dealing with the outer world; they tend to function best when they can be systematic, methodical, and scheduled. People who prefer a Perceiving attitude when they are extraverting enjoy gathering as much information about the outer world as is possible; they tend to function best when they can take a flexible, adaptable, and spontaneous approach to the world. Remember that J points to a person's preferred judging function, shown in the third letter of a person's type (T or F), while P points to a person's preferred perceiving function, shown in the second letter of a type (S or N). Thus,

- E or I refers to the direction of a person's energy flow
- S or N refers to a person's preferred form of perception
- T or F refers to a person's preferred form of judgment
- J or P refers to a person's preferred function when he or she is extraverting

The Form of Each Function

The Dominant Function We typically want to devote most of our attention and activity to our dominant function. This is our preferred form of judgment (either Thinking or Feeling) or our preferred form of perception (either Sensing or Intuition). We tend to use our dominant function primarily in our preferred attitude or orientation of energy, either Extraversion or Introversion. So if your dominant function is Thinking and you prefer the Extraverted attitude, you probably enjoy spending much of your time making logical judgments, reaching conclusions, and accomplishing things out in the world.

Dominant Extraverted Thinking ———▶ Logical judgments, conclusions, accomplishments *in the world*

If your dominant function is Intuition and you prefer the Extraverted attitude, then you probably enjoy spending much of your time coming up with new ideas and possibilities for projects out in the world and letting others know about your enthusiasm.

Dominant Extraverted Intuition ———▶ New ideas, possibilities for projects, enthusiasms *in the world*

The Auxiliary Function A second, or auxiliary, function complements the dominant function in two ways. First, the auxiliary function is always from the other pair of functions—that is, if the dominant function is a judging function, then the auxiliary function will be the preferred perceiving function; if the dominant function is a perceiving function, then the auxiliary function will be the preferred judging function. Second, the auxiliary function will tend to operate primarily in the less-preferred attitude—either Extraversion or Introversion. Thus, if the dominant function is extraverted, then the auxiliary function will be introverted; if the dominant function is introverted, then the auxiliary function will be extraverted.

So, if your dominant function is Extraverted Thinking, your auxiliary function will be either Introverted Sensing or Introverted Intuition, whichever function you prefer. If your auxiliary preference is Introverted Intuition, the information you gather is likely to emphasize internal ideas, hypotheses, and theories.

Auxiliary Introverted Intuition ———▶ *Internal* ideas, hypotheses, theories

Your dominant Extraverted Thinking judgment will focus on that kind of internal information in order to create models and systems and ways to implement them in the world. Because your dominant, driving function, Extraverted Thinking, attracts you to accomplishing things in the world, implementing your ideas will be more appealing to you than the ideas themselves.

Dominant Extraverted Thinking
    +   = *Implementation* of ideas
Auxiliary Introverted Intuition

If your dominant function is Extraverted Intuition, your auxiliary function will be either Introverted Thinking or Introverted Feeling, whichever you prefer. If your auxiliary function is Introverted Feeling, the conclusions you reach about which ideas to pursue will probably be oriented to your values, the things that are most important to you.

Auxiliary Introverted Feeling ⟶ Value, things of importance

Your dominant Extraverted Intuition will therefore generate ideas and possibilities about your important values. And because your dominant, driving force, Extraverted Intuition, attracts you to exploring ideas in the world, coming up with the ideas will be more appealing to you than implementing them.

Dominant Extraverted Intuition
+ = *Exploration* of ideas
Auxiliary Introverted Feeling

The dominant and auxiliary functions complement each other by providing balance between perception and judgment and Introversion and Extraversion. Myers believed that this kind of balance was necessary for good type development.

The Judging Versus Perceiving Attitude   Myers used the fourth pair of opposites, implied but not made explicit in Jung's writings, to enable us to determine type dynamics. The Judging versus Perceiving distinction indicates one's attitude toward the outer world—that is, whether the preferred perceiving function (either Sensing or Intuition) or the preferred judging function (either Thinking or Feeling) is used when a person is extraverting, regardless of whether Extraversion is the person's preferred attitude. In the examples of dominant and auxiliary functions that were just discussed, the person whose dominant function is Extraverted Thinking has a Judging attitude (J) toward the outer world; she extraverts her Thinking. The person whose dominant function is Extraverted Intuition has a Perceiving attitude (P) toward the outer world; he extraverts his Intuition.

Here is an example to show how Myers used the J–P concept to identify type dynamics. We begin with ISTJ—a type that prefers Introversion, Sensing, Thinking, and a Judging attitude.

Looking at the type ISTJ, we see the following:

- The preferred attitude or orientation of energy is Introversion.
- The preferred way of perceiving is Sensing.
- The preferred way of judging is Thinking.
- The preferred function to use while extraverting is the Judging function, in this case, Thinking.

Remember that for any four-letter type, one of the two middle letters is the dominant function and the other middle letter is the auxiliary function. And remember also that one of the middle letters operates primarily in the Extraverted attitude and the other operates in the Introverted attitude. The method that follows will help you identify which middle letter is dominant and which is auxiliary, and which middle letter is extraverted and which is introverted.

First, look at the last letter of the four-letter type. It is J, which tells us that an ISTJ extraverts the preferred judging function, which is the third letter, T for Thinking. To remind us that T is the extraverted function, we'll put a small "e" beside the T.

$$I S T_e J$$

We know that if one middle function is extraverted, the remaining middle function is introverted, so we'll put a small "i" beside the S (Sensing), the remaining middle letter.

$$I S_i T_e J$$

We now need to know whether an ISTJ type prefers Extraversion or Introversion as an attitude. So we look at the first letter of the type. It identifies Introversion as the attitude preference for ISTJ. We know that people use their dominant function in their preferred attitude of Extraversion or Introversion, so we match the preferred attitude shown in the first letter (I) with the function that has an "i" beside it. For ISTJ, that is Sensing. For ISTJ, therefore, Sensing that is introverted (commonly referred to as *Introverted Sensing*) is the dominant function. The auxiliary function is identified by the remaining middle letter, T, which has an "e" next to it. Thinking that is extraverted (or *Extraverted Thinking*) is the auxiliary function for ISTJ.

There are two functions whose letters don't appear in the type code—N for Intuition and F for Feeling. In any type, the two missing letters designate the tertiary and inferior functions. By definition, the *inferior function* is the polar opposite of the dominant function—that is, it is opposite in both function and attitude. So for the dominant Introverted Sensing ISTJ, the inferior function is Extraverted Intuition, as shown:

The tertiary function is always the function opposite the auxiliary function. For ISTJ, whose auxiliary function is Thinking, it is Feeling.

There is some disagreement about the attitude associated with the tertiary function, so no attitude for the tertiary function is shown above. The view taken by Myers and McCaulley (1985), and continued in Myers et al. (1998), is that the tertiary function shares the same attitude as the auxiliary and inferior functions—that is, the dominant function takes the preferred attitude, with the auxiliary, tertiary, and inferior functions all taking the less-preferred attitude. However, two alternative views have been suggested.[9] Because of these differences of opinion, the attitude of the tertiary function is not considered in this book.

Now let's look at the dynamics of a type that prefers Extraversion. For an easy comparison, we'll look at ESTJ, the type that shares all but the E–I preference with ISTJ. Once again, we determine what function the person uses when extraverting by looking at the last letter of the type, which for ESTJ is J for Judging. And, once again, we find that the person prefers Thinking. Using our previous notation system, we have the following:

$$E\ S\ T_e\ J$$

We assign a small "i" to the remaining middle letter, S for Sensing:

$$E\ S_i\ T_e\ J$$

The first letter in the type tells us that this person prefers the Extraverted attitude, and the letter that has an "e" attached to it for ESTJ is T for Thinking. Thinking that is extraverted (or *Extraverted Thinking*) is thus the dominant function for ESTJ. The remaining middle function, designated by S for Sensing, is the auxiliary function, and we see that it is introverted. Thus the auxiliary function for ESTJ is *Introverted Sensing.*

To complete the picture, we identify the inferior function as the polar opposite of the dominant function—that is, Introverted Feeling—and the tertiary function as Intuition, as shown:

Differing Dynamics and Their Effects

Now that you understand the underlying theory of type dynamics and have a system for identifying the dynamics in any type, we can explore what difference these dynamics make in people's personalities. For example, how are ISTJs and ESTJs different?

Based on their shared preferences for Sensing and Thinking, we might safely assume that an ISTJ and an ESTJ would prefer the same kinds of information-gathering approaches and decision-making methods. We would also expect both to be comfortable with structure and closure. Both have the same two letters, F and N, missing from their four-letter type. So we should not expect the two types to pay a great deal of attention to Feeling values and future possibilities.

However, the function that is dominant for the ISTJ (Introverted Sensing) is the auxiliary function for the ESTJ; the function that is auxiliary for the ISTJ (Extraverted Thinking) is the dominant function for the ESTJ. Thus the amount of energy available to the Sensing and Thinking functions of these two types differs and, according to the theory, will influence the degree of differentiation of these functions. Further, you will have noted that the inferior functions of these two types are different: For the ISTJ (dominant Introverted Sensing), Extraverted Intuition is the inferior function; for the ESTJ (dominant Extraverted Thinking), Introverted Feeling is the inferior function. Of course, their tertiary functions are different as well: For the ISTJ (auxiliary Extraverted Thinking), Feeling is the tertiary function; for the ESTJ (auxiliary Introverted Sensing), Intuition is the auxiliary function. As we shall see throughout this book, these differences in type dynamics lead to important and predictable differences in the ways these two types experience and express their personalities. Equally important and notable differences occur for other types who share three letters in their four-letter type.

How the Dynamics of ISTJ and ESTJ Are Shown

Jung and Myers specified that the dominant function is the function that is the most differentiated, energized, and under a person's conscious control. The auxiliary, tertiary, and inferior functions are progressively less developed and have less conscious energy available.

Thus, for the ISTJ, dominant Introverted Sensing would be the most differentiated and energized and therefore the most consciously directed function. We would expect an ISTJ to first process information internally and to be quite confident about the accuracy of her perceptions. Auxiliary Extraverted Thinking would be less developed but quite accessible. We would expect this person to be somewhat less confident about communicating logical conclusions. Tertiary Feeling is less developed than auxiliary Thinking, so she might not have ready access to her Feeling values. Inferior Extraverted Intuition would be virtually undifferentiated and unconscious. We would expect her to pay little attention to possibilities in the outside world.

For the ESTJ, Extraverted Thinking is the most energized and differentiated function. We would expect an ESTJ to make judgments about the outside world quickly and with great certainty. Introverted Sensing is next in line; the ESTJ's second concern would be with processing the data relevant to his decisions. Tertiary Intuition might be expressed through reluctant or occasional attention to possibilities. Inferior Introverted Feeling—undifferentiated and unconscious—would result in little or no attention to the Feeling values in a situation.

This is true for other types who share the same functions and attitudes, but for whom the dominant and auxiliary functions differ. Research by Mitchell (1992b) suggests that the following model may form the basis for differences in dominant versus auxiliary differentiation.

If Introverted Feeling is my dominant function and your auxiliary function, I should use Introverted Feeling more often than you do and with greater confidence and facility. Most likely, I will also have developed all or most of the personality characteristics associated with habitual use of the preference and have a fair amount of comfort and facility in using them. In contrast, your auxiliary Introverted Feeling will be expressed less often and with less confidence and facility. And you may have developed only some of the attributes associated with a preference for Introverted Feeling and have somewhat less comfort and facility in using them.

Examining the Effects of Type Dynamics

The remainder of this chapter describes some of the important effects of type dynamics. These include differences related to which function is used first; whether the dominant function is a judging or a perceiving function; whether the dominant function is extraverted or introverted; using the dominant function in the less-preferred attitude; and an alternative way of looking at the J–P attitude pair.

Which Function Is Used First?

An ENFP (dominant Extraverted Intuition, auxiliary Introverted Feeling) and an INFP (auxiliary Extraverted Intuition, dominant Introverted Feeling) were the coleaders of a seminar. During the afternoon session, both noted and commented to the other that there was something amiss in a particular segment of the lesson. They agreed to review it later. As soon as the seminar ended, the ENFP said, "Okay, we need to talk about that now and figure it out." The INFP said, "But I'm not ready yet. I need some time to evaluate it by myself before I'll be ready to talk about it."

The ENFP wanted to explore the possibilities first and then reach a conclusion. The INFP needed to get a feel for (make a judgment about) what happened before being ready to consider possibilities that could confirm or negate her conclusions. Thus, each person's dominant function was engaged first. In this way, the dominant function seems to serve as a kind of default mechanism in the psyche, much like the default settings in a computer program.

Is the Dominant Function a Judging or Perceiving Function?

An ISTJ (dominant Introverted Sensing, auxiliary Extraverted Thinking) and an ESTJ (dominant Extraverted Thinking, auxiliary Introverted

Sensing) were business partners. After investigating the various computers available, they agreed on one. But just as they were about to purchase it, one of their customers told them about another machine that had additional features that might be useful in their business. The ISTJ was ready to switch to the new option; the ESTJ gave many reasons for sticking with the original decision and played down the alleged assets of the alternative machine. It took several days to convince him to alter his decision.

Dominant Judging types (those whose dominant function is either Thinking or Feeling) tend to be more reluctant to change a decision in the face of contradictory evidence than are dominant Perceiving types. For the latter (those whose dominant function is either Sensing or Intuition), the data (perceptions) are primary; conclusions (judgments) are less important. So when new information alters a previously held conclusion, dominant Perceiving types find it fairly easy to change a decision, even if they were comfortable with it. For dominant Judging types, the conclusion is primary, and a good deal of energy is invested in it. In the face of contradictory evidence, they find it more difficult to give up their initial conclusion. They may doggedly question the new data before reluctantly altering their decision.

Is the Function Extraverted or Introverted?

A common area of difficulty for people learning about type is the difference between extraverting and introverting a particular function. Here are some examples that highlight such differences.

Is Sensing Extraverted or Introverted? Myra, an ESFP (dominant Extraverted Sensing), and Bonnie, an ISFJ (dominant Introverted Sensing), went to the Bahamas together. Neither had been there before. Bonnie came prepared with an itinerary of specific things to see and do and time estimates for doing them. Myra objected to this imposed structure. She wanted to have the fullest possible range of experiences and to remain open to any sensory exploration that came her way. The two succeeded in compromising by alternating days of doing things "Myra's way" with days of doing them "Bonnie's way." But neither was quite comfortable with the other's preferred mode of operation.

Extraverted Sensing types take in the widest range of available sensory messages from the environment, receiving pleasure from their intensity and breadth and having little or no restrictions on what are acceptable data. Introverted Sensing types, in contrast, seem to operate with an established inner structure within which incoming sensory information is classified and ordered. The data are then readily available in all their detail for the appreciation of and use by the Introverted Sensing type.

Is Intuition Extraverted or Introverted? Yolanda, an ENFP, feels that she is frequently criticized and put down for her ideas. As a dominant Extraverted Intuitive type, she talks about her ideas as they are being formed, before she subjects them to her own critical judgment. In contrast, Hal, an INFJ (dominant Introverted Intuitive type), keeps his ideas to himself for a long time before sharing them. He wants to ensure that his ideas are seen as only ideas, and not as finalized, worked-out systems. When he does talk about his ideas, he uses disclaimers, emphasizing their tentative nature.

Dominant Introverted Intuitive types tend to focus primarily on ideas and possibilities at a conceptual level and to focus on the essence of those inner ideas that are certain. Introverted Intuition is tuned in to inner interconnected possibilities that may take the form of complex theories, models, and the like. Their relevance to the outer world is usually secondary, so only well-thought-out and important ideas are shared with others.

Dominant Extraverted Intuitive types tend to be more attracted to a wide range of possibilities in the outer environment, readily sharing them with others as ideas to be explored and applying those ideas in the outer world. So Yolanda, in sharing her ideas before she has critiqued them herself, risks being misunderstood by others. Hal, in initially keeping his ideas to himself, misses out on feedback that might help him further shape his ideas.

Is Thinking Extraverted or Introverted? Two INTP (dominant Introverted Thinking) researchers were discussing possibilities and plans for continuing their research. They explored many wide-ranging possibilities, discussing each with great enthusiasm. At one point in their discussion, their ENTJ (dominant Extraverted Thinking) project manager came in briefly and listened with great interest as they discussed their ideas. Two months later, the two INTPs were surprised and rather vexed when they discovered that their project manager had applied for a grant to do the research project he had listened in on!

For the INTPs, their discussion was "just tossing around ideas." The particular idea that their project manager overheard them discussing was no more important than ten others they talked about that day. To the ENTJ, their enthusiasm about it (and the fact that it also appealed to him) was sufficient motive for taking action. Extraverted Thinking types use their judgment in the arena of the outer world, critically evaluating what is happening (if their auxiliary function is Sensing) or the potential for effective outcomes (if their auxiliary function is Intuition) with a goal of logic and coherence in the outer world. They are oriented to acting on their conclusions. The critical judgment of Introverted Thinking types operates internally, as they figure out what is going on or what is possible with a goal of inner logic and coherence. Actualizing their conclusions is secondary.

Is Feeling Extraverted or Introverted? George, an ENFJ (dominant Extraverted Feeling), hired Ellen, an INFP (dominant Introverted Feeling), to edit his book manuscript. Ellen was gratified to learn that the edited manuscript had been accepted for publication by a prestigious university press. This news confirmed her feeling that she had done a good job. She was embarrassed, however, when George, who had already paid her for her work, took her out to dinner and presented her with an expensive gift to show his appreciation. Rather than increasing her confidence in her work, this seemingly excessive display of gratitude made Ellen distrust George's judgment of her. His unbounded enthusiasm seemed to indicate to her a lack of discrimination.

This is a good example of how Introverted Feeling types focus on inner harmony and being at peace within themselves, whereas Extraverted Feeling types devote their energy to maintaining harmony in the outer world. George was merely sharing his delight in his success with someone he felt had contributed greatly to it. He would have been puzzled and shocked had he known about Ellen's reaction, which she did not reveal to him.

What Happens When the Dominant Function Is Used in the Less-Preferred Attitude?

The examples above show that much misunderstanding can arise between people whose dominant functions operate in opposite attitudes. Von Franz

(1971) reiterates Jung's observation that we have more difficulty with people who use their dominant function in the "other" attitude than we do with people whose type is the complete opposite of our own. We may become impatient with others on whom we project our own discomfort with using a less-preferred attitude.

Thus, Introverted Thinking types may find their Extraverted Thinking colleagues to be lacking in depth and conceptual clarity, too quick to reveal their thinking process to others, and likely to not think things through well enough. Extraverted Thinking types may see their Introverted Thinking type counterparts as obtuse, obscure, esoteric in their interests, unnecessarily complex, and perhaps withholding and unwilling to share their thoughts with others.

Introverted Feeling types may see their Extraverted Feeling associates as insincere and nondiscriminating in their expression of Feeling values, intrusive and overbearing in their focus on establishing and maintaining harmony for the people in their environment, and likely to choose breadth rather than depth of feeling. Extraverted Feeling types may feel unsure about the values of their Introverted Feeling friends and colleagues. They may experience doubts about whether they are appreciated, may feel criticized, and may perceive (often accurately) the Introverted Feeling type's judgment that the Extraverted Feeling type lacks depth.

By the same token, when people use a function in their own less-preferred attitude, they may experience a sense of "wrongness" or discomfort with themselves. You will recall that the Jung-Myers approach specifies that we are free to use each of the four functions—S, N, T, and F—in *both* the attitudes of Extraversion and Introversion at least some of the time. Such flows of energy are necessary for good adaptation in an active, dynamic psychological system. Thus, an INFP may have a *preference* for introverting Feeling and extraverting Intuition, but is free to extravert Feeling on occasion and to introvert Intuition when that is desirable. For example, an INFP may speak to a group of people about his or her strong values and may spend time thinking about new ideas, theories, and possibilities without communicating them to others in any way. He or she is also free to introvert inferior Thinking (typically extraverted in an INFP) and to use tertiary Sensing in either the Extraverted or Introverted attitude. Similarly, an ESTJ, whose typical type dynamics suggest habitual use of Extraverted Thinking and Introverted Sensing, is able to introvert

Thinking by silently considering the logical consequences of a decision and to extravert Sensing by seeking out sensory experiences in the outside world as fully as possible. Nevertheless, *because* attitude determines the sphere in which a function operates—the outer world or the inner world—when we use a function in the less-preferred attitude we find ourselves in a foreign land, full of uncertainty and lacking in confidence. We feel and behave differently and may appear different to others. This is especially true when the function in question is the dominant one.

The Perceiving Function in the Less-Preferred Attitude   Introverts who typically introvert Sensing or Intuition may feel overwhelmed or unfocused when they extravert that function. Exposing their perceiving process to others may interfere with their confidence in their ability to concentrate and direct their train of thought. Their ideas may appear disjointed to both themselves and others, as their inner processing is likely to be much faster than their speech. As a result, much of the detail and complexity of their inner perceptions will not be communicated.

The effects of introverting Sensing or Intuition in people who normally extravert these functions are less apparent. Extraverted Sensing types and Extraverted Intuitive types describe having great difficulty staying focused on inner perception. Their attention wanders and they become confused and somewhat disoriented. They may feel lost in internal complexity and be unable to communicate what is going on inside them.

The Judging Function in the Less-Preferred Attitude   Introverts who typically introvert Feeling or Thinking may feel they are overdoing it, telling too much or providing too much detail when they extravert that function. Other people may confirm the Introvert's fear that he or she has revealed too much. Because that function is usually used internally, Introverts may have difficulty knowing just how much of their inner processes to reveal to others.

The effects of introverting a normally extraverted function are less readily apparent to observers. But Extraverts report that when they introvert their typically extraverted Feeling or Thinking, they can become quite confused and circular in their reasoning. They need to talk out their process and receive feedback from others in order to feel comfortable with their decisions.

Another Way of Looking at the J–P Attitude

When people discuss the J–P distinction, they usually talk about the attitudinal and behavioral differences that result from extraverting one's preferred judging process versus extraverting one's preferred perceiving process. In this section we will examine another aspect of J and P by comparing the function that is extraverted with the corresponding function that is introverted. We will look at what attitudinal and behavioral differences result from J types introverting their preferred perceiving process and P types introverting their preferred judging process.

Extraverting Versus Introverting the Perceiving Process   Bill, an INTJ (dominant introverted Intuition), and his wife, Arlene, an INFP (auxiliary extraverted Intuition), spent a week at an artist's colony in New England. Later, Arlene remarked that she had enjoyed participating, at least peripherally, in some of the more unconventional activities at the colony and thought she could get caught up in it for a while if she spent more time there. Bill saw his wife's statement as evidence of a possible character flaw, suggesting a failure on her part to maintain strong, unalterable values. He indicated that he had no such urges and was immune to any dubious attraction to what he termed "immoral" behaviors.

How can we account for the different reactions of Bill and Arlene? Remember that the people who extravert their perceiving function are those whose type ends with the letter P. These are ENTP, ENFP, ESTP, ESFP, INTP, INFP, ISTP, and ISFP. Of course, all of these types introvert their judging function. But the external focus of their perception makes it likely that they will easily change and adapt to a changing outer environment, even having a "chameleonlike" tendency to take on the behaviors and values of people in different contexts.

The people who introvert their perceiving function are those whose type ends with the letter J. These are ENTJ, ENFJ, ESTJ, ESFJ, INTJ, INFJ, ISTJ, and ISFJ. Because these types' perceiving focus is internal, their inner perceptions have a constancy and predictability from one circumstance to the next. All of these types extravert their preferred judging process.

Bill seemed to confuse Arlene's openness to new data with a readiness to change her basic moral standards (as embodied in her dominant Introverted Feeling). He did not experience the "pull" of the outer environment himself, for his own perceiving focus is internal and not easily amenable to outside influences.

The fact that J types, who extravert their judging function, like to control and regulate and are more comfortable in a predictable environment is reinforced by their introverting of their perceiving function. This makes the outer environment less salient than it is for those who extravert their perceiving function. For the Extraverted Perceiving types, who introvert their preferred judging function, the basic decision-making structure (Thinking or Feeling) remains constant and secure. But in their efforts to fully observe or experience their environment, they may appear to have shifting and unreliable judgments.

Extraverting Versus Introverting the Judging Functions The phone rang. It was Carla, Rosa's ENFP daughter. (Rosa is an INTP—a dominant Introverted Thinking type.) Carla was attending college in another state. "Mom, I have a chance to move out of the dorm and into a six-bedroom house with four girls and a guy," she said excitedly. "It's a great house, right next to campus, and it will even be cheaper than the dorm! It's okay with you, isn't it?"

Rosa quickly thought, she's too young to live off campus. It seems to me it's against the rules for freshmen, anyway. She probably doesn't know the prospective roommates very well, and her judgment about people can be really off. It sounds like a bad idea to me. She said to Carla, "Tell me some more about the house and your friends. How did you hear about it? Are the others freshmen, too?"

Just then, Rosa's husband, Mario, an INTJ (dominant Introverted Intuitive type with auxiliary extraverted Thinking), came into the room. "It's Carla," said Rosa. Mario picked up the phone. Carla repeated her exciting news. Mario immediately said, "That's a terrible idea. You're too young to live off campus. Isn't it against the rules for freshmen? And who are these people, anyway? You know you're not a very good judge of people!"

Carla burst into tears, accused her parents of treating her like a child, and angrily hung up the phone. The next day, after everyone had calmed down, Carla gave her parents information about the house, the roommates, and the college rules. Both parents were satisfied and relieved, and Carla was ecstatic when they agreed to her request.

This story demonstrates an interesting consequence of opposite attitudes of the judging process. Remember that people whose type ends with the letter J extravert their judging function. People whose type ends with P extravert their perceiving function, so their judging function is introverted. In the example above, whether the judging function was dominant or auxiliary didn't matter.

Later, in discussing what had happened, Mario and Rosa noted that they had had very similar judgments about their daughter's plans. But Rosa's introversion of her judging function made her keep her concerns to herself, while her extraversion of her perceiving function encouraged her to ask for more information. Mario's extraversion of his judging function encouraged him to state his concerns up front. He acknowledged that after Carla had hung up, he realized he was missing a lot of information about her plans.

There are many other effects of differing type dynamics, both dramatic and subtle, and we can use them to make specific behavioral predictions. The dynamic character of typology teems with possibilities for observing individual similarities and differences. This is a far more fruitful approach than a concept of type that stays at the simplistic level of "I'm an INTP, so I like mathematical models. You're an ENFJ, so you like people to get along!"

4

The Dynamics of the Hidden Personality

THIS CHAPTER PROVIDES the context for recognizing and understanding how the hidden part of personality, the inferior function, is manifested. It will discuss the following:

- Purposeful use of the less-preferred functions
- The conditions for the eruption of the inferior function
- The nature of the inferior function
- The role of the inferior function in **self-regulation**
- The role of the tertiary function
- The contribution of the inferior function to personal development and individuation
- The roles of the tertiary and auxiliary functions
- The importance of the inferior function in **midlife**

Purposeful Use of the Less-Preferred Functions

We are all capable of using our tertiary and inferior functions when a particular task requires them. When our least-preferred process is being used consciously, we may best think of it as our *fourth, or least-preferred, function.* When this process is engaged unconsciously and operates outside our control, it serves as our *inferior* function. As we discussed in Chapter 3, the tertiary is the function that is opposite our auxiliary function. When it is under conscious control, however, we may think of it as our *third function.* We may even have developed tactics that help us use it more easily and effectively, or we may have learned to ask for expert input from friends or colleagues whose dominant or auxiliary function is our third or fourth function. As we will see, however, this purposeful use of the less-preferred functions is quite different from the involuntary occurrence, or "attack," that we describe as being in the grip of one's inferior function.

Many people become quite comfortable and skillful in using their less-preferred functions. The more our life situations call for this use, the easier it becomes and the more effective we become at it, especially if our less-preferred functions serve the goals of our preferred ones. As an INFP researcher, I had to use Sensing and Thinking a good deal of the time. And although it was difficult and fatiguing at first, it became easier over time and I became better at those aspects of my work. I was very motivated to use my third and fourth functions well because they provided the Sensing data and logical data analysis that permitted me to use my dominant Feeling and auxiliary Intuition. The research topics were important to me, and I very much enjoyed developing hypotheses and extracting meaning from the results of the research.

However, no matter how experienced, skilled, and comfortable we may be in the conscious use of our third and fourth functions, *this does not seem to alter its eruption as an inferior function.* Given the right preconditions that make us vulnerable to being "taken over by the other side," we will likely fall into our inferior modes. Conscious skill and experience with a function does not prevent us from falling into the grip. With sufficient fatigue or stress, our inferior function will take over, quite beyond our control. And even with considerable skill and familiarity with our less-preferred functions, excessive use of them can serve as a trigger for a full-blown "grip" experience.

Conditions for Eruption of the Inferior Function

The primary precondition for eruption of the inferior function is a lowering of our general level of consciousness. Jung referred to this process as an *abaissement du niveau mental* (Samuels et al., 1986). It permits a transfer of energy from the more conscious and developed dominant and auxiliary functions to the relatively unconscious tertiary and inferior functions. Several circumstances encourage this transfer of energy; the most common ones are fatigue, illness, and stress, and the use of alcohol or other mind-altering drugs.

The process that occurs when one or more of these preconditions is in effect seems to be the following: The tired, ill, stressed, or drug-altered person becomes careless and ineffective in using her usually reliable dominant function. Perhaps her perception is dulled or her usual good judgment is faulty. So her normal, comfortable orientation to herself (i.e., her security in her dominant and auxiliary functions) is threatened.

People typically respond to this threat by trying harder and harder, using their dominant function to the point of one-sidedness or exaggeration. One-sidedness involves all the person's energy going to the dominant function, with no balance provided by the auxiliary or other functions. Such exaggerated, unbalanced efforts inevitably lead to further failure and distress. It is as if the psyche then says, "This isn't working the way it's supposed to in spite of my best efforts. I'd better try a different approach entirely, the most different approach possible. Maybe that will work." The most different approach possible is likely to be the least familiar, most undeveloped and unused aspect of personality, the inferior function (and often the tertiary function as well).

For example, an ENTP who is becoming stressed may show exaggerated Extraverted Intuition by frenetically tossing out many ideas while making no attempt to select among them with his auxiliary Thinking. As his efforts are met with inevitable frustration and failure, his inferior Introverted Sensing will take over his personality. He may latch on to a minor detail and insist that it alone is the cause of the difficulties he is encountering.

Much of the time people engage in positive and adaptive behavior in response to fatigue and stress, taking a break, seeking advice, asking for help, or getting a good night's sleep, for example, as an effective way of dealing with difficult situations. These coping mechanisms seem to be general human responses to stressors and cut across all types. It is hard to predict just how much stress, fatigue, or illness is enough to stimulate one-sided type exaggeration or a full-blown inferior function experience. One's type, however, may influence not only the frequency and intensity of these experiences, but the very definition of stress. What is very stressful for some types can be exciting and energizing for others. Further, what each type finds energizing and stressful corresponds very well to the qualities of their dominant and inferior functions, respectively. Freedom to use one's dominant function is energizing; being forced to use one's inferior function is stressful.

The Nature of the Inferior Function

The inferior function phenomenon has a number of distinctive features that are generally associated with the form in which it appears and certain telltale characteristics associated with its activated state. Jung (1976b) described the nature of the inferior function in this way:

> The inferior function is always associated with an archaic personality in ourselves; in the inferior function we are all primitives. In our differentiated functions we are civilized and we are supposed to have free will; but there is no such thing as free will when it comes to the inferior function. There we have an open wound, or at least an open door through which anything might enter. (p. 20)

Clues to the Form

You can get a pretty good idea of what your inferior function looks like by reading the description of your opposite type. However, in the grip of your inferior function, you don't become a mature, well-functioning opposite type, since your experience and facility with your less-preferred functions is relatively limited. So you turn into a rather sorry example of your opposite. Instead of the positive, adaptive character of those qualities when they are developed, there is a negative cast to your "hidden personality." Of course, this is typically not the case when you are purposefully engaging your third and fourth functions or using them in a playful or relaxed fashion.

There are other methods of identifying the form of an individual's inferior function. I often ask people, "What are you like when you are at your worst, when you don't feel like your usual self?" Typically people describe their experience of their inferior function. Another way to identify the inferior function is to think about which function fatigues you most when you use it, or which one you are most sensitive about. Alternatively, you might think about which function energizes you most and is most satisfying to use. Chances are that the opposite of that function is your inferior function.

Since in the Jung-Myers theory the inferior function is a process rather than a structure, we can describe its form but we cannot specify a content for a particular person. Often, however, the content that accompanies an inferior function episode comes from the person's unconscious, more specifically, from his or her **shadow.**

The Inferior Function and the Shadow   Many people confuse the inferior function with the concept of the shadow and use the terms interchangeably (Quenk, 1982). In Jung's system, the shadow is an archetype, one of our innate modes of responding to important universal psychological realities. The shadow includes those things people are unable or unwilling to acknowledge about themselves, such as undesirable character traits, weaknesses, fears, and lapses in morality, or desirable qualities such as intelligence, attractiveness, and leadership skills. The shadow is a key component of a person's **personal unconscious,** a layer of the psyche that is more accessible than its much larger counterpart, the collective unconscious.

Although they are not the same concept, the relationship between the inferior function and the shadow is very important. In effect, one's shadow supplies the personal contents that appear when the inferior function is **constellated,** or evoked. Metaphorically, the inferior function is the skeletal form and the shadow is the flesh that gives it substance and life.

As Jung said in a quotation cited earlier, the inferior function serves as a doorway through which the contents of both the personal and collective unconscious may enter. This can be recognized in the repetitive content "themes" that we experience when we are in the grip of our inferior function or when we observe others in this state. For example, couples often fight about the same things over and over again, typically making the same complaints and accusations, even using the same words on repeated occasions. To the extent that stress provokes or exacerbates such fights, it is likely that two unconscious inferior functions are in operation (see Chapter 14 for more on this topic).

Projection of the Inferior Function   Often the first sign of an activated inferior function is its appearance in the form of a projection. When we project our inferior function onto someone else, we are in effect saying, "I don't have this childish, untrustworthy, and unreliable characteristic. You have it, or she has it, or they have it!"

Perhaps to "prepare" for times when they will need to project to maintain their psychological balance, people become skilled at identifying their opposite type. Or they may devote much time and energy to pointing out annoying, unacceptable characteristics in a particular person or in a particular "type of person." Often, when a person says, "I can't stand the kind of person who . . . ," the description that follows comes remarkably close to the form of his or her own inferior function. Even more important, projection is the mechanism underlying our biases about people who have opposite type preferences. For example, it accounts for the arrogance many Intuitive types direct at Sensing types and the disdain many Sensing types express toward Intuitive types. "See how obsessed that guy is with controlling every detail of his business; what a waste of time!" scoffs the Intuitive, who, when in the grip, becomes obsessed with irrelevant details. "What a lot of harebrained, crazy notions she has about what might happen; what a waste of energy!" proclaims the Sensing type, who, when in the grip, is overwhelmed with ungrounded possibilities.

Character of the Inferior Function

There are certain predictable features of the inferior function, regardless of which function it is or the personal history of the individual possessing it. Although the following characteristics may also accompany other psychic manifestations, such as unconscious **complexes,** they often characterize a person's expression of his or her inferior function.

Tunnel Vision An important characteristic of all inferior functions is *tunnel vision*. This is what makes whatever is being experienced seem real and believable. We can compare this with how we would react to the same thing when we are not in the grip. We think, "How could I have believed that?" or "I must have been blind not to have seen that!" When we focus on a limited piece of reality, what we perceive or conclude may certainly be true, valid, logical, and real. But its import and impact are likely to be out of proportion because all the information that lies outside the tunnel is not available to us. This larger body of data or thought usually tempers the perception or judgment made within the tunnel. The issue on which we focus when in the grip may appropriately be seen as trivial or without substance when viewed in a broader context.

Loss of Sense of Humor All types generally report losing their sense of humor when in the grip of their inferior function. To see anything humorous in our exaggerated, atypical behavior, we would have to be standing outside it, looking at it from a broadened perspective. This is possible when our grip experience is a minor episode, but not when we are fully in the grip of our unconscious inferior function. It is for this reason that people who are very upset or angry are often unable to tell when someone else is joking or teasing them. Even if we are aware that we are in the grip, we usually are unable to fully appreciate the extremity of our distorted perceptions and judgments. It is therefore generally not a good idea to tease people, make light of their reactions, or dismiss their concerns with observations such as, "You're overreacting," or "You're just in the grip of your inferior function."

All-or-None Statements The unconscious has a black-and-white notion of the world. It is nondiscriminating; the shades of gray characteristic of conscious and differentiated psychological functioning are absent. When someone starts making categorical, all-or-none statements, chances are the statements come from the person's unconscious. When an Intuitive type says, "You always forget to balance the checkbook," or a person with a Thinking preference says, "You never say you're sorry!" you are probably hearing from the inferior function or some other aspect of the person's unconscious.

Role of the Inferior Function in Self-Regulation

> We know that three of the four functions of consciousness can become differentiated, i.e., conscious, while the other remains connected with the matrix, the unconscious, and is known as the "inferior" function. It is the Achilles' heel of even the most heroic consciousness. (Jung, 1959, p. 237)

Jung believed that the auxiliary and tertiary functions could achieve some degree of differentiation, but he was quite clear that it was necessary that the inferior function remain outside conscious control. In this form it is able to provide access to the vital contents of the unconscious, the source of growth and development of the personality. Thus, for Jung (1976b) the inferior function was a powerful tool for self-regulation, the necessary element that makes our completion possible:

> I do not believe it is humanly possible to differentiate all four functions alike, otherwise we would be perfect like God, and that surely will not happen . . . we would lose the most precious connection with the unconscious through the inferior function, which is invariably the

weakest; only through our feebleness and incapacity are we linked up with the unconscious, with the lower world of the instincts and with our fellow beings. (pp. 97, 98)

Myers was more sanguine than Jung regarding development of the less-preferred functions. With her primary focus on conscious adaptation through type development, she seemed to describe the possibility of increasing the degree of conscious control over one's functions and of learning to call them into play at will. Where Jung stressed the compensatory role of the inferior function, Myers (1980/1995) gave it a more complementary position in her typological system. She paid considerably less attention than Jung to the inferior function as the link to unconscious knowledge and thus to its transformative capability, choosing instead to focus on its ability to offer a new and useful perspective:

> Because [the less-preferred functions] were necessarily neglected while the preferred processes were developed, they are immature and cannot be expected to offer great wisdom....A person can, however, profitably accept them as younger members of the family, who are entitled to speak up in family councils before decisions are made. If they are given assignments that use their respective gifts and if their help is appreciated and their contributions seriously considered, they will, like children, grow steadily wiser, and the quality of their contributions will steadily improve. (p. 202)

The Compensatory Process

If it were possible to make the unconscious inferior function conscious, its compensatory role as a safety valve for the psyche would be eliminated. When we are too comfortable and secure in our conscious approach, when we believe that we are fully defined by our dominant and auxiliary processes, or when we are excessive or one-sided in any way, we risk overconfidence, rigidity, and stagnation. We need to uncover new information about ourselves or find a different perspective. This valuable knowledge or perspective may be awaiting access through the inferior function.

The inferior function serves as a signaling device in the psyche, warning that something important is out of alignment, in need of attention, or being misperceived or miscalculated. Sometimes the message is merely that we need to stop doing whatever we are doing, rest, and take a look around. Whatever its impetus, it helps reorient us and provides alternative perspectives and points of view. And it does so in such a forceful and dramatic manner that it cannot be ignored, dismissed, or permanently transferred to someone else (by projection).

Looking at alternative perspectives and new information is often what a psychotherapist does for a client who is locked into a particular way of perceiving or judging and cannot see other options. So we can imagine the inferior function as a person's "resident therapist," available to share the broader vision that is possible when unconscious information is accessible to consciousness.

A major consequence of being in the grip of the inferior function is a loss of confidence in what is familiar, valued, or taken for granted. The "flip" into the opposite has shock value—it makes us look at ourselves differently and acknowledge things we previously ignored or rejected. We sometimes integrate the necessary information by having our consciousness literally raised. We become more cautious, more self-doubting, more appreciative of previously disparaged qualities, and so on. The inferior function experience thus expands consciousness in an adaptive manner.

Avoiding the Grip

There are times when we are able to recognize that we are out of sorts or our perspective is off and we can avoid falling into the grip of our inferior function by ignoring or denying it, or by labeling it as just a reaction to stress and fatigue. Do we then miss the opportunity to get new information by avoiding the experience? Or do we simply recognize that we are overreacting because of an altered state and, in a healthy manner, refuse to take the distorted information seriously? Both explanations are possible, but the second probably becomes more prevalent as we grow older and have ample experience of ourselves. We learn to recognize our reactions and develop adaptive ways of dealing with them. If the psyche is truly self-regulating, we can count on any needed new information getting to us sooner or later. Inappropriately avoiding it will serve only as a temporary solution.

Role of the Tertiary Function

Because the inferior and tertiary functions are both relatively unconscious, engagement of either one may constellate the other. If an INFP is in the grip of inferior Thinking, accusing himself of all manner of incompetencies, his weak tertiary Sensing can easily "prove" that even the most minor and routine activity or the simplest directions are beyond his ability. Alternatively (assuming the necessary preconditions), failure or difficulty in performing a Sensing task may quickly lead him to generalize his incompetence to all arenas, not just the present task.

Similarly, an ENFP's inferior Sensing may emerge as obsessiveness about something someone said to her at work, but if it is combined with her tertiary Thinking, it might cause her to reach the illogical conclusion that she will therefore not receive a desired promotion.

The tertiary function influences the expression of the inferior function and thus provides additional predictive and explanatory information. This is apparent in comparing manifestations of the inferior function in people who have opposite auxiliary (and therefore tertiary) functions. Although there is a fair amount of similarity between ENFPs and ENTPs, for example, or between ISTPs and INTPs, the differences between each pair are very consistently related to their different auxiliary and tertiary functions.

Contribution of the Inferior Function to Personal Development and Individuation

Jung (1970a) said that "the 'other' in us always seems alien and unacceptable; but if we let ourselves be aggrieved, the feeling sinks in, and we are the richer for this little bit of self-knowledge" (p. 486).

Von Franz (1971) described the inferior function as slow, touchy, tyrannical, and childish. But she saw the tremendous charge of emotion that accompanies the inferior function as providing us with a new potential for life, noting that

> the behavior of the Inferior Function is wonderfully mirrored in those fairy tales where there is the following structure. A king has three sons. He likes the elder sons but the youngest is regarded as a fool. The king then sets a task in which the sons may have to find the water of life, or the most beautiful bride. (p. 8)

What then occurs in this fairy tale scenario is familiar. The king (dominant function) assumes that the two competent older sons (auxiliary and tertiary functions) will succeed at the task. They try but fail miserably. The youngest son begs to be given a chance. In his foolishness and naiveté, he comes up with an unorthodox but effective solution and thus succeeds where his "betters" have failed. He wins the prize, is recognized as valuable, and takes on a significant role in ruling the kingdom wisely.

Thus, the inexperience and innocence of an inferior function can hold the key to the new awareness necessary for an innovative solution to a work or life problem. Solving the problem—winning the prize—leads to acknowledging the value of one's neglected and unappreciated inferior function. As a result, it can take its rightful place in one's life, helping to rule the kingdom wisely.

The inferior function also appears during important transitional periods in our lives. People report that memorable encounters with their inferior function have often preceded or accompanied significant developmental changes. Moving out of one's childhood home, graduating from high school or college, getting married or divorced, and experiencing the death of a loved one are the kinds of transitional events people mention.

Sometimes an intense inferior function experience results in a renewed appreciation of parts of ourselves that we have taken for granted. Familiarity with our strengths may lead us to minimize them, thereby not developing them to their fullest potential. We may then start to overvalue our less-preferred characteristics and people in whom those qualities are well developed. Ultimately, becoming aware of an unrecognized or unappreciated aspect of oneself releases energy that is then available for constructive growth.

Another way in which the inferior function broadens our knowledge of ourselves results from its attachment to the less-preferred attitude, be it Extraversion or Introversion. Not only is the opposite, inexperienced function activated; the less-preferred attitude is as well. The combination of the two introduces two "alien" factors.

When an Extravert is forced to introvert while in the grip of the inferior function, an uncomfortable situation results, regardless of which function is being introverted. The Extravert's typical and natural ways of dealing with things—talking to people, asking for advice, taking action, and engaging in some energetic activity—become inaccessible because energy has been transferred from the outer world to the inner world. Perhaps this accounts for the observation that depression is harder on Extraverts than it is on Introverts in that depression involves turning inward to the Introverted mode of being. This turning inward is a comfortable arena for Introverts, while it is a more alien, uncomfortable one for many Extraverts.

Though painful and somewhat alien, new and welcome awareness often results when Extraverts seek out or find themselves in an Introverted mode. In fact, it is likely that formal meditation techniques are very helpful and adaptive for Extraverts because they encourage entering and remaining in an Introverted mode.

For the Introvert forced to extravert while in the grip of the inferior function, the discomfort and sense of losing one's bearings can be equally disruptive. The Introvert is less able to keep things inside or reflect in the privacy of his or her own mind. Rather, what would ordinarily stay inside and safe from external scrutiny is inevitably blurted out, acted on, or shared (often with inappropriate people). This can lead to fear of public humiliation. Operating in the Extraverted world for any length of time can feel alien and disconcerting to many Introverts. On the other hand, extraverting can stimulate many satisfying and positive experiences for Introverts, which are similar to those experienced by Extraverts when they achieve greater comfort while introverting.

One Introvert said that when he becomes stressed, he compulsively seeks people out, engages them in long conversations, or gets involved in various activities with them. Often this leads him to new insights into himself or recognition that things he habitually rejected as irrelevant or unimportant to him were quite the opposite. Often Introverts in their teens or early twenties report enjoying the release from social inhibitions that being in the grip encourages. Similar benefits of being forced into the opposite attitude are reported by Extraverts forced into Introversion. They are able to recognize their own inner richness and experience an unfamiliar pleasure in solitude.

Roles of the Tertiary and Auxiliary Functions

What accounts for the termination of an episode of the inferior function and the subsequent return of equilibrium? Does it require actual restoration of balance and correction of one-sidedness—that is, does some message have to be received? People report that the length of time they may spend in the grip of their inferior function varies a great deal—from minutes to weeks or even longer.

Remember that an inferior function experience creates something like chaos in a personality, shifting the influence of each typological element, energizing aspects that usually have little energy, putting aside usually reliable and trustworthy parts of ourselves. When such an episode has run its course or served its purpose, we somehow return to "normal" and no longer feel and seem "beside ourselves."

Exactly how this happens is difficult to observe precisely, but the process or mechanism whereby equilibrium is achieved seems to occur through constellation, or activation, of the tertiary function and, even more noticeably, the auxiliary function. This process enables the gradual reestablishment of trust and confidence in oneself. The grip of the inferior function diminishes first through activation of the tertiary function, then through increased energy and attention to the auxiliary function, and finally through reexperiencing the confidence, competence, and centeredness of one's dominant function.

Sometimes we can be astute and observant enough to see this kind of progression from tertiary to auxiliary and, finally, to dominant function. Often, however, we are not able to capture the movement to the tertiary but do notice the auxiliary function coming back into play and forming a helpful bridge or link to the dominant form of our personality. With the dominant and auxiliary functions restored to their former ascendance, our essential character structure is back in control and able to function effectively.

Importance of the Inferior Function in Midlife

Victor Hugo (1988) wrote that "forty is the old age of youth; fifty the youth of old age." Hugo's observation underscores the importance of our forties—and with a steadily increasing life expectancy, our fifties—as transitional decades often aptly distinguished by a "midlife crisis." As a period of transformation, it can be both enhancing and destructive in causing people to come to terms with the neglected aspects of their psyche. The often frequent eruptions of the inferior function that occur during midlife can provide the crucial awareness necessary for our transition from the follies of youth to the wise acceptance of old age.

We spend the first half of our lives establishing our identity in two important areas: love and work. We appropriately need awareness, control, and consciousness to succeed in these two worlds. Thus, competence at this point in our lives is best achieved by using our most conscious and developed processes, our dominant and auxiliary functions.

Assuming adequate success in the tasks of the first half of life, the goal of midlife and beyond is completion of one's personality. We strive to become the best and most complete version of ourselves possible. So, in the natural scheme of things and without conscious effort, we find the neglected, undeveloped sides of ourselves increasingly compelling. Previously unimportant and uninteresting things become appealing in ways unimagined during the first half of life.

In typological terms, those things that were unimportant, uninteresting, or unvalued in the first half of life are embodied in the inferior and tertiary functions. Accordingly, people consistently report that, beginning around middle age, they find themselves attracted to pursuits requiring their less-preferred processes. Previously unappealing things become a source of excitement, renewal, and relaxation. Sometimes older or retiring people develop a new career based on a former hobby that may have involved less-preferred processes.

Von Franz (1971) described incorporation of the inferior as follows:

> To the general outline of the inferior function belongs the fact that it is generally slow, in contrast to the superior function. . . . If you think of the turning point of life and the problems of aging and of turning within, then this slowing down of the whole life process by bringing in the inferior function is just the thing which is needed. So the slowness should not be treated with impatience; . . . one should rather accept the fact that in this realm one has to waste time. (p. 8)

However, some older people do not appear to follow this path. They do not mellow as they get older by gradually integrating their tertiary and inferior functions. Rather, this second group of older people become more rigidly committed to their dominant and auxiliary processes, which they use in an exaggerated, extreme manner.

Slowly integrating previously neglected functions furthers the task of completion and individuation. Stubborn adherence to the consciously developed processes appropriate to the tasks of early adulthood seems to impede progress toward that goal. Older people in this position may look like caricatures of their type. Even well-developed perception and judgment can be maladaptive when applied compulsively and exclusively.

People with different personality types show consistent patterns of development within their type. Careful study reveals the influence of their tertiary and inferior functions as they contribute to completion of personality and the individuation process. However, as is true in so many arenas, the ways in which different types approach the task of integrating formerly ignored aspects of themselves can differ greatly. Some, most notably those who prefer Intuition and a Perceiving attitude (NP types), enjoy the natural unfolding of their midlife development. They have little desire to actively direct it, preferring instead to experience the surprise associated with discovering yet another new aspect of themselves. Others, often (but by no means always) those who prefer Sensing and a Judging attitude (SJ types), may take an active part in developing previously neglected parts of themselves. Their tendency to seek out information and methods for stimulating their own midlife development is characteristic of their predominantly experiential and pragmatic approach to life tasks.

A Caveat About Midlife Development

The natural course of type development that was just described assumes that an individual has been free to devote the first half of life to living in his or her particular dominant and auxiliary functions. But suppose that for one or another reason a person was forced to operate out of the tertiary and inferior functions in the first half of life—choosing a life partner and career from these perspectives rather than to satisfy the goals of naturally preferred functions? What is the task of the second half of life for this person?

For people with such a course of development, the transformative energy available at midlife can offer the opportunity to engage and live out their dominant and auxiliary functions, perhaps for the first time in their lives. In such a scenario, midlife changes in career or relationship represent an energizing of natural, preferred processes—a chance to allow the less natural, nonpreferred tertiary and auxiliary functions to recede into the background so that the dominant and auxiliary functions can become fully engaged. Given this alternative scenario of midlife development, it is wise to be cautious about making too facile an interpretation of someone else's "midlife crisis."

THE HIDDEN

PERSONALITY

IN ACTION

5

Approaching the Hidden
Personality of the Sixteen Types

THIS CHAPTER PROVIDES brief descriptions of the areas covered in Chapters 6 through 13, each of which is devoted to one of the dominant types. Each of these eight chapters presents a dominant function with its preferred attitude and two opposite auxiliary and tertiary functions. Because this orientation chapter gives the rationale for the subsections in the type chapters, it is important that you read it before you proceed to any of the next eight chapters.

Each chapter on the dominant functions covers six topics relevant to the inferior function. The brief discussions of these areas in this chapter summarize and expand on the discussions in Chapter 4.

The Dominant Function Versus the Inferior Function

This section contrasts effective use of the dominant function of the type in question with effective use of the dominant function of the opposite type (e.g., Extraverted Thinking types are compared with Introverted Feeling types). This information is divided into two subsections: "Important Features of the Dominant Function" and "Important Features of the Opposite Type's Dominant Function."

Important Features of the Dominant Function

A brief type description highlights qualities of the dominant function that are important to understanding aspects of its inferior manifestations. It also helps us contrast the typical behavior of people of that type with their behavior when in the grip of the inferior function for either brief or extended periods.

The Dominant Function at Work

A significant portion of a person's life is spent working either outside or inside the home. As we shall see, characteristics of a type's dominant function are reflected in what kinds of work people of that type choose and what energizes them in work situations.

The two different auxiliary functions are often important in the differences reported in energizing and stressful work attributes, and these differences are noted in this section. In addition, where there were sufficient data to suggest reliable observations, gender differences observed for people of the same type are also mentioned.

Important Features of the Opposite Type's Dominant Function

Each of the next eight chapters lists three qualities associated with the dominant function of the opposite type that are relevant to a prediction of its form as an inferior function. These qualities will alert you to later descriptions of these same features in their inferior form. For example, the three qualities of dominant Introverted Feeling are listed in the chapter that presents Extraverted Thinking types. Also included are suggestions for reviewing the characteristics of people with the dominant function of the opposite type and references to other relevant discussions in this book. This review provides the background needed to explore the various ways in which the inferior function is expressed for the types in question.

Everyday Manifestations of the Inferior Function

The influence of the inferior function can be seen in two areas of everyday behavior: (1) what people are particularly sensitive about and (2) what people typically project onto others. It can also provide a welcome break from our everyday behavior when expressed through interests and hobbies.

Typical Sensitivities and Projections

Our least-preferred, or inferior, process influences us even when we are not in its grip. This section centers on the two ways in which our inferior function affects our everyday lives.

Typical Sensitivities We tend to lack confidence in areas in which we are inexperienced. When we are forced to use our least-developed function or other neglected parts of ourselves, we are likely to feel uncomfortable, insecure, nervous, and vulnerable. Von Franz (1971) made the observation that

> people are very easily influenced when it is a question of their inferior function. Since it is in the unconscious, they can easily be made uncertain of their position, whereas in the realm of their superior function they generally know how to act when attacked. . . . As soon as you feel strong you are quite willing to discuss things or to change your attitude, but where you feel inferior you get fanatical and touchy and are easily influenced. The expression on a friend's face can affect the feeling of a thinking type because his feeling is unconscious and therefore open to influence. (p. 53)

The particular sensitivities of each type are consistent and predictable. They are often evident in people's descriptions of the more stressful aspects of their work lives. A description of these sensitivities is included in each of the next eight chapters.

Typical Projections Each type projects the inferior function in characteristic ways. Remember that projection involves attributing to others our own unacknowledged and unconscious qualities. Because inferior function episodes often involve projection, this information is helpful in becoming aware of one's own and others' impending "altered states." This section identifies typical projections of the type being described.

Expression Through Interests and Hobbies

Exercising an unfamiliar process can be relaxing and enjoyable, especially when one's competence is not an issue of concern. If we need a break from using our dominant and auxiliary functions, a hobby using our inferior or tertiary function may be just the right thing. This section identifies some of the ways people of each type engage their inferior and tertiary functions for rest, relaxation, and recreation.

Eruptions of the Inferior Function

The two subsections included here introduce the type-related circumstances that tend to provoke inferior function reactions and the form in which the inferior function of the type is manifested.

Typical Provocations or Triggers

Chapter 4 described the general conditions for eruption of the inferior function for all types. This section deals with some typical type-related situations, events, or contexts that provoke or trigger the experience. As we might expect, these often involve having to use one's less-preferred processes or being around people or in situations where those processes predominate. When such conditions persist over long periods, predictable chronic inferior function responses are likely to be observed.

Triggers and Stressors at Work

Not surprisingly, the particular work-related stressors each type mentions often require using less-preferred functions with little opportunity to engage preferred processes. The qualities of their inferior function are often evident in what people of a particular type find especially provoking and stressful at work.

Because ongoing and pervasive work stress has become endemic the world over, the workplace provides a convenient and useful laboratory for studying the ways in which the inferior function is triggered for different types at work as well as for observing the effects of chronic stress on the everyday functioning of healthy personalities. In this section, the influence of the two different auxiliary functions is mentioned, and where there were sufficient data to suggest reliable observations, gender differences in provocations and stress reactions for people of the same type are also mentioned.

The Form of the Inferior Function

Chapter 3 described each inferior function as having a predictable form. The form of the inferior function roughly corresponds to the qualities associated with that function when it is a dominant function—but with a negative, primitive, and undifferentiated cast to it. Regardless of whether an episode is brief, stimulated by short-term stress, or chronic and pervasive, in response to long-term stress, the form in which an inferior function is expressed encompasses the same arena of out-of-character qualities.

To help you understand the forms of each inferior function, the three salient qualities listed under "Important Features of the Opposite Type" are listed again in this section, but in their negative, inferior, form. Because the tertiary function is usually activated along with the inferior function, relevant tertiary characteristics are also identified. A table then compares the three features in their dominant and inferior forms. This table is followed by descriptions and brief examples of each of the three forms of the inferior function.

Lengthy Episodes in the Grip

Short-term grip episodes are less intrusive and distressing because individuals "return to themselves" relatively quickly. They and others typically recognize the "aberration" as a temporary occurrence. This section examines what happens when stress continues over long periods with little or no respite. This may very well be the case for those who experience chronic illness or pain or are caregivers to chronically ill people, and for anyone who experiences long-term unemployment, homelessness, or the like. Any unremitting drain on one's energy, especially if one is forced to use less-preferred functions and attitudes to survive, is likely to keep a person in a chronic grip state.

A person in such circumstances may not notice the gradual alteration in his or her personality. Others may assume that the person's "grip" behavior is natural and habitual—especially if they have never known the chronically stressed person in nonstressful circumstances. This is likely to be true of caregivers in hospitals or nursing homes, for example, or of colleagues in high-stress work settings.

Grip Experiences

This section consists of stories about people's experiences of their inferior function. Some of the stories describe relatively brief episodes, while others explore responses to long-term stress related to either work situations or other kinds of chronic stressors. In addition to striking variations in their essential nature, the examples provided by the eight dominant types reveal some basic type differences. These influence the style, length, and number of different elements that appear in their stories. For this reason, the number of stories needed to illustrate various aspects of different inferior functions varies from chapter to chapter. Some chapter stories are brief and focus primarily on one expression of the inferior. Others are more complex, illustrating the interactions of all three salient features in one experience.

Where the information was available, the individual's assessment of the importance of the experience in his or her life is included. Often, however, the value of inferior function episodes is not immediately apparent. For some people, the experiences are too unpleasant and painful to think about. For others, such awareness comes later, sometimes in conjunction with other similar episodes. For still others, a lengthy period of being in the grip can stimulate significant new awareness and life-changing decisions.

Return of Equilibrium

An inferior function experience cannot fulfill its self-regulating purpose if we deny it, reject it, or try to get rid of it. Yet we often resort to such "solutions" because we feel uncomfortable, anxious, embarrassed, or perplexed by our out-of-character behavior. However, the dynamics of the inferior function suggest that most episodes come to an end naturally, regardless of whether we profit from them. Once the inferior function is constellated, a natural progression occurs that ends in a return to our normal equilibrium.

This progression often engages first the tertiary, then the auxiliary, and finally the dominant function. Moderately persistent stress, as often occurs in the workplace, seems to follow such a progression. However, where a person is chronically in the grip, a natural progression out of it may not occur. Often a crisis forces the individual to recognize that he or she has lost touch with the central qualities of his or her dominant and auxiliary functions. Only then may the person reassess the situation and find effective ways of regaining equilibrium.

People who have the same inferior function report consistencies in how their return to equilibrium occurs. This section describes typical ways people extricate from their out-of-character selves, as well as the helpful or detrimental things others may do to contribute to their return to equilibrium. Sometimes the influence of the different tertiary and auxiliary functions is notable as people come back to being themselves; such observations are mentioned in this section. Included also is a discussion of how different types try to deal with the kind of chronic and pervasive stress that may lead to lengthier experiences in the grip

Expressions in Midlife

Jung put a heavy emphasis on the developmental tasks associated with the second half of life. Remember that the chief task of adulthood is to establish oneself in work or career and in significant relationships. We therefore rely heavily on our dominant and auxiliary functions during our young adult and adult years. Our later years are accompanied by a natural movement toward completion, which occurs through attention to and gradual integration of our tertiary and inferior functions.

Whether the ideal and the real are congruent, however, varies widely among older people. As described in Chapter 4, some aging individuals appear to become stuck in their type, with increasing exaggeration and rigidity of their dominant and auxiliary functions accompanied by strong resistance to even minimum inclusion of their tertiary and inferior functions.

Older people whose natural development permits incorporation of previously neglected functions seem to mellow in the expression of their personalities. Previously ignored aspects of life are added; formerly crucial goals and behaviors become less compelling. The subordinate tertiary and inferior processes are thus added to the personality; they do not replace or in any way supersede the developed dominant and auxiliary processes.

This section describes different ways of responding to the aging period by individuals of that type.

Knowledge from Grip Experiences

Although new awareness from grip experiences can take some time to integrate, people of each type tend to agree on the general enhancing effects of repeated experiences of this kind. This section briefly summarizes the new knowledge gained by individuals of that type.

Summary

The last section of each chapter gives a brief synopsis of the provocations, triggers, and stressors that push people into the grip, the forms in which the inferior function is likely to appear, how equilibrium is regained by using approaches that are effective for the type, and the kinds of new information typically acquired through grip experiences. A table summarizes these features.

Some Cautions and Caveats

Here are a few cautions and caveats to keep in mind when reading the next eight chapters, especially the ones that discuss your own type and the types of people closest to you.

"I Don't Relate to Any of These!"

Some people don't find themselves in the description of their inferior function, or, for that matter, in any of the eight inferior functions. This is often the case with young people whose type differentiation and development are still in process. Sometimes people who don't identify with any inferior function are well-functioning people for whom psychological type is not the most helpful or salient set of personality descriptors. Others are individuals with psychological difficulties that inhibit recognition and expression of their type. For such people, type is but one aspect of personality that remains unclear and undifferentiated. (For a discussion of this and related issues, see N. L. Quenk, 1984, 1985b, 2000a; A. T. Quenk, 1985; and Myers et al., 1998.)

Some people clearly identify with one of the sixteen types but don't experience any of the inferior functions with notable frequency or intensity. Again, their particular mode of adaptation or developmental path may be outside this system of explanation. Others may experience the identified inferior function but in an unusual manner. They may not recognize their expression of the inferior in the descriptions provided. All of these variations on the theme add to an already rich diversity of individual differences among human beings.

"I Experience All of Them!"

Some people find themselves well described by two or more inferior functions that are manifested either together or equally frequently. There are several possible explanations for this. For one thing, it is fairly common to experience negative expressions of one's tertiary function as well as one's inferior function, often at the same time. And those people whose dominant and inferior functions are not well differentiated (i.e., where both use an equal share of the available energy) may concurrently or alternately experience both as inferior functions. (For a discussion of the latter, see N. L. Quenk, 1985a.)

Bear in mind also that the inferior function is the doorway to the unconscious and all its contents. Once the door is opened, a wide variety of unpleasant, undesirable, and ignored "stuff" may emerge. This is one major source of the confusion, distress, and distraction we experience when we are not ourselves. We are faced with all kinds of repressed, neglected, and otherwise unfamiliar parts of ourselves.

You may find in reading about your type that some things are very true for you, while others simply don't apply. This is to be expected when we are describing individuality. It is the same with general type descriptions. Some aspects of our type are simply more salient than others.

Reality and the Inferior Function

There is no necessary relationship between being in the grip of your inferior function and the reality of your perceptions or judgments at the time. The two are often independent of each other. So if you are in the grip of an inferior function whose form focuses on incompetence, the particular incompetence you notice may actually be there! You or some other person may in fact have made a mistake or performed some task in an inadequate manner.

It is in the reaction to the error that the operation of the inferior function can be identified. We will see an overreaction, a single-minded focus, a high level of emotion, and a readiness to generalize and expand single incidents into global or eternal "truths." When these kinds of responses occur, we are likely to be experiencing or witnessing the state of being "beside oneself."

The reality of other kinds of responses may be somewhat different, however. An example is a situation in which a headache triggers obsessive concern that one has a brain tumor. The headache is real; the conclusion regarding the brain tumor is likely to be unfounded. However, there may be a different "truth" embodied in this kind of inferior function manifestation. Perhaps the person's readiness to imagine a life-threatening illness portends an underlying distress or despair about a current life situation. An astute person might examine the possible roots of the overreaction and then reassess important relationships, career goals, or the like.

Reading the Next Eight Chapters

Many readers will start with the chapter about their own type. Others may read the chapters in the order in which they appear, beginning with Extraverted Thinking types and ending with Extraverted Intuitive types. Whichever method you choose, ideally your reading will be satisfying and enlightening and greatly increase your understanding of yourself and others.

6

Extraverted Thinking Types

ESTJ and ENTJ

<u>BASIC TYPE DYNAMICS</u>

DOMINANT EXTRAVERTED THINKING

AUXILIARY INTROVERTED SENSING OR INTUITION

TERTIARY INTUITION OR SENSING

INFERIOR INTROVERTED FEELING

Extraverted Thinking Versus Introverted Feeling

THIS CHAPTER EXAMINES the way effective Extraverted Thinking types experience their inferior function and the temporary transformation they make into ineffective, inferior Introverted Feeling types when they are either briefly or chronically "in the grip." A review of the characteristics of Extraverted Thinking and Introverted Feeling will be helpful to our discussion.

Important Features of Dominant Extraverted Thinking

Extraverted Thinking types enjoy making decisions. They like to be in control of things and value efficient and effective decision making. They are comfortable in leadership positions and readily accept responsibility for making things happen. They want things to be logical, so they require rationality in most situations. They expect goals to be reached in a competent manner and they want to be recognized for their accomplishments. Being respected is therefore of greater importance to them than being liked.

Critiquing comes naturally to them, and they often solicit constructive criticism of their work from trusted colleagues. However, they do not appreciate critical comments about their personal qualities, critiques that are personal attacks on their competence or integrity, or unsolicited criticism by people they don't know or respect. They are seen by others and see themselves as having rigorous standards that typically take precedence over both their own and others' personal needs. Their communication style is honest, direct, and to the point, and they prefer others to be similarly candid with them.

With their dominant focus on truth, accuracy, and productivity, Extraverted Thinking types can be seen as one-sided in their commitment to work. The high value ESTJs and ENTJs place on critical analysis, competence, and forthright communication may foster a perception that they don't care about people. Others are therefore often surprised to discover that Extraverted Thinking types are typically quite devoted to family and friends. They energetically strive to ensure the well-being and happiness of their loved ones.

Whether at work or at home, ESTJs and ENTJs are adept at dealing with crisis situations that don't engage their inferior Introverted Feeling. They readily take charge, organize people for effective action, and communicate a sense of calm, security, and confidence.

Extraverted Thinking Types at Work

Extraverted Thinking types love working, and competence at work is a central aspect of their self-image, especially in organizational settings. They are energized by events, situations, and people that encourage them to take leadership positions. In general, Extraverted Thinking types welcome the challenges and opportunities for achievement that accompany their work lives, and ENTJs in particular report little work-related stress as compared to other types. Though both of these types generally seem to enjoy their work lives and report fewer dissatisfactions than other types, ENTJs appear to be more satisfied with more work characteristics than any other type.

Consistent with their auxiliary Intuition, ENTJs enjoy variety, complexity, ingenuity, cleverness, and having open communication in their environment. For one ENTJ woman, "creativity, challenge, autonomy, clear goals, consistent and congruent leadership, variety, and an opportunity to shine" were listed as the most energizing work characteristics. An ESTJ who is an independent consultant said, "I love organizing my day and my work with lists. I like to handle some routine administrative work where I can sort through details quickly. I enjoy presenting material in very clear ways with lots of examples. I like helping people move to action."

Important Features of Dominant Introverted Feeling

The qualities associated with Introverted Feeling that are relevant to our discussion of its form as an inferior function are an emphasis on

- Inner harmony
- Economy of emotional expression
- Acceptance of feeling as nonlogical

For a detailed description of dominant Introverted Feeling, read the beginning of Chapter 7, "Introverted Feeling Types: ISFP and INFP," and the type descriptions for ISFP and INFP that appear in Appendix A. This will provide the background needed to explore the various ways inferior Introverted Feeling is expressed in ESTJs and ENTJs.

The Everyday Introverted Feeling of Extraverted Thinking Types

The inferior function affects Extraverted Thinking types in several different ways. These include everyday sensitivities, projections, and ways of relaxing, as well as the dramatic manifestations that can be seen when the inferior erupts and a full-blown episode occurs or when an ESTJ or ENTJ is chronically in the grip because of long-term stress.

Typical Sensitivities and Projections

When Feeling types talk about things they care about (their Feeling values), an expression of emotion may accompany their expression of the values involved. For Introverted Feeling types, the emotion may be somewhat muted, but it is still a way of emphasizing the importance of whatever is being discussed. Extraverted Thinking types may not differentiate between Feeling as a judging process and a Feeling type's use of emotion. They may confuse using Feeling for rational decision making with sentimentality and emotionality. This occurs because they experience their own Introverted Feeling as sentimental and emotional—as *inferior* Introverted Feeling. Being in the presence of Feeling values and emotion brings ESTJs and ENTJs uncomfortably close to their own unconscious Feeling and can disrupt or hamper their ability to be effective as themselves, i.e., as Extraverted Thinking types.

When experiencing the all-or-none quality of a largely unconscious process, ESTJs and ENTJs may express seemingly excessive emotion in response to sad movies or true stories about pain and suffering. "I get all choked up by those really sentimental greeting cards," said one ENTJ, "and it feels out of control, overly sentimental, and illogical. I want sad stories to have a happy ending, even if it isn't true to life."

Extraverted Thinking types may see Feeling types as overly sensitive to criticism and as needing frequent reassurance. They may be dubious about the effectiveness of these people, fearing that their judgment may be faulty or that their emotions will inappropriately influence their decisions—again confusing rational Feeling judgment with emotion. Since Extraverted Thinking types distrust their own judgment when emotion rules them, they assume the same unreliability is true for dominant Feeling types.

ESTJs and ENTJs report being quite uncomfortable with their own and others' Feeling judgment. "It seems mushy and chaotic and scary, not crisp and precise like thinking," said one ENTJ. An ESTJ described her uneasiness about expressing appreciation or complimenting others verbally: "I never know how much is appropriate. It always feels gushy." She found writing thank-you notes to be much more satisfying both personally and to the recipients, who recognized the genuine depth of her feelings.

Because their opposites, Introverted Feeling types, are so hard to "read," Extraverted Thinking types may judge Extraverted Feeling types, who readily express their dominant Feeling, more harshly than they do Introverted Feeling types. Introverted Feeling types are more muted in their expression of Feeling. ESTJs and ENTJs tend to see people who readily express Feeling as excessive, phony, and manipulative. When they are around an Introverted Feeling type, they may feel off-balance, needing to "walk on eggshells," and afraid of being misunderstood or of unintentionally offending the person. But more often they may ignore Introverted Feeling types because they don't express themselves directly. As we will see, the sensitivities of Extraverted Thinking types toward both of the dominant Feeling types (Extraverted Feeling types and Introverted Feeling types) are reflected in the expression of their own inferior Feeling.

Expression Through Interests and Hobbies

The Introverted Feeling values of Extraverted Thinking types may be seen in their intense passion for a particular cause. This may take the form of tireless devotion to a civic cause such as prevention of child abuse, aid to the homeless, or some church or community activity. The Extraverted Thinking type is likely to contribute to the chosen arena by doing what he or she loves most—that is, providing effective leadership and constructive critical judgment.

A similar expression may occur in the religious and spiritual realm, or in the kind of music, art, and literature the person prefers. These areas may play to his or her more romantic, dramatic, and emotive sensibilities, giving free rein to his or her other, typically unexpressed, side. Here again, ESTJs and ENTJs may not only gain aesthetic pleasure but also often contribute time and energy to the organizations that are affiliated with the music, art, and literature. They may chair a philanthropic board, manage fund-raising projects, and the like. Sometimes their contribution makes use of the special talents of their dominant function and also engages their inferior Feeling function in a gratifying way. Often the most meaningful hobbies serve this kind of dual purpose. As one ESTJ explained, "The volunteer work itself is very enjoyable. I like being able to contribute what I know. But the sense of community, the connectedness with others on something larger than any one of us, is even more important."

Like other Extraverted types, Extraverted Thinking types can find excessive solitary time unpleasant. One ENTJ reported that she tends to feel sad and lonely when she spends too much time alone. Her hobbies of sewing, quilting, and other craft activities, which activate her tertiary Sensing, seem to alleviate her negative reactions to being alone. For her, tertiary Sensing may moderate the negativity of inferior Introverted Feeling.

Many Extraverted Thinking types report that they don't have outside interests and hobbies, that their work is their passion, and that working provides them with their greatest pleasure. The husband of one ESTJ worried that his wife might never retire. The only way he could get her to go on vacation was by planning such exciting trips that she couldn't possibly refuse to participate in them.

In spite of this, however, some Extraverted Thinking types identify specific activities or times when things other than work hold a special appeal. One ENTJ reported that she sometimes gives herself permission to be entirely unrestrained, often when she is dancing. She plans to be spontaneous when she dances and does so with great expression and abandon.

Eruptions of Inferior Introverted Feeling

When one or more of the preconditions for an eruption of the inferior function are present, Introverted Feeling appears in its more exaggerated and disruptive form. In addition to the general conditions described in Chapter 4, Extraverted Thinking types are vulnerable to the type-specific factors described below.

Typical Provocations or Triggers

Like their dominant Introverted Thinking counterparts, Extraverted Thinking types tend to be quite selective in their choice of areas in which to invest their Feeling. They are intensely passionate about only a few things, so when one of their cherished values is disregarded, ignored, or unappreciated, their inferior Feeling is likely to be constellated.

One ESTJ who felt type was very useful in understanding people purposely omitted his type on his evaluation of a type conference, only to be told that his evaluation would not be counted unless his type was specified on it. He had not indicated his type because he felt the reputation ESTJs have for being "critical" had led to his opinions being ignored in the past. He lashed out at the evaluator and was immediately embarrassed. Later, in recounting the incident to friends, he explained that he felt discounted, dismissed, and ignored: "It's as if they were telling me that my strong commitments were worthless simply because of my type." An ENTJ said that his inferior function can be provoked "when someone misinterprets my good intent as having an evil or a selfish motive."

Accusations of coldness and lack of concern for others can serve as a trigger for the inferior function, as can fears of having been excessively harsh with someone. A spouse bursting into tears or other expressions of strong emotion from people they care about can also set the stage for an eruption of Extraverted Thinking types' inferior Introverted Feeling. An ENTJ woman cited having "been bossy and dictatorial and [feeling] I hurt someone in the process," and another mentioned "being told that I offended someone or hurt their feelings" as provocations to their inferior function.

Triggers and Stressors at Work

ESTJs and ENTJs want to be challenged at work, but not by uncooperative, controlling, difficult people. These kinds of people create great stress at work for both ESTJs and ENTJs. ESTJs find lack of control in the workplace and an overwhelming workload stressful as well. They want their roles and responsibilities to be clearly defined, and they prefer tangible results to intangible ones. An ESTJ woman said she found it stressful "when procedures keep changing and when there are projects without defined criteria and benchmarks."

Both ESTJs and ENTJs find dealing with incompetence, illogical behavior, and ill-defined criteria to be stressful work conditions. ENTJs in particular are stressed by criticism that is not constructive and by unfairness to themselves and others. For one ESTJ, what is stressful is "when I'm dealing with incompetence. When nothing seems to be getting completed. When people are being uncooperative and unhelpful."

Events, situations, and people that are directly or indirectly connected to Introverted Feeling also serve as stressors for Extraverted Thinking types. These include being around people who are expressing their Feeling values as well as being around strong emotion, especially when it seems irrelevant to the situation at hand. "Doing too much Feeling stuff gets in the way of the task," said an ENTJ. "Dealing with petty emotional problems at work is really stressful," said another.

Their opposites, dominant Introverted Feeling types, enjoy a work environment that permits flexibility and change, in which performance criteria are geared to individual needs and goals. Extraverted Thinking types, however, find that flexibility and shifting criteria interfere with their ability to maintain control of their time and achieve goals efficiently. What an ISFP or INFP may consider an interesting diversion that may stimulate new information and worthwhile ideas may be an unwelcome distraction for an ESTJ or ENTJ. An Introverted Feeling type's ideal work environment can be an Extraverted Thinking type's "nightmare" work environment. As we shall see in the next chapter, the same holds true for an Introverted Feeling type in an Extraverted Thinking type's ideal work environment.

In a work situation in which the particular triggers and stressors for Extraverted Thinking types continue over long periods, ESTJs and ENTJs may respond quickly and intensely to the triggers described here. This increases the likelihood that their subsequent demonstrations of "grip" behavior will be frequent and pervasive. When persistent stress causes them to be chronically in the grip of inferior Introverted Feeling, they are likely to lose touch with their natural competence and become increasingly self-doubting, ineffective, and depressed.

The Form of the Inferior Function

One of the manifestations of any inferior function is diminished effectiveness in the use of the developed dominant function. For Extraverted Thinking types, there may be a loss of ability to think logically and take effective action, or an inability to recognize the relevance of logic in a situation. One ESTJ said, "I bounce from task to task with no results. I have internal arguments with myself, but I can't come to any conclusion." And an ENTJ observed, "The feeling that I am unappreciated becomes the central thing, and I can't consider anything else." An ENTJ said that she "becomes disorganized and loses things. I'm late to meetings and miss deadlines, and I focus on nonpriority activities and tasks. I procrastinate and do only what is due immediately."

Others report being unable to think, having tunnel vision, and being easily fatigued at work. What they normally do very easily requires great effort. An ESTJ described being unable to organize the structure for a work assignment. An ENTJ felt powerless to influence future events significantly. Another reported that, when under great stress, he would lose the capacity for verbal expression and would have difficulty getting his words out. In general, there is an uncharacteristic reduction in productive work accompanied by a feeling of failure.

In the initial stages of the process, ESTJs may lose access to their auxiliary Sensing, while ENTJs may lose access to their auxiliary Intuition. They seem to function only "from the neck up," as one ENTJ described it, operating entirely out of their heads. This results in an exaggeration of their Thinking, which they and others experience as the excesses of their natural approach. It is an example of how a dominant process operates without the balancing effects of the auxiliary. As dominant and auxiliary functions continue to recede into the background, the qualities of inferior Introverted Feeling become manifested in hypersensitivity to inner states, outbursts of emotion, and a fear of feeling. For ESTJs, tertiary Intuition appears in the form of negative possibilities, and ENTJs' tertiary Sensing emerges in the form of undeniable facts—both serving to confirm their inner turmoil and fears of being unappreciated and unworthy. The comparison between dominant and inferior Introverted Feeling is shown in Table 2.

Von Franz (1971) captures all three aspects of inferior Introverted Feeling (hypersensitivity to inner states, outbursts of emotion, and fear of feeling) in the following statement, which also describes the all-or-none, often one-sided expression of inferior Introverted Feeling in Extraverted Thinking types:

Table 2 Dominant and Inferior Expressions of Introverted Feeling

As Dominant Function of ISFPs and INFPs	As Inferior Function of ESTJs and ENTJs
• Inner harmony	• Hypersensitivity to inner states
• Economy of emotional expression	• Outbursts of emotion
• Acceptance of feeling as nonlogical	• Fear of feeling

The hidden introverted feeling of the extraverted thinking type establishes strong invisible loyalties. Such people are among the most faithful of all friends, even though they may only write at Christmas. They are absolutely faithful in their feelings, but one has to move towards it to get to know of its existence. . . . [But] unconscious and undeveloped feeling is barbaric and absolute, and therefore sometimes hidden destructive fanaticism suddenly bursts out of the extraverted thinking type. (p. 40)

Hypersensitivity to Inner States   Effective dominant Introverted Feeling types use a finely developed awareness of their inner values as a reliable guide for judging themselves and others. In the grip of inferior Introverted Feeling, Extraverted Thinking types become hypersensitive to their own and others' emotions, often misinterpreting comments from others as personal criticism. In their dominant approach, they typically interpret objectively offered criticism by respected colleagues as an appropriate means to promote excellence. In the grip of their inferior Introverted Feeling, they may easily take offense and overreact to such criticism. Unaware of the Extraverted Thinking person's vulnerable "altered" condition, however, colleagues, family members, and friends may communicate criticism as directly as usual. Even mild negative comments may provoke hurt feelings when the Extraverted Thinking type is in this state. ESTJs and ENTJs report having difficulty acknowledging, even to themselves, but particularly to the person who has helped bring about the situation, that their feelings have been hurt. They may lash out at others instead, as the examples below illustrate.

"I feel that I am being criticized unfairly," said an ESTJ. "I blame others for my own faults and find fault with others over nothing. I become demanding because I am in a panic about possibly missing deadlines. I watch the clock. I think lots of negative thoughts, put myself down, and feel that others dislike and reject me. My self-esteem about my abilities gets lower and lower." Note the illogical progression of his thoughts.

"I think I'm pretty confident about my abilities as a trainer," said an ENTJ. "But when I've worked very hard preparing for a training session and am especially tired out, I am plagued with the thought that the trainees don't like me, that they like my colleagues better, especially if the colleague I'm teaching with is a Feeling type."

Another ENTJ described "feeling like a victim—persecuted, unappreciated, and used. I don't see things clearly and I can't seem to think.

I take things personally and am hypersensitive. I will say something without thinking, then become defensive and feel threatened."

An ESTJ made this observation: "I find myself taking a martyr role, alone and unloved, totally unappreciated. Then I shut down." An ENTJ described being "particularly sensitive to any signs of being excluded from important roles. When that happens, I feel that my contributions are not being valued." And another ENTJ described "feeling isolated or excluded and having a sense that people don't respect me, especially people Irespect."

In a variation on this theme, some ESTJs and ENTJs describe situations in which they effectively apply their usual action-oriented, logical problem solving. But later (perhaps even years later), if they are in a vulnerable state, they will recall a specific incident and beat themselves up for not being conscious of other people's feelings. One ESTJ recalled thinking, "Why did I say that to Ellen at that party five years ago? How stupid and insensitive of me!"

Some Extraverted Thinking types are painfully aware of the dilemma they face in dealing with relationship issues within a task-oriented setting. Focusing on others' feelings inhibits their ability to take effective Thinking action, though it prevents negative feedback from others about their lack of caring concern.

Outbursts of Emotion   Effective dominant Introverted Feeling types show an economy of emotional expression. They are typically quite selective and discriminating in revealing their deepest and most cherished values and feelings. Extraverted Thinking types in the grip of inferior Introverted Feeling lack control and discrimination when expressing their inner emotional states. However, their fear of having others witness their rejected, irrational selves strongly motivates them to stay in control if at all possible. They especially worry about losing control in public, particularly at work. Avoiding a public display often results in an even stronger outburst of affect at home, directed at family members, since the emotions have to be released somewhere.

An ENTJ said, "I feel lost and out of control. I know I am not myself, but I can't help it. I don't want company or to be touched. I want to be left alone and I want to escape."

"I will get a headache or shoulder ache and feel really tense. I feel like crying but try to hide it. I hide my feelings inside and push them down, and then become angry, depressed, and withdrawn," recalled an ESTJ.

Both ESTJs and ENTJs report sometimes feeling suddenly tearful for no apparent reason, and crying in private. However, if the worst happens and they lose control, they may explode in public. This may begin as expressions of intense anger about others' incompetence but may quickly evolve into tearful recriminations about a lack of appreciation and recognition.

In recalling one such incident, an ESTJ said, "I am normally not an emotional person; at least I don't show my emotions. I am a very steady person externally. My outburst was quite unlike me." One ESTJ said she is "more emotional and not calm—I'm irritable, can easily snap at people. Another ESTJ woman commented, "I get so emotional I can't stand myself."

As is the case for all the inferior function expressions, anger is a commonly mentioned response for both ESTJs and ENTJs. This is as true for women of these types as it is for men. ESTJ and ENTJ women list "emotionality" as their most frequent grip reaction, and although men of these types mention this much less frequently, they often report episodes of emotionality in describing inferior function experiences.

An ENTJ minister worked hard over a period of five years and saw his church grow from a few hundred to more than a thousand members. Throughout this stressful time he managed all facets of his work calmly and effectively. But one day at a church board meeting, he broke down sobbing, lost all control, and was unable to function in his job. It took him several months to recover completely, during which time his grateful and concerned church officials carried on his work for him.

Extraverted Thinking types may be on shaky ground in situations that call for expressions of feeling. One ESTJ described her difficulty with intimate relationships this way: "I'm normally gregarious and outgoing with people. But if I get into a one-on-one relationship that's significant, especially romantically, I can't express what I feel or what I'm experiencing. Eventually, I blurt out some really exaggerated emotion at exactly the wrong time. I feel childish and silly and don't want to ever do that again."

Fear of Feeling Talking about innermost values, feelings, and concerns is quite difficult even for dominant Introverted Feeling types. Jung (1976a) observed that "the very fact that thoughts can generally be expressed more intelligibly than feelings demands a more than ordinary descriptive or artistic ability before the real wealth of this feeling can be even approximately presented or communicated to the world" (p. 388).

Effective dominant Introverted Feeling types accept the nuances of feeling they experience as natural and welcome evidence of their own inner complexity. But feelings and emotions intruding into the consciousness of an Extraverted Thinking type who is in the grip of inferior Introverted Feeling are experienced as so alien and overwhelming that they are inexpressible. From a Thinking point of view, the eruption of "illogical," uncontrolled, and disorderly feelings is like being at the mercy of strange and overwhelming forces that threaten a person's equilibrium, if not his or her whole existence. As a result, Extraverted Thinking types are rarely able to communicate their distress to others, often maintaining their typical controlled demeanor while fearing that they will lose control of their emotions. In extreme instances, they may be terrified that they are going crazy.

To fend off the feared result, initial attempts involve maintaining cool and detached effectiveness and objectivity. Casual observers will not detect the intense inner battle for control. More careful observation, however, may reveal uncharacteristic silence, withdrawal, moodiness, or flat and depressed affect. Men and women of both types typically report becoming uncharacteristically quiet and withdrawn. An ESTJ described feeling "a swirling in the pit of my stomach and a desperate attempt to figure out why and to define my reaction logically."

Because the Extraverted Thinking type has few resources for communicating what is going on inside, potential helpers may remain largely unaware of any distress, even when the person is in serious trouble. The despair, sense of isolation, and feeling of worthlessness may become so extreme that the person may become severely depressed, sometimes requiring medication or hospitalization. Acquaintances and colleagues may be surprised to learn that such an episode has occurred because until final control is lost, the ESTJ or ENTJ may appear fairly "normal." "I'm calm on the outside, in control, very logical, solve problems, yet it ties me up inside," said an ENTJ. This manifestation of the inferior is an exaggeration of the dominant Introverted Feeling type's "economy of emotional expression."

Two Extraverted Thinking types described their experiences with their inferior functions in these ways after their episodes had run their course:

"I became overly sensitive and tried to cover it with biting sarcasm. My energy was focused inside and I felt shaky. I wanted to be alone. I put on a front of being a strong soldier, but it was really only a protective shell to hide my vulnerability."

"I was different in being very negative. Everything appeared bleak. I was disoriented and aggressive. I talked to myself more. I got emotional (angry or sad, tearful or despondent). In very bad cases, I even contemplated suicide."

Lengthy Episodes in the Grip

The types of episodes described above are experienced by ESTJs or ENTJs as temporary states during which they are vulnerable to the three forms in which their inferior functions are expressed. However, when an Extraverted Thinking type is chronically in the grip of inferior Introverted Feeling, inferior function behavior may become habitual. Both the individual and others are likely to believe that hypersensitivity, negativity, frequent expressions of anger, and emotional outbursts are a part of the natural makeup of the ESTJ or ENTJ. Since the process of becoming chronically in the grip is often gradual, even people who have known the person in a nonstressed state are likely not to notice what, in retrospect, will be recognized as a radical alteration of personality. The Extraverted Thinking type will appear to be a rather exaggerated, poorly developed Introverted Feeling type.

However, there are also occasions when a lengthy time in the grip of inferior Introverted Feeling can stimulate new awareness and positive growth toward completion and individuation. Remember that Jung saw the inferior function as the doorway to the unconscious and an important part of the self-regulating capacity of our psyches. The last story in this chapter illustrates such a situation.

Grip Experiences

The stories included in this section illustrate one or more forms of inferior Introverted Feeling as experienced by ESTJs and ENTJs. These types report that significant or long-lasting experiences of the inferior function are rare. They tend to be reluctant to recognize and acknowledge them unless they appear in an extreme form, and they prefer to interpret them within a logical framework.

"You Won't Have Me to Kick Around Anymore!"

Dr. Wong, an ENTJ university professor, had once again obligated himself to too many professional and civic projects. One of them was conducting an evening seminar for graduate students. Throughout the semester, the students had often complained to him about his overbearing and officious lecture style. They requested a more collegial, participative approach. Dr. Wong listened dispassionately to these requests but did little to accommodate the students.

Finally, in protest, the students boycotted the seminar, and for two weeks in a row no students showed up. Incensed and hurt, Dr. Wong wrote a memo to each student berating each personally for a lack of gratitude for his hard work and what he was giving up to teach, and gross insensitivity to his needs. He further informed them that he was resigning his faculty position because of their vicious attack on him and would no longer be available as a victim of their immature and petty nastiness.

After a week of fuming, during which time he discussed the incident with colleagues, he realized that he had overreacted, wrote a brief note of apology to the students, and reconvened the seminar for the next week. "I learned a lot about the logic of emotion from that episode," he said. "I was really able to understand how the students experienced my style. I realized that they wanted a more collegial relationship because they respected me. We were able to talk directly and honestly to each other at the next seminar, which was probably the best we'd ever had."

"How Do I Love Thee?"

The loss of an important relationship often triggers an inferior function response, as the next story illustrates. After thirty years of marriage, Mike's wife, Alicia, an ISFP, insisted they get a divorce. She told Mike, an ESTJ, that although she loved and admired him, she had also put up with too many years of emotional coldness from him.

Mike became flooded with strong and disturbing feelings. He wrote gushingly sentimental poetry and love letters to Alicia extolling her virtues and the spiritual nature of their relationship. He frequently cried and begged her to change her mind. She became so concerned about his out-of-character reaction that she made an appointment for both of them with a marital therapist to "help him deal with the divorce."

When he had calmed down from his initial extreme reaction, Mike recognized that his responses were quite out of character. But his experience of intense despair and isolation allowed him to empathize with Alicia's reactions to his habitual coldness. The couple reached a mutual decision to divorce but afterward were able to enjoy each other's company and their shared memories for the first time in many years.

"But It's Illogical!"

The roles were somewhat reversed in a similar situation where Rona, an ESTJ, and her INFP husband, Ralph, decided to divorce. Though they enjoyed each other's company, the couple agreed that they did not love each other but rather lived as congenial roommates. They therefore began settling their affairs and arranged to renovate and then sell their house. Ralph dragged his feet, as was his habit. Rona worried that he was having a hard time, but she finally took charge and filed the divorce papers.

To her chagrin, she found herself weeping uncontrollably at unpredictable times both day and night. It took enormous effort not to break down in front of her clients, and she finally took a week off to collect herself and to seek help from a therapist.

"My decision is right, it's logical, it's what we both want. Why is this happening to me?" she wailed. "It's illogical! And what makes it even worse is that Ralph is doing just fine. He's rented an apartment, has bought new furniture, is going out with friends—and here I am a basket case!"

Because Rona was already familiar with type, she welcomed the typological clarification that an explanation of her inferior function provided. She found it reasonable and logical. But she still wept.

"Shouldn't it go away now that I know that people of my type are like this when they're stressed?" she asked.

Rona's intellectual understanding of her reaction was helpful but not sufficient to alleviate her distressing emotional reaction. Her therapist suggested that her out-of-character response to a perfectly logical decision was providing her with an opportunity to grieve the loss of a relationship that was important to her, to acknowledge the depth of her feeling, and to become aware of her very real sadness. Surrendering to these deep feelings was not easy for her, but after about a month she began to feel like herself again and was no longer overcome by emotion.

A Time to Weep

Jenny's company was in great upheaval; it was undergoing a major reorganization and had had several takeover threats from other companies. Employees were worried, demoralized, and increasingly ineffective. As an ESTJ high-level manager, Jenny was responsible for holding everything together, making efficient management decisions, and allaying the fears of everyone who worked under her.

To anyone observing her, Jenny appeared to be dealing with this difficult situation with cool detachment and efficient determination. She was able to calm others down, suggest practical alternatives to people who felt stuck in negativity, and provide support for her management colleagues as they, too, took on the stress of the situation.

But every afternoon when Jenny left work and got into her car to drive home, she burst into tears, weeping throughout the entire half-hour drive. She was unable to control her reaction no matter how hard she tried. After several months, with no hope of significant improvement in her work stress, she acknowledged to herself just how devastated she was by the distress around her. After careful investigation of alternatives, she sought and accepted a position with another company.

Her decision turned out well for her. Reflecting on her reaction to stress at her other job, she said, "I'm being more careful to acknowledge my feelings, at least to myself. Though this job can become pretty stressful, too, I think I can avoid getting into the extreme state I was in before."

"But the Audience Never Knew It!"

Frank, an ENTJ, related the following incident:

> My boss asked me to do a presentation about volunteerism for his church congregation. I would be the guest speaker they often scheduled between the two church services. I was under great time pressure on a number of work tasks and was somewhat uneasy because I perceived this church audience as quite judgmental. But I was secure in my knowledge of my material and wished to accommodate my boss, so I agreed to do it.

About three minutes into my talk, I noticed a man in the third row who many years ago had been extremely critical of me, causing me great distress during a particularly difficult period of my life. I immediately felt out of control internally and feared that I would be unable to go on. But the audience never knew it. I was on automatic pilot for the rest of the time. A friend who was sitting in the front row later told me that the only indication of my discomfort was that I turned beet red for a few minutes, but my voice did not waver at all.

Frank reported being so shaken by his exaggerated emotional reaction that he had to think about the meaning of the man's criticism of him. He discovered a connection between that incident and one that had occurred during his grade school years. This awareness helped Frank understand other puzzling feelings he had experienced over the years. In the end, he was pleased and energized by his insight.

"It Was a Lovely Wedding!"

Margo's son Andy, an INFP, was getting married. Andy and his fiancée, Sue, an ESFP, wanted their large wedding to be very special and meaningful. The couple took great care in selecting invitations, music, decorations, food, guests, and entertainment. Every aspect of their celebration was to have significance. Margo knew that it was particularly important to Andy and Sue that their families, especially their mothers, be fully involved in the event. Sue's family was delighted and readily threw themselves into the spirit of things, but Margo, an ENTJ, was rather beside herself.

"I felt like I was in a foreign country," she said later. "I felt inept, awkward, unable to tell what was important and what I was supposed to do. It was so alien. Almost everyone else seemed excited and in tune with all the preparations, and that made me feel even more out of touch. Yet I very much wanted to please Andy, knowing how important it was to him. Now I understand why I eloped when I got married. It let me avoid dealing with this kind of thing!"

In spite of her discomfort, Margo persevered and the wedding came off beautifully. At the actual event, she was able to relax and enjoy herself and the fruits of everyone's labors. "I'd rather not have to go through this again," she said, "but if I do at least I will have learned from this experience that I'm not as bad at it as I first thought, and it can be fun once you get into it!"

Growth from Grief

An ESTJ in her early fifties offered the following poignant account, which shows how the fruits of a chronic grip experience were incorporated into and expressed through her natural type.

> I've had a number of friends and relatives die over the last few years. I always take the time to write a long letter to their loved ones, describing in great detail the qualities of their loved one, complete with many examples illustrating their wonderful qualities. A number of the recipients have told me how they've read those letters over and over again both to themselves and to their relatives. I can easily recall many details of my relationships with these people—I have a good memory, and I'm happy to put that to use for others.
>
> One close friend died recently of cancer. For the last three and a half years of her life, I was part of a Healing Circle for her—a support group of friends who developed healing "rituals." We met every two to three weeks over the time period. Looking back, it was a big commitment, but it didn't seem so at the time. It just seemed like a natural thing to do. I've helped several Healing Circles get started for others. I began to look for books on similar support groups and found a few, but in language that was way too metaphorical for me and without much structure. I've started to gather stories and put together a "how-to" book for others to start Healing Circles of their own. I'm signed up to teach a class in how to develop your own personal Healing Circle at a nonprofit center for people in health crises.

Return of Equilibrium

Some of the ways people regain the comfort and security of dominant and auxiliary functioning are common to all types, such as a change of scenery or engaging in a physical activity. As described in Chapter 5, however, the auxiliary function and, less obviously, the tertiary function seem to serve as a bridge in the natural process of regaining equilibrium.

Extraverted Thinking types report needing to be left alone for a period of time both during and after an incident occurs. ESTJs say that solitary physical activity and attending to their own needs and comfort is helpful, as is a change of scene and a focus on things outside themselves (Sensing). One ESTJ said, "I must get alone—rationalize what is happening and look at the situation as a problem. I can then readjust my reaction and find the energy for a solution." "I need time to think things through," said an ENTJ. "My close friends can help by encouraging me to vent." An ESTJ said, "I love to complain to people about the situation causing the stress, taking no responsibility for my part in the stress at that point! Just let me vent and agree with me, please!" An ENTJ reported that what helps her most is retreating to her bed with snacks and some light reading. The next morning, after a good night's sleep, she usually has many new ideas (Intuition), which permit her to reconnect with important projects and plans.

Some Extraverted Thinking types need to experience the depths of their Feeling side and talk about their experience with trusted people. If others intrude too aggressively, they will be rebuffed and almost snubbed by the Extraverted Thinking person. But a more gentle approach can encourage the expression of difficult feelings. Silent support, a nonjudgmental approach, and avoidance of direct attacks on the problems at hand are most appreciated. One ESTJ acknowledged that "others should not be logical but should take care of the logical needs in my situation. Be there to listen and understand my feelings, if I am able to express them."

Perhaps more than any other types, many ESTJs and ENTJs report very few or quite minor eruptions of their inferior function, and these tend to last minutes or hours rather than the days and weeks reported by other types. Some explain that their dislike of such experiences encourages them to develop methods of avoidance, since an outburst becomes just one more problem or interference to be dealt with. They therefore use practiced techniques for recognizing and diverting an impending "loss of self." The meaning of the experience, however, may not be lost for them. Early signs of an impending episode remind them of their humanity and vulnerability, and they respond to this by tempering a perhaps overly task-oriented approach to life. One ENTJ was described by his wife as rarely staying in a bad place for very long. His only inferior function manifestation was an occasional irrational emotional outburst that appeared extremely out of character for him. The episodes didn't last long, however. She reported that he took them in stride and did not seem to dwell on them.

At times, the distraction of new input (even something as simple as a phone call from a friend or an interesting article or TV program) can be enough to stimulate a return to equilibrium. However, in more extreme and lengthier episodes of the inferior function, simple distractions are likely to be ineffective.

Perhaps because problem solving is energizing and challenging to them, Extraverted Thinking types often learn to recognize early signs that they are reacting to persistent work stress in an inferior function manner. They then treat their reaction to the stressful situation as a problem that they can solve, using Extraverted Thinking techniques. Their first response, therefore, will likely be to confront the problem head-on and try to solve it. ESTJs and ENTJs of both genders report that reframing the issue that led to their grip reaction is useful, and ENTJ women in particular use an analytical, problem-solving approach to deal with persistent stressors at work.

"I break down larger projects into smaller ones. I concentrate on who can help on the project and thus relieve the stress—and I leave my work assignments at work," said an ENTJ. Another said, "I invest significant energy in planning and communicating with everyone involved and contributing to the work product. I maintain regular communication to offer support, check on progress, remind people, if necessary nag them." An ESTJ stated that the way she handles her work stress is by "meeting deadlines and bringing a project to completion. Others can help by either offering to take over some aspect or else getting out of my way."

One ENTJ said that others can help him by "making it safe to talk about what is going on inside me, letting me know it's perfectly okay, that I'm okay and normal." And an ENTJ student in her early twenties described needing "time to think things through. My close friends can help by encouraging me to vent."

A major stress reducer for ESTJ men is exercise or other physical release, such as participating in a sport, while ENTJ men more often mention engaging in relaxing hobbies or seeking a change of scenery. A regular exercise routine is appealing to ENTJs of both genders as well. Leading techniques for ESTJ women include reframing and problem solving, as well as talking to others about their feelings. ENTJ women also find talking to others helpful but by far prefer a problem-solving, reframing approach to work stress. ESTJ and ENTJ men seem less likely to choose talking to others as a stress reducer.

Expressions in Midlife

As described in Chapters 4 and 5, midlife can take two alternative tracks for people of each type. Some Extraverted Thinking types become "stuck" in their type, perhaps having failed to satisfactorily accomplish the tasks of adulthood. Other ESTJs and ENTJs, however, temper their type through gradual integration of inferior Feeling and tertiary Intuition or Sensing. Like other Extraverted people, ESTJs and ENTJs report a previously unfamiliar pleasure in solitude and silence. However, those who substitute rigidity for growth become inflexible in their insistence on private time. They may organize their lives around invariable routines, becoming irritable and accusatory when unaccustomed events or unexpected people intervene.

Adult children of rigid Extraverted Thinking types get a message that the grandchildren are tolerated but not enjoyed, and that family visits are necessary but unwelcome burdens. The ESTJ grandfather of a newborn showed no interest in the child, reluctantly holding him briefly only when cajoled by his daughter. A 65-year-old ENTJ insisted that her five children and twelve grandchildren spend Christmas morning at her home but complained for weeks before and after the event about how much trouble it was.

Older Extraverted Thinking types who add Feeling to their lives, however, often delight in the newfound pleasures of warm and close relationships with their children and grandchildren. Friendships with peers may also become increasingly important and enjoyable. Unlike their less-developed counterparts, who often become depressed if forced to retire from work or home activities, they welcome new relationships and the challenge of new activities. This is in marked contrast to their earlier disinterest in hobbies and nonwork activities.

Having good role models who have opposite preferences seems particularly helpful to Extraverted Thinking types, although this is generally true for all types. The converse is also true: If an opposite preference comes to be associated with a negative role model, it is less likely to be welcomed and developed during our middle and advanced years.

Sometimes spending a lengthy period in the grip of inferior Introverted Feeling can serve as an important stimulus to midlife development for Extraverted Thinking types. The combination of the natural upheaval of midlife and the disruption and distress of a chronic grip experience may push an ESTJ or ENTJ into serious examination of goals and values, which may lead to significant changes in the way the second half of life is lived.

Knowledge from Grip Experiences

In addition to learning to recognize and circumvent the kind of stress and fatigue that may lead to a grip experience, Extraverted Thinking types report a greater recognition of their important relationships and more tolerance for others' points of view and ways of approaching life. They are better able to temper their very high standards for themselves and others, to "slow down a little and lighten up," as one ENTJ expressed it. Many also become aware that others can see them as invulnerable, not knowing of the ESTJ's or ENTJ's distress unless told of it. When stress is extreme and persists over time, Extraverted Thinking types often cope adequately by taking a problem-solving approach to their situation. However, at times they remain in the grip of their inferior function and, when they finally become aware of their habitual out-of-character state, may drastically alter their work or home situation.

Summary

In the grip of inferior Introverted Feeling, Extraverted Thinking types become sensitive to relationship issues, have outbursts of extreme emotion, and experience a loss of self-worth or a sense of inner turmoil. Auxiliary Sensing or Intuition serves as a buffer against the inferior function's incompetence and aids them in reestablishing equilibrium. Extraverted Thinking types typically have difficulty expressing their internal distress directly and try to hide their inner experience. ESTJs use factual reality to maintain or regain control of their inner state; ENTJs address hypotheses and possibilities that take them beyond and outside their distress.

Important inferior function experiences remind Extraverted Thinking types of their limitations, their basic connection with the more "irrational" ways of being human, and the importance of close companions and

Table 3 Inferior Function of Extraverted Thinking Types: ESTJ and ENTJ

Triggers for the Inferior Function	*Forms of the Grip Experience*
• Disregard of their deep values	• Hypersensitivity to inner states
• Others' emotional expressions	• Outbursts of emotion
• Remorse for their own harshness	• Fear of feeling

Ways of Returning to Equilibrium	*New Knowledge*
• Experience the depth of their feeling	• Recognition of own limits
• Silent suport from others	• Acceptance of the irrational
• Talking to a trusted person	• The importance of intimate relationships

intimate relationships to their sense of competence and well-being. A brief overview of the major features of their inferior function experience appears in Table 3.

7

Introverted Feeling Types
ISFP and INFP

BASIC TYPE DYNAMICS

DOMINANT INTROVERTED FEELING

AUXILIARY EXTRAVERTED SENSING OR INTUITION

TERTIARY INTUITION OR SENSING

INFERIOR EXTRAVERTED THINKING

Introverted Feeling Versus Extraverted Thinking

THIS CHAPTER EXAMINES the way effective Introverted Feeling types experience their inferior function and the temporary transformation they make into ineffective, inferior Extraverted Thinking types when they are either briefly or chronically "in the grip." A review of the characteristics of Introverted Feeling and Extraverted Thinking will be helpful to our discussion.

Important Features of Dominant Introverted Feeling

Introverted Feeling types are flexible, open, complicated, mild, modest, and often self-effacing. Though difficult to get to know, they are seen as trustworthy confidants who are tolerant of a wide range of differences. Their habitual approach to people is nonjudgmental, understanding, and forgiving. They place a high value on affirming both their own and others' individuality and uniqueness. They seek to affirm all parties in a controversy and thus readily see the validity of contradictory points of view. Underlying their characteristic tolerance is an overarching natural curiosity. They find the diversity in the world immensely appealing. ISFPs want to experience as much of the environment, especially the natural environment, as possible; INFPs' desire for broad experience, especially human experience, may be secondary to their need to understand it.

Both Introverted Feeling types may find it difficult to take a firm stance on issues that are not centrally important to them. As a result, they may see themselves and be seen by others as indecisive and lacking in conviction. In matters in which they hold strong values, however, they are firm and uncompromising in expressing and enacting their beliefs.

Introverted Feeling types focus on what is good in others, so they tend to downplay others' faults, often forgiving them for slights or minor hurtful behavior. At their best, they accept their own mistakes and imperfections as well, achieving some success in maintaining the inner harmony that is so important to them.

In crisis situations, they typically will hold back to see if others will solve the problem competently. They are then content to follow someone else's lead. But if adequate leadership is absent, ISFPs and INFPs may assume a dominant role, acting swiftly, confidently, and competently to handle the difficult situation.

Introverted Feeling Types at Work

Work is energizing for Introverted Feeling types when it enables them to enact important values, especially by helping others grow and develop as individuals. Their own growth and development is equally important. Thus they flourish in an environment that offers the freedom to complete projects within a flexible time frame and focuses more on people than on the "bottom line." An ISFP said he was particularly energized by "successfully completing a task or mission when I am assisting someone else." An

INFP is energized by "working one to one with people, helping them discover themselves."

Having the freedom to be creative in a relaxed atmosphere is important for both Introverted Feeling types, but their respective auxiliary Sensing and Intuition influence their preferred focus. ISFPs tend to enjoy accomplishing concrete projects, such as "interesting, hands-on work that I know has a purpose and gives me a sense of accomplishment" or "hands-on materials, creating things, lack of boundaries." INFPs' auxiliary Intuition emerges in a liking for innovation, particularly in the context of helping people. The following description typifies energizing work for INFPs: "growing and developing yourself and others and creating new programs." INFPs generally find difficult tasks appealing, while many ISFPs appreciate simplicity in their work assignments. One INFP is energized by "doing something I enjoy that is difficult but has the end result of being something productive and helpful." Another expressed feeling energized "when I take on a hard problem that can be solved in a new way that allows me to use my creativity and feel as if I've done something."

Important Features of Dominant Extraverted Thinking

The qualities associated with Extraverted Thinking that are relevant to our discussion of its form as an inferior function are an emphasis on

- Competence
- Truth and accuracy
- Decisive action

For a detailed description of dominant Extraverted Thinking, read the beginning of Chapter 6, "Extraverted Thinking Types: ESTJ and ENTJ," and the type descriptions for ESTJ and ENTJ that appear in Appendix A. This will provide the background needed to explore the various ways inferior Extraverted Thinking is expressed in ISFPs and INFPs.

The Everyday Extraverted Thinking of Introverted Feeling Types

The inferior function affects Introverted Feeling types in several different ways. These include everyday sensitivities, projections, and ways of relaxing, as well as the dramatic manifestations that can be seen when the inferior function erupts and a full-blown episode occurs, or when an ISFP or INFP is chronically in the grip because of long-term stress.

Typical Sensitivities and Projections

Like their Extraverted Feeling counterparts, Introverted Feeling types may be concerned about their intellectual abilities, often viewing others, particularly Thinking types, as smarter and more knowledgeable than themselves. Because they are likely to be somewhat uneasy about their skill in logical analysis, they tend to be hypersensitive to illogic, dishonesty, and inaccuracy in others. They are quick to detect insincerity or phoniness, and they readily take offense when faced with the hyperbole typical of television commercials and candidates running for political office. One INFP who hated magic shows and card tricks gave as her reason for this her dislike of "being fooled."

Introverted Feeling types also may be somewhat disdainful of people who act quickly on the basis of insufficient information, seeing their own careful, reflective, and restrained approach to problem solving as inherently better. They may be quick to point out the errors made or opportunities missed by people who reach conclusions hastily.

Projection of the inferior function is revealed in a readiness to notice and comment on mistakes made by others. "I start noticing that there are an unusual number of rude and incompetent drivers on the highway," said one INFP. An ISFP commented that she becomes "very aware that people at work are not following procedures and are making the same mistakes over and over again. But when I think about it later, I have to admit there are no more mistakes than usual."

An extreme, even passionate, focus on the evil and wrongdoing in the world may also indicate Introverted Feeling types' hypersensitivity to the "Thinking" issues of truth and justice. Their often-noted idealism about the perfectibility of humanity may also reflect their discomfort with the harsh reality of an imperfect world. This kind of all-or-none approach is a reflection of the unconscious, black-and-white character of their inferior function.

Because their opposites, Extraverted Thinking types, can be experienced as intimidating, ISFPs and INFPs are sensitive to perceived negative messages from these types. They may project their own black-and-white critical judgments onto them, seeing ESTJs and ENTJs as hypercritical, controlling, demanding, and intrusive. Straightforward comments from an Extraverted Thinking type may therefore be taken as global criticism and simple requests as dictatorial commands.

Expressions Through Interests and Hobbies

Introverted Feeling types may select hobbies that engage their Thinking function. One INFP thoroughly enjoys computer games that require logic and strategy. Another relaxes by analyzing companies for possible investment. An ISFP spends many hours developing software programs to automate the computer entry of his pharmaceutical data. An INFP is a skilled equestrian, devoting much of her spare time to learning precise and intricate riding techniques. An ISFP who is prone to intense headaches finds that grooming her cats and dogs invariably alleviates her pain.

As an INFP psychotherapist, I find that cleaning the house, organizing drawers, or alphabetizing spices can provide a relaxing and welcome break from seeing clients, theorizing, doing research, and writing. This gives my dominant Feeling and auxiliary Intuition a rest when they have been used particularly intensively. Another INFP engages her tertiary Sensing in her detailed, photorealistic drawings of objects and people, and many INFPs mention crafts as a hobby. An ISFP relaxes most successfully while doing the Sunday *New York Times* crossword puzzle. He enjoys being able to put the many facts he knows into the logical order of the English language and giving his tertiary Intuition free rein to fill in the gaps in the puzzle.

People whose daily work requires them to use less-preferred functions may use their preferred processes in their leisure time. An ISFP business manager described suppressing her dominant Feeling and auxiliary Sensing at work, where Thinking and Intuition are more highly valued. She spends as much of her free time as possible enjoying the outdoors. This comes naturally to her and is the most comfortable and relaxing place for her to be. There is a similar tendency for Extraverted Feeling types to engage their preferred functions in leisure activities.

Eruptions of Inferior Extraverted Thinking

When one or more of the preconditions for an eruption of the inferior function are present, Extraverted Thinking appears in its more exaggerated and disruptive form. In addition to the general conditions described in Chapter 4, Introverted Feeling types are vulnerable to the type-specific factors described below.

Typical Provocations or Triggers

Introverted Feeling types frequently mention that an atmosphere of negativity and excessive criticism provides a fertile context for an eruption of their inferior function. Even if the criticism is not directed at them, it brings out their Extraverted Thinking in a black-and-white form. They harshly attack the people who are being negative and critical—for being negative and critical!

As an important part of her job, an INFP nursing supervisor critiqued the records and charts of the nurses who worked under her. One nurse, also an INFP, invariably became furious when his charts were reviewed. He accused his supervisor of gross insensitivity and pettiness and of being unfit for her job. Though the supervisor tried valiantly to view these attacks in context, they would often "send her into a tailspin" and she would be filled with self-doubt, guilt, and a sense of incompetence about her performance. In the context of each having to use less-preferred processes, these two INFPs constellated their own and each other's inferior functions.

Fears of impending loss and separation from people who are important to them can serve as triggers for ISFPs and INFPs. One INFP said he is most likely to fall into the grip of his inferior function "when something very dear to me is threatened and I'm afraid I'll lose my most valued connections with life." An ISFP said that for her it is "when my attachments to people are demeaned and invalidated."

Introverted Feeling types quickly fall into their inferior mode when an important value has been violated. One INFP said:

> I put my feelers out to detect more and even unrelated violations. Once when reviewing my manuscript, which had been typed by a new typist, I found he had made all kinds of really stupid errors. Just after that, I called a colleague at a hotel where I was to meet her. The operator connected me with a wrong room three times. I concluded that the hotel was badly managed and all the staff were incompetent. I went back to the manuscript and found more mistakes and blamed the typist. But this time they were my mistakes!

An INFP said he gets in the grip "when someone really steps on my core values, i.e., accuses me of being dishonest." Another INFP said, "Unfairness, social injustice, manipulation; when someone is unwilling to discuss problems that need to be resolved and not left to just 'go away'; when someone is not authentic and honest in a relationship."

Another trigger for the inferior function of Introverted Feeling types occurs when they project their own unrealistic standard of competence onto others and feel they have not lived up to other people's expectations. "I know I should have been better prepared for that one scene in the play," said an INFP. "It ruined the whole thing." Obsessing on this one perceived inadequacy could quickly lead to a full-fledged experience of inferior Extraverted Thinking.

A highly regarded ISFP office manager persistently berated himself for his imperfect filing system. "Even though I do everything else adequately, I know my boss is disappointed in my overall performance," he said. As a chronic focus for his imagined inadequacy, he was hypersensitive to any reference to the files, readily seeing criticism in the most innocent comments and quickly generalizing it to be a negative assessment of his overall performance and his acceptability as a person.

Triggers and Stressors at Work

Work environments that offer little opportunity for fulfillment of Introverted Feeling values are inherently stressful for ISFPs and INFPs, even if other stressors are absent. If such limited opportunity is accompanied by conflict, difficult and controlling people, and a bottom-line atmosphere oriented to deadlines and rigid rules and procedures, the workplace can become intolerable for Introverted Feeling types. An ISFP finds it stressful to "work with people who are very focused on regulations and rules," and another said, "I dislike strict deadlines and like to move at my own pace." One INFP said she was stressed by "office politics that are out of line with my personal values, not being heard, and disregarded." Another INFP's stressors included "dealing with details, making arrangements, applying policy to a situation and balancing that with my personal values; having to do paperwork that meets the mandate of my organization but not my 'personal mandate.'" The following description by an INFP includes many Introverted Feeling stressors: "constant interruptions and demands on my time; a hostile environment; dysfunctional relationships; unappreciative managers and disgruntled, complaining co-workers and clients."

In a work situation in which the particular stressors for Introverted Feeling types persist over a long period, an ISFP or INFP may be pushed into the grip very quickly and powerfully by the triggers described here. His or her subsequent demonstrations of "grip" behavior are likely to be frequent and pervasive. When persistent stress causes them to be chronically in the grip of inferior Extraverted Thinking, Introverted Feeling types are likely to lose touch with their inner values, believing them to be muddled and untrustworthy. They may eventually begin to feel hopeless and despairing about themselves and the human condition.

The Form of the Inferior Function

Being out of character can be temporarily enjoyable when inhibitions are lessened, freeing up energy to explore unfamiliar but intriguing parts of oneself. Introverted Feeling types sometimes report becoming more sociable and outgoing. This is particularly true for male ISFPs and INFPs in their early twenties and somewhat less so for older males of these types. Women generally do not report this kind of lowering of inhibitions, perhaps because any such "positive" expression is likely to be eradicated by the negative expressions of anger and criticality that are the hallmarks of inferior Extraverted Thinking. Women may find these inferior function expressions to be more unacceptable than do men.

However, over time the characteristic tolerance, flexibility, and quiet caring of Introverted Feeling types diminishes as the energy available to their dominant Introverted Feeling dwindles. "I lose my concern for harmony, my connection with my inner values," said an INFP. An ISFP said he "searches for conflict and forgets about others' feelings." ISFPs may also lose access to their auxiliary Sensing function. "I react quickly without finding out any facts," said one. INFPs may similarly lose sight of their auxiliary Intuition. One INFP said that she "cannot process information, thoughts, or ideas" and becomes "focused on detail, making elaborate plans that are unnecessary."

Initially, INFPs and ISFPs may control their urge to blurt out hostile thoughts by engaging in destructive fantasies directed at just about anyone

Table 4 Dominant and Inferior Expressions of Extraverted Thinking

As Dominant Function of ESTJs and ENTJs	As Inferior Function of ISFPs and INFPs
• Competence	• Judgments of incompetence
• Truth and accuracy	• Aggressive criticism
• Decisive action	• Precipitous action

available. Alternatively, they may employ biting sarcasm and cynicism. As these tactics fail, the negative Extraverted Thinking of their inferior function becomes manifested in judgments of incompetence, aggressive criticism, and precipitous action. For ISFPs, tertiary Intuition may be revealed in their being plagued by the negative possibilities they imagine will be the inevitable, logical consequences of their incompetence. For INFPs, tertiary Sensing provides all the "facts" necessary to support their overwhelming sense of failure.

The comparison between dominant and inferior Extraverted Thinking is shown in Table 4.

Jung (1976a) alludes to these inferior manifestations in the following statement:

> Just as introverted thinking is counterbalanced by a primitive feeling, to which objects attach themselves with magical force, introverted feeling is counterbalanced by a primitive thinking, whose concretism and slavery to facts surpass all bounds. (p. 388)

Judgments of Incompetence In the early stages of expression of their inferior function, Introverted Feeling types often project their unconscious fears of their own incompetence. They become hypersensitive to others' mistakes. Because of the Extraverted attitude of their inferior function, the projections often extend to large segments of the outer world, encompassing much of humanity. Once caught up in this state, they see incompetence in employees, bosses, colleagues, strangers on the street, the person on the other end of the telephone, drivers on the highway, local and national institutions, and major world figures.

Introverted Feeling types in this state may complain loudly about others' gross ineptitude. ISFPs and INFPs seem to turn into the very opposite of their accepting, nonjudgmental, and flexible selves, coming across as harsh critics and judges whose standards of competence are too extreme to be met.

Inferior Thinking often comes out in an unrelenting search for accuracy—in a precise, nitpicky logic and focus, and an almost legalistic standard of validity. One INFP said, "I home in on precise logic and truth and am very critical, detailed, picky, frustrated, and irritable. I'm nitpicky and see only what is in front of me." An ISFP said, "I'm in a bad mood and show it. I cut myself off and am critical, judgmental, bitchy; I am not accepting, happy, optimistic, nice, or understanding. Usually, I am friendly and always have time for people. When I'm tired and vulnerable, I can get into this state by remembering some incredibly dumb thing I did—an embarrassing moment. Or somebody else's incompetence that reflects on my own will set me off."

When this projection of their sense of incompetence fails to take care of whatever has triggered it, the negative energy of the inferior function takes the form of critical self-judgment. Introverted Feeling types become focused on their own incompetence, extending it both backward and forward in time and including the world at large in their conclusion. In the words of one INFP:

> I become overwhelmed by an awareness that I am totally incompetent at everything I do, that I always have been and always will be—and that the whole world knows it! The truth of this is beyond doubt. I am mortified at not recognizing this before, and of compounding the offense by acting as if I were competent. I am unable to verbalize my despair to others for fear I will make a fool of myself by acknowledging my former ignorance of my true lack of ability. I view my advanced degrees and other achievements as the result of people feeling sorry for me— I was too emotionally fragile to be told the truth.

"Everything seems impossible," said an ISFP. "I begin to lose faith in my ability to do even the simplest task, and I especially distrust my ability to make competent decisions about my life." An INFP said, "I become rigid and think I am stupid, hopeless, etc. I often play a mental videotape of all the times I remember getting things wrong." Another INFP described being "very arbitrary, loud, direct, hateful. I become inflexible, rigid, and most intolerant. I make snap judgments and become quite self-condemning. I think it's all over; I'm no longer worthwhile."

When feeling vulnerable, another INFP worried about whether his teachers had paid sufficient attention to his work to properly evaluate it. "Maybe they were so wrapped up in their own work that I slipped through undetected," he said. An ISFP said, "I review all the mistakes I ever made in my life and then conclude that I am a bona fide failure at everything I attempt to do, despite any evidence to the contrary."

Aggressive Criticism   We know that effective dominant Extraverted Thinking types make useful critical judgments about the world. In the grip of inferior Extraverted Thinking, Introverted Feeling types make judgments that are overly categorical, harsh, exaggerated, hypercritical, and often unfounded. In marked contrast to their typically gentle, self effacing manner, they become so aggressively judgmental that they come across as caricatures of their opposite types, the Extraverted Thinking types. Depending on the nature and intensity of the precipitating circumstances, the excessive criticism may be immediately directed at themselves or may focus first on the objectionable qualities of others, only later culminating in severe self-criticism. Such alternating criticism of others and self is evident in some of the preceding comments describing "incompetence."

One ISFP said, "My humor becomes biting and cynical and I take an 'army-navy' dictatorial approach to communicating with others. I am very negative." Another described becoming "very short-tempered. I react quickly and sometimes not rationally. I yell at people and have very little patience." "I'll be loud, critical, and rash, talk about people behind their backs, or be unreasonable," said another.

An INFP becomes "more intense. I tend to lash out at people with great anger. I am blaming and accusatory. I get vicious 'Ben Hur'–type images with a lot of violent action. I feel cold, intolerant, uncaring, rigid, straitjacketed, focused, and terrier–like."

"I snap at people and I don't care about their reactions to this. I criticize people, especially for their incompetence. I generalize this to thinking that the whole world is incompetent and has screwed up values, and I stop caring about my own values," explained another INFP. "I become self-critical, doubting, irritable, inflexible, and more picky. I focus on details. Usually, I am flexible and quiet and like new challenges, new ideas, and working with people."

When one ISFP becomes especially irritated with her husband's chronic indecision, she provides him with lengthy, logical accounts of his available choices, adopting a combative, lawyerlike tone. One INFP makes almost vicious attacks on people who fail to live up to his ethical standards. "One winter I found out the gas company had turned off service to my disabled neighbor, who couldn't pay her bill. I flew into a rage, called the president of the company, and threatened to expose him to the newspapers. Even I was surprised at the language I used," he said.

Precipitous Action   Introverted Feeling types in the grip are often overwhelmed by the urge to take some action, usually to correct some imagined mistake or incompetence of their own. But where the dominant Extraverted Thinking type uses differentiated judgment in deciding what action to take, if any, the Introverted Feeling type's actions often exacerbate the problem. A difficult situation may be created where there initially wasn't one.

At her engagement party, Sylvia, an INFP, was kissed playfully by a former boyfriend while both were alone in the kitchen. Later that night, she remembered that a friend of hers had passed by the kitchen door and might have seen the kiss. She called her friend and begged her not to tell anyone. She interpreted her friend's puzzled response as evidence that she had already told several other people. Sylvia then called four more close friends to warn them not to tell. By this time, the innocent kiss was common knowledge to virtually everyone who had been at the party. Of course, Sylvia's fiancé found out about the kissing incident and was hurt and angry. Sylvia's precipitous "fixing" created an unnecessary problem that required a great deal of real correction.

The urge to take action can also be seen in attempts by Introverted Feeling types to take control. One INFP reported that when things seem out of control, he attempts to put them in order, organize them, and piece together data in an orderly, logical, linear fashion. An ISFP responds to such episodes by taking charge of people and ordering them around. Others make lists, organize the list contents logically, and methodically check off the items once they are accomplished.

Undertaking large household cleaning projects, reorganizing, and moving furniture are also ways of responding to increasing stress. They are usually accompanied by concerns about one's abilities—perhaps indicative of attempts to ward off inferior Thinking by acting in a decisive, controlled way.

Lengthy Episodes in the Grip

The types of episodes described above are experienced by ISFPs and INFPs as temporary states during which they are vulnerable to the three forms in which their inferior functions are expressed. However, when an Introverted Feeling type is chronically in the grip of inferior Extraverted Thinking, inferior function behavior may become habitual. The typical and "normal" moderate dissatisfaction of ISFPs and INFPs with themselves, others, and life in general relative to their ideals takes the form of automatic cynicism, distrust of others' motives, and pervasive anger toward the world and everyone in it.

INFPs are more likely than ISFPs to leave a highly stressful work situation, even though ISFPs try to avoid stressful situations if at all possible. Perhaps the INFPs' auxiliary Intuition helps them imagine alternatives and their generally greater self-confidence allows them to risk new work situations. ISFPs may pay a high price for their lower stress tolerance and persistence in stressful work situations: they self-report the highest incidence of hypertension and heart disease of all the types and are also highest in experiencing emotional burnout and depersonalization when they are stressed at work. INFPs, in contrast, are among the least likely types to experience these stress effects.

Chronic grip behavior may lead both the individual and others to believe that cynicism, negativity, and sarcasm are a part of the natural makeup of the ISFP or INFP and that the person has always been mean-spirited, hypercritical, and fault-finding. Since the process of becoming chronically in the grip is often gradual, even people who have known the person in a nonstressed state are likely not to notice what, in retrospect, will be recognized as a radical alteration of personality. The Introverted Feeling type will appear to be a rather exaggerated, poorly developed Extraverted Thinking type, as the last story in the next section illustrates.

However, there are also occasions when a lengthy time in the grip of inferior Introverted Feeling can stimulate new awareness and positive growth toward completion and individuation. Remember that Jung saw the inferior function as the doorway to the unconscious and an important part of the self-regulating capacity of our psyches.

Grip Experiences

The stories included in this section illustrate one or more forms of inferior Extraverted Thinking as experienced by ISFPs and INFPs. Characteristics of dominant Introverted Feeling types come through in the telling of these episodes—their deeply held values, unassuming approach, and readiness to take responsibility for themselves and others.

Out of the Depths Comes Appreciation

Jack, an INFP, related the following story:

> As part of a professional training program I was enrolled in, I had to complete a take-home exam that required me to integrate the complex information in the course. I had never written a take-home exam before, and I looked forward to it, as the questions were challenging and I enjoy writing. But I had great trouble answering the questions. I thought everything I wrote was either wrong, trivial, or irrelevant. I was in the depths of despair, seriously questioning my competence and professional skills. I kept thinking it would get better if I kept at it, but over the six weeks I worked on the exam, it only got worse.
>
> Several days before I was to turn in my examination, I realized that I had unwittingly defined the take-home exam as a requirement to cite chapter and verse, and to provide carefully substantiated facts leading to logical conclusions. This was not my comfortable approach to problem solving. I depended largely on my ideas and insight to guide my work. I realized that in writing the exam, I had been treating my ideas as if they had to be facts, and I was expecting my conclusions to have the status of truth. No wonder I couldn't tell if my ideas were any good: I was evaluating them from an inappropriate perspective.
>
> I was able to easily redefine the task, set aside the books I was consulting, and answer the questions with confidence and satisfaction. I got an A+ on the exam.

"But There Have to Be Rules and Procedures!"

Mona, an ISFP owner and operator of a fabric store, had a relaxed, easygoing management style. Her five full-time and part-time employees enjoyed a friendly, cooperative relationship with her. Mona's style of keeping records, ordering stock, doing the accounting, and attending to other business activities was equally casual. Everything would be taken care of eventually, though perhaps not in the most efficient fashion.

During a time of financial stress when business appeared to be waning, Mona decided that she needed to put her business activities in order. She spent two evenings writing out detailed and elaborate "rules of law," specifying how her employees must conduct business affairs and interpersonal relationships with each other and with customers. She called an early-morning meeting to convey the new requirements.

"They all listened quietly and attentively," Mona remembered. "Each said something like, 'Uh, huh,' 'Sure, Mona,' or 'Fine, that's okay.' But then they totally ignored my rules and conducted themselves and the business as usual!

"Later, several of them told me they figured I was stressed and wasn't acting normally, so they thought the best thing to do was to humor me until I came out of it. They were right. When I did come out of it, I looked at my two evenings' worth of rules and regulations and was flabbergasted. I couldn't understand how I could have possibly thought any of it was appropriate!"

Embarrassing Error or Earache?

An INFP philosophy professor related the following experience that had occurred years earlier while he was a graduate student.

> I was invited to deliver a lecture on my area of specialization in philosophy at an annual philosophical society meeting. Although I was somewhat anxious, as this would be my first major presentation, I was excited about it and quite pleased with my professors' high opinion of me.
>
> I was told that several philosophers who were experts in my area might be attending my presentation. The lecture was attended by over 100 people. I introduced my talk with a brief overview of the philosophical system underlying my approach. I had been speaking for about ten minutes when a man at the back of the room began shaking his head vigorously.
>
> In that instant I knew that he was one of the "experts"—that I must have made some egregious error, was making a fool of myself, and was in danger of continuing to do so. All my thoughts flew from my head! My choice was either to persevere and forge ahead with a high risk of making further stupid statements or to mortify myself by being unable to continue. Under the circumstances, the first option was the lesser evil. I recovered and continued, though with quite a bit of uneasiness.

At the end of my lecture, the man who had been shaking his head came up to me and said, "I'm sorry to ask you to repeat something you said during your lecture, but I have a terrible ear infection and I couldn't clear my ears enough to be able to hear you."

I realized that his head shaking was an attempt to unclog his ears—not a negative comment on what I was saying. However, my readiness to distrust my knowledge was clearly a sign that I was insecure and thus basically incompetent. I interpreted my quickness to "lose it" as a way of unconsciously chastising myself for my arrogance in thinking too well of myself.

Years later, I recognized that my expectations of myself had been unrealistic. I had wanted to explain my philosophical approach perfectly and was afraid of making any kind of error. Thinking about this made me reflect on the realistic consequences of making a mistake in public. Would one error really be so terrible? Wasn't an important aspect of competence the ability to accept one's errors and learn from them?

As a result of this experience, I am better able to accept my mistakes as natural consequences of being human. They do not interrupt my train of thought, nor do I overreact to them as I once did.

"I Wasn't Good at That Anyway"

Ben, an ISFP, had majored in physical education in college and planned to teach at the high school level. But because he was unable to find a position in his field, he took a job in the drafting department of a large manufacturing firm. His minor in college had been art, and he had always enjoyed the creative outlet his artwork provided him. He liked designing teaching materials for the company's training department and was particularly good at improving on other people's designs, putting to good use his fine sense of color, shape, and texture.

As a result of his excellent work, Ben was promoted to a project manager position. His job now required him to read and evaluate reports and decide what kinds of training materials were appropriate. After two weeks in this new position, Ben developed stomach problems, back pain, and headaches. He was unable to concentrate at work and responded to requests by saying, "I can't do that," or "I don't know how."

"I feel really stupid, incompetent, and worthless," he told a career counselor. "My boss agrees. He says I am totally uncreative because I can't come up with original training designs. He's right. Before, I was good at improving on other people's designs—not coming up with my own. Now

I don't think I can even do that. I don't think I was ever really good at that anyway. The rest of the team made up for my lack of talent."

Promoted to a position beyond his level of expertise, Ben lost contact with his real sources of competence, which, abetted by his boss, he now devalued. When he eventually moved into a position that again made use of his particular talents, his sense of self gradually returned. "I realize now that I don't have to accept other people's idea of creativity. I can be happy with my own definition," he said.

"Go Ahead, Make My Day!"

After thinking about it for a long time, Suzanne, an INFP, decided on a career change that required an advanced degree. She applied to a graduate program at a university in a nearby state and, because the deadline for admission to the fall program had passed, hoped she would be admitted for the spring semester.

Early one morning during the last week of August, Suzanne received a phone call from the head of the graduate department informing her that because her qualifications for the program were so outstanding, the department was offering her a full tuition scholarship as well as a sizable fellowship to help defray her living expenses. And even though the semester had already started, they wanted her to enroll for the fall semester rather than wait until spring. How soon could she come?

Suzanne was overwhelmed. She had been planning to complete various projects in the next few months, but they would have to wait. The offer was too good to turn down. Suzanne felt pleased and affirmed by the university's recognition of her accomplishments. After considering how much time she needed to fulfill current commitments, she informed the department head that she could start in ten days.

By the following day, however, the stress of moving to another state, the prospect of finding a place to live that would accept her three cats, the concern about needing to supplement her fellowship money, and the countless other details that came into her mind utterly changed her initial happy mood. Her thoughts raced: What if they just had this fellowship left over and had to get rid of it and I was the only person available? What if it's not that I'm so great, but that everybody else in the program is mediocre? What if I get there and can't catch up with the work I've missed? I shouldn't be making a precipitous decision like this. The last time

I decided on a move quickly, it turned out to be a big mistake. And there won't be any good places to live because the semester has started. And what if I don't like it and I quit and disappoint these people who are going out of their way for me? And what if I don't live up to their expectations? And what if . . .

Suzanne disregarded reassurance from others, descending further into negative judgments of herself, her competence, and her decision-making abilities. Finally, she gained sufficient perspective to recall that her current negativity was "standard operating procedure" when she felt uprooted and disconcerted by all the practical details facing her. She was then able to accept putting up with her discomfort until she moved and her life situation became more settled.

The next story highlights the effects of using less-preferred functions for a lengthy period.

"But He Sure Acted Like an ESTJ!"

The first-year students in a graduate program often commiserated with one another about the way Dr. Parks, the longtime chairman of their department, treated them. He ran a tight ship, insisting on strict adherence to detailed requirements and procedures. The students also complained of his inaccessibility and refusal to treat them in the collegial manner they thought appropriate to graduate training in a human services field. The more advanced students told their junior colleagues that this was just the way he was and they'd have to get used to it.

Some of the first-year students were familiar with personality type and shared the description of ESTJ with their classmates as well as with the more advanced students. All agreed that Dr. Parks must be an ESTJ— though not a very well developed one, they believed.

At the end of the next year, the department sponsored an MBTI presentation and all students and professors took the assessment. When sharing of type occurred during the session, the students were astounded to hear Dr. Parks verify that he was an INFP! They got a clue to his dynamics (and their error in assessing his type) when he volunteered the information that he found his administrative duties burdensome and stressful and was looking forward to retiring at the end of the year.

Apparently, Dr. Parks's notion of a "good" department chairman (perhaps based on prior role models) fit the profile of his opposite type and was unnatural and uncomfortable for him. He behaved in a rigid, unfeeling, and distant manner, suppressing his natural affinity for friendly relationships and a flexible approach to learning. Because he had been in the position a long time, students never had an opportunity to experience him as himself—to their and his own detriment.

Return of Equilibrium

As the preceding stories illustrate, some time is required for things to play out before equilibrium is restored in a person who has been in the grip. However, as the last story shows, chronically being in the grip may force a person to permanently leave the stressful situation.

The following comments were made by some Introverted Feeling types about how they typically disengage from inferior function experiences. Note that for both ISFPs and INFPs, it is important that they be able to spend some time alone when emerging from the grip and not be "helped" by others. This appears to be less crucial for female ISFPs, who are likely to welcome talking to others early in the process. Female INFPs find talking to others helpful, but not usually right away. Male Introverted Feeling types mention talking to others less frequently. Engaging in relaxing, distracting activities and hobbies is helpful for both genders.

"I need to get away and think things through," said an ISFP. "People should just let me be," he added. An INFP said she needs to "go with the flow, get away from the situation for a while. I need to talk about it without being censored (or taken too seriously)." And another INFP agreed that "I don't like it when others help. I'll just be with myself and work out solutions or compromises."

"It has to expire on its own," said an ISFP. "If someone else says something about it, it can make it worse—unless I am already coming out of it. If someone I respect but am not emotionally close to says something, I may check it out. It depends on how it is said."

"I need to go with the flow and allow myself time to experience it. Others need to be patient and empathic. They need to allow me time to reflect," said another ISFP.

"Exercise helps, and so does talking to someone. But others need to listen and not try to reason with me or be logical. Having my feelings validated is important."

A consistent theme that seems to signal that the experience is winding down is an often painful awareness of the effect their inferior function is having on people. "We become aware of the damage to relationships caused by the episode and are thankful it's over," reported a group of Introverted Feeling types. One INFP said, "I become aware of being out of sorts, take a deep breath, chill out (after being embarrassed). Others need to give me space and be forgiving when I ask forgiveness." Another INFP reported that "It helps if others let me have my say, don't get defensive, and don't challenge my 'truth' at that moment. Acknowledge that you understand what I'm saying. We can talk about it when I'm myself again."

The process of becoming "oneself again" can be aided by auxiliary Sensing or Intuition. ISFPs find it helpful to satisfy their Sensing need for sleep, or to simply "zone out" by watching a lot of television. Later, starting a craft project that uses established skills may signal the diminishing effects of an inferior function episode. Engaging in distracting activities, hobbies, and recreation is helpful. INFPs also can find new energy and motivation by coming up with an intriguing thought or a new approach to an ongoing project.

INFPs report that the process of emerging from their grip experience happens simultaneously with the new learning or awareness that occurs. In line with their overriding focus on growth and development, they seem to welcome any opportunity to expand their self-awareness, even when it is painful. This happens for other types as well, but it seems to be more noticeable for those who have Intuition as their auxiliary function. Often the new knowledge comes in the form of a previously unrecognized idea or new insight. This is what occurred for the person who realized he had approached the take-home exam from the wrong perspective.

Expressions in Midlife

Midlife is not always accompanied by a positive and progressive integration of inferior Extraverted Thinking. Nor do we see evidence of the inclusion of tertiary Sensing or Intuition in the personality of all aging Introverted Feeling types.

The aging process finds some Introverted Feeling types becoming stuck in their type rather than broadening their perspective. They may appear to others to be perpetually searching for self-fulfillment, changing jobs or careers, assuring others and themselves that this next time will be the last and "right" choice. This may also take the form of repetitive searching for a "soul mate," resulting in failed marriages and partnerships and dissatisfying romantic affairs.

Some Introverted Feeling types may incorporate inferior Thinking and tertiary Sensing or Intuition into their personalities, but in a somewhat rigid, extreme, and stereotypical way. They seem hypercritical of others, obsess about minor details, and lose their former facility with ideas and possibilities. Rather than simply adding appropriate Thinking to their repertoire, they seem to delete Feeling. Aging finds them frequently in the grip of inferior Thinking and tertiary Sensing or Intuition.

Introverted Feeling types whose course of development is more fortunate reveal increased confidence in their own values, a new interest in activities that involve their tertiary Sensing or Intuition, and an attraction to analytic approaches. They report more comfort in logical decision making, less concern about hurting others' feelings, and greater impatience with sentimental expressions of feeling.

In contrast to Extraverted Thinking types, whose positive midlife expressions include being more willing to let go of things that don't fit their image of what is correct and logical, Introverted Feeling types become more confident and forthright in stating their convictions to others. They are more willing to tell other people what they need and want and are less concerned about fulfilling others' expectations. They may also enjoy doing things in an orderly, logical sequence and appreciate the beauty of the universe as expressed in the laws of physics and chemistry. This may emerge in as common an activity as cooking. An INFP cook, who had habitually deviated from recipes as a young adult, discovered in his fifties that following the order and precision of a detailed recipe was quite appealing. He was intrigued with the particular mix of ingredients and the logic of their proportions. This INFP's midlife change contrasts with that of an ISTJ cook described in Chapter 12, who, having adhered strictly to recipes in her youth, dispensed with them entirely in midlife.

Positive incorporation of inferior and tertiary functions can appear in the career area. One 47-year-old INFP said,

> I think that in the last ten years or so I have gained psychological reassurance that I am competent at some things. It needed to come first in my chosen professional arena—through gaining confidence as a professional, as a faculty member training students, and then as a bit of an

authority in certain theoretical areas. Then I could play with areas in which I had never sought competence before. I recently took a night course in electrical rewiring and practiced it in my own home. But the secure base of my preferred world (teaching and writing) needed to be there, as well as in my personal life (as a partner and a parent), before I could have energy to devote to such things as mastering electrical circuits. It had to happen at the right time also. I could never have done it in my twenties or younger.

Sometimes spending a lengthy period in the grip of inferior Extraverted Thinking can serve as an important stimulus to midlife development for Introverted Feeling types. The combination of the natural upheaval of midlife and the disruption and distress of a chronic grip experience may push an ISFP or INFP into serious soul searching and reconsideration of long-standing goals, which may lead to significant changes in the way the second half of life is lived.

Knowledge from Grip Experiences

In addition to learning to recognize and avoid the stress and fatigue that may lead to a grip experience, Introverted Feeling types report a greater ability to temper their idealism without resorting to despair and cynicism. This may allow them to willingly remain in stressful situations they might otherwise see as intolerable and therefore leave. In work situations, they are more willing to acknowledge their leadership skills and to deal with overwhelming work demands by remembering that they usually manage to get everything done somehow. When they are not able to meet their own or others' expectations, they are better able to take it in stride and accept their frailties without feeling inadequate.

When stress at work or at home is extreme and persistent, Introverted Feeling types are likely to suffer through as long as their important values are engaged and there is some hope of eventual reduction in stress. When they have been in the grip for a lengthy period and finally become aware of their habitual out-of-character state, perhaps by becoming ill or seriously depressed, they are likely to drastically change their work or home situation or simply leave.

Summary

In the grip of inferior Extraverted Thinking, ISFPs and INFPs focus on their own and others' incompetence, are hypersensitive to signs of dishonesty, and take precipitous action, often aimed at correcting an imagined error. The new awareness that occurs, often in conjunction with the process of regaining their Introverted Feeling equilibrium, tends to engage their auxiliary extraverted Sensing or Intuition. Discovery of facts that explain puzzling reactions occurs for ISFPs; significant insights that stimulate a new point of view are helpful to INFPs. As a result of important inferior function experiences, Introverted Feeling types are able to accept and value their own competitiveness, need for achievement, or desire for power and control—motives that their conscious Introverted Feeling values tend to reject and deny. They are also better able to accept and acknowledge their own competencies, as well as their insecurities and failings. They are thus able to temper their sometimes excessive idealism with more realistic goals. A brief overview of the major features of their inferior function experience appears on the following page in Table 5.

Table 5 Inferior Function of Introverted Feeling Types: ISFP and INFP

Triggers for the Inferior Function	*Forms of the Grip Experience*
• Negativity and excessive criticism	• Judgments of incompetence
• Fear of impending loss and separation	• Aggressive criticism
• Violation of values	• Precipitous action

Ways of Returning to Equilibrium	*New Knowledge*
• Expires on its own	• Acceptance of power needs
• Have feelings validated	• Acknowledgment of competence
• Avoidance by others of trying to reason with them	• Moderated idealism

8

Introverted Thinking Types

ISTP and INTP

BASIC TYPE DYNAMICS

DOMINANT INTROVERTED THINKING

AUXILIARY EXTRAVERTED SENSING OR INTUITION

TERTIARY INTUITION OR SENSING

INFERIOR EXTRAVERTED FEELING

Introverted Thinking Versus Extraverted Feeling

THIS CHAPTER EXAMINES the way effective Introverted Thinking types experience their inferior function and the temporary transformation they make into ineffective, inferior Extraverted Feeling types when they are either briefly or chronically "in the grip." A review of the characteristics of Introverted Thinking and Extraverted Feeling will be helpful to our discussion.

Important Features of Dominant Introverted Thinking

Introverted Thinking types maintain the utmost objectivity. They approach people and events as dispassionate observers, with the goal of arriving at the most comprehensive truth possible. The process of objective analysis is a source of great enjoyment for the Introverted Thinking type, with its outcome often of much lesser importance. Introverted Thinking types typically do not take constructive criticism and disagreement personally. They often welcome tough, unrelenting critique as an aid to achieving the highest levels of accuracy and objectivity.

Because they do not take criticism personally, ISTPs and INTPs are often surprised to discover that others are hurt or offended by their constructive criticism. Others often see them as distant, unfeeling, disinterested in people, and arrogant—all characteristics that they disavow. The fact that they may appear to have these qualities is a function of their basic typological approach, which applies objective analysis to most things, including people.

In a crisis that does not provoke their inferior function, Introverted Thinking types take the same detached, objective approach typical of their nonstressful problem solving. They don't tend to report the internal (and undetectable) turmoil described by the Introverted Sensing types, and they appear to experience little or no emotional response to objectively experienced crises.

Introverted Thinking Types at Work

Achievement and satisfaction at work are as central to the identity of Introverted Thinking types as they are for their Extraverted Thinking counterparts. In general, however, ISTPs and especially INTPs report less satisfaction with their work situations than do ESTJs and ENTJs. A corporate environment that emphasizes management of people, observable team efforts, and outer-world results often forces Introverts to use their less-preferred form of energy. This can be particularly difficult for Introverted Thinking types because they are most energized when they can work independently and with intense focus on challenging problems. ISTPs' auxiliary Sensing function motivates them to prefer clear, stable structures and responsibilities at work. In that context, they enjoy active involvement in concrete, tangible efforts. One ISTP likes "breaking down problems into manageable steps and finding solutions that work for everyone," another likes "solving problems and building things," and a third favors "a variety of issues requiring my attention; a fast-paced environment with lots of problem-solving requirements." "Solving problems and building things" is most energizing for an ISTP in his early twenties.

INTPs' auxiliary Intuition emerges in their desire to be creative, independent, and resourceful in solving problems. An INTP said, "I love doing good, competent work that makes a difference for my clients. I enjoy the collegial and intellectually rigorous environment." An INTP in her early twenties mentioned "having a challenge that I successfully overcome." INTPs enjoy devising new systems and putting ideas together in different ways. Both of the Introverted Thinking types want the highest level of autonomy and the freedom to solve problems in their own way. As one ISTP explained, "I want the freedom to use my time in my own way, to spend as much time as necessary thinking."

Important Features of Dominant Extraverted Feeling

The qualities associated with Extraverted Feeling that are relevant to our discussion of its form as an inferior function are

- Comfortable inattention to logic
- Sensitivity to others' welfare
- Sharing of emotions

For a detailed description of dominant Extraverted Feeling, read the beginning of Chapter 9, "Extraverted Feeling Types: ESFJ and ENFJ," and the type descriptions for ESFJ and ENFJ that appear in Appendix A. This will provide the background needed to explore the various ways inferior Extraverted Feeling is expressed in ISTPs and INTPs.

The Everyday Extraverted Feeling of Introverted Thinking Types

The inferior function affects Introverted Thinking types in several different ways. These include everyday sensitivities, projections, and ways of relaxing, as well as the dramatic manifestations that can be seen when the inferior erupts and a full-blown episode occurs or when an ISTP or INTP is chronically in the grip because of long-term stress.

Typical Sensitivities and Projections

Introverted Thinking types may notice and comment on what they consider to be inappropriate, irrelevant, even histrionic communication styles
and behavior, which they often attribute to Extraverted Feeling types or
Extraverted Intuitive types with auxiliary Feeling (ENFPs). They may treat
such people with disdain and in turn may be seen as hypercritical, dismissive, and lacking in social graces.

An INTP father was chastised by his wife and children—all of whom
had a preference for Feeling—because, when he was told by his son that
he had crashed his bike into a wall, his first question was, "Is the bike badly
damaged?" The family members agreed that he should have first asked
whether his son was hurt. The father replied that he had already determined by looking at him that his son was not hurt and therefore
had chosen the condition of the bike as the next logical priority. This
father was quite puzzled by his family's perception that he cared more for
a bicycle than for his son. He assumed that his love for his family was self-
evident.

Introverted Thinking types may assess behavior based on subjective
values as "noise in the system" that interferes with the accurate appraisal of
situations and is therefore a waste of time. Extraverted Feeling types can
seem out of control to them. The higher value that ESFJs and ENFJs place
on harmony over logically determined truth arouses distrust in the Introverted Thinking type, who then doubts these types' intellectual abilities.
Like their Extraverted Thinking counterparts, Introverted Thinking types
may therefore interpret other peoples' need for frequent personal validation as weakness and insecurity.

Because Introverted Thinking types value logical Thinking and objective analysis of situations, they do not see much value in idle conversation
and social small talk. They may feel inept and awkward when situations
require this of them, and their discomfort, inexperience, and lack of
understanding of this kind of social interaction often leads them to "put
my foot in my mouth and say exactly the most inappropriate thing," as one
INTP expressed it. "I then feel really inadequate and foolish and I can
dwell on my ineptness for days," he explained.

As for expressing their own Feeling side, Von Franz (1971) states that

> the feeling of the introverted thinking type is extraverted. He has the
> same kind of strong, loyal and warm feeling described as typical for the

extraverted thinking type, but with the difference that the feeling of the introverted thinking type flows toward definite objects. (p. 41)

Those definite objects may be people, causes, spiritual arenas, and so on. In their raw, inexperienced form, these Feeling expressions come out as clichés and sound sentimental and excessive. Sensing this, Introverted Thinking types hesitate to express them and may do so only in the relative safety of close one-on-one relationships.

Expressions Through Interests and Hobbies

Many ISTPs and INTPs have a passion for challenging but primarily solitary physical activities. They may be avid mountain or rock climbers and serious hikers or backpackers. They describe having a deep emotional and spiritual reaction to wilderness experiences and their oneness with the universe. The mountain, trail, or rock can become the "other" in their experience of intense feeling.

One INTP mountain climber writes emotionally evocative poetry describing his reactions to his climbing experiences. An ISTP police lieutenant loves listening to music of the Romantic era, especially Wagner. Another ISTP enjoys reading romance novels and an INTP reads spiritual literature. Another INTP covers both auxiliary Sensing and inferior Feeling in her relaxation activities. She described her pleasure in a "sensory trip" to a nearby small town, where she quickly checks out the bookstore, listens to music, sits in the park, eats ice cream, and reflects on the week. She also engages in deep conversation with an ESFJ friend and makes special cards to express her appreciation or love to special people.

Tertiary Sensing often shows in the hobbies of INTPs. They mention gardening, cooking, knitting, and playing golf or other sports that require individual skill. ISTPs may engage tertiary Intuition through such activities as visiting museums or reading art books. One ISTP's elaborate model train boards create complex, evocative scenes, complete with stories about the tiny figures and their lives in the towns he depicts.

Eruptions of Inferior Extraverted Feeling

When one or more of the preconditions for an eruption of the inferior function are present, Extraverted Feeling appears in its more exaggerated, disruptive form. In addition to the general conditions described in Chapter 4, Introverted Thinking types are vulnerable to the type-specific factors described below.

Typical Provocations or Triggers

Being around people who are expressing strong emotions can serve as a trigger for Introverted Thinking types, especially if those people are criticizing the personal characteristics of the ISTP or INTP. Dealing with incompetence also serves as a major trigger. And, as is the case for Extraverted Thinking types, ISTPs and INTPs can be pushed into the grip when their own strong values and feelings are not recognized or affirmed.

Others' insensitivity to an Introverted Thinking type's need for silence and solitude—"not enough time to recharge," said one INTP—can also provoke the experience. The short-term, intense stress of a crisis situation, especially if others are expressing strong emotions and the ISTP or INTP is expected to respond to the emotion, is also a stimulus to the inferior function. Introverted Thinking types may themselves react with an uncharacteristic display of emotion or readily take offense at such times.

Other triggers are feeling controlled by arbitrary situations that limit their freedom of choice and action, and feeling that others are intruding on their space. Being treated unfairly and feeling unheard, unvalued, and excluded from important decision-making discussions can also push these types into their inferior function. An INTP covered many triggers to inferior Extraverted Feeling in her description: "other people becoming very emotional, excessive control from other people, others encroaching on my responsibilities, having to rely on others who—I feel—are not competent."

In projecting their inferior Extraverted Feeling onto others, Introverted Thinking types can readily see others' easy expression of emotion as hysterical and out of control. Because of their fear of being consumed by strong, uncontrollable emotions, they assume that any expression of emotion is similarly out of bounds. ISTPs and INTPs may try to leave a situation in which highly charged feelings are being expressed, and if that is not possible, they may react with a full-blown episode of their inferior function.

Triggers and Stressors at Work

Introverted Thinking types find being micromanaged, supervising and working with incompetent, uncooperative people, and dealing with an overwhelming workload to be major sources of stress and dissatisfaction at work. Deadlines and an excessive workload can interfere with their need for time to focus in depth on the problems they are trying to solve for their organization. Incompetent people inhibit their reaching a solution or acquiring necessary information, and onerous, rigid supervision wastes their time and insults their sense of competence. One INTP listed as stressful "paperwork, especially if the purpose is unclear; overly directive managers and situations in which my autonomy is compromised; pointless meetings; and large 'networking' events." An ISTP said, "Don't tell me I can't do something and try to restrict my freedom."

Both types, especially INTPs, find it stressful when they don't have sufficient time to be alone and introvert, which makes multiple meetings and meandering agendas particularly noxious for them. Both types are also stressed when strong emotions are displayed at work, an event that often engages their inferior Extraverted Feeling. An INTP described her stressors as "emotionalized situations and interpersonal conflict." An ISTP said he finds it stressful "when individuals get hung up on their personal preferences—refusing to let their emotions take a backseat, which becomes an obstacle."

In a work situation in which the particular stressors for Introverted Thinking types persist over a long period, an ISTP or INTP may be pushed into the grip very quickly and powerfully by the triggers described here. His or her subsequent demonstrations of "grip" behavior are likely to be frequent and pervasive. When persistent stress causes these types to be chronically in the grip of inferior Extraverted Feeling, episodes of intellectual inefficiency and poor use of logic can become habitual. Their typical and "normal" moderate dissatisfaction with their work situation can also become chronic. They may complain continually about others' incompetence and the irrationality of management. They are likely to feel singled out for victimization and may imagine elaborate but baseless "conspiracies" being hatched by co-workers or supervisors that are designed to make the ISTP or INTP look bad and exclude him or her from decision-making roles at work. One INTP described this as "feeling paranoid."

INTPs tend to find more areas of life to be stressful than do ISTPs, and they have fewer available ways of coping with stress than any other type. However, ISTPs report the second-highest frequency (ISFPs being first) of hypertension and heart disease. INTPs, like INFPs, report these conditions relatively infrequently.

The Form of the Inferior

Like Introverted Feeling types, Introverted Thinking types often report becoming uncharacteristically sociable, outgoing, and expressive of feelings as part of their inferior function experience. This is reported by both males and females of these types and by individuals of all ages. However, the loss of social inhibition is likely to emerge eventually in easily expressed anger, being loud and perhaps inappropriate and obnoxious. Introverted Thinking types seem to report less pleasure in losing their inhibitions than do Introverted Feeling types, perhaps because they are uncomfortable extraverting their normally introverted critical Thinking. It may be that their naturally unspoken critical stance emerges more quickly than it does for ISFPs and INFPs.

As the Introverted Thinking type's conscious control of differentiated Thinking starts to diminish, use of that dominant function along with auxiliary Sensing or Intuition becomes increasingly difficult. The internal struggle for control may be largely unobserved by others. But as time goes on, others may notice a certain slowness, vagueness, and distractibility replacing the sharp acuity that they are used to seeing in the ISTP or INTP. Introverted Thinking types report becoming illogical, inefficient, unfocused, and scattered. An INTP described becoming "emotional, edgy, disorganized, obsessive about details, confused, closed. Usually I am easygoing, centered, and creative and see lots of options." An ISTP reported becoming "confused, disorganized, unable to focus. I lose track of my organizational strategies and get messy." A young ISTP described himself as "slow and dimwitted, forgetting stuff all the time." And a youthful INTP said, "I lack the mental energy and clarity that I ordinarily maintain. I'm not able to concentrate at all. I become completely illogical."

As inferior Extraverted Feeling becomes more prominent in the demeanor of the Introverted Thinking type, it comes out in the form of logic being emphasized to an extreme, hypersensitivity to relationships, and emotionalism. For ISTPs, tertiary Intuition may aid and abet these

Table 6 Dominant and Inferior Expressions of Extraverted Feeling

As Dominant Function of ESFJs and ENFJs	As Inferior Function of ISTPs and INTPs
• Comfortable inattention to logic	• Logic emphasized to an extreme
• Sensitivity to others' welfare	• Hypersensitivity to relationships
• Sharing of emotions	• Emotionalism

forms, appearing as a conviction of some imagined "pattern" of others' uncaring neglect of the ISTP's needs and feelings. For INTPs, tertiary Sensing takes the form of an obsessive review of the facts and details that prove that others neglect the INTP's needs and feelings.

The comparison between dominant and inferior Extraverted Feeling is shown in Table 6.

Jung (1976a) touched on a combination of these characteristics as they can be seen in their inferior form:

> Because of the highly impersonal character of the conscious attitude, the unconscious feelings are extremely personal and oversensitive, giving rise to secret prejudices—a readiness, for instance, to misconstrue any opposition to his formula as personal ill-will, or a constant tendency to make negative assumptions about other people in order to invalidate their arguments in advance—in defense, naturally, of his own touchiness. (p. 350)

Logic Emphasized to an Extreme Effective dominant Extraverted Feeling types are quite comfortable making decisions that are not logical. Introverted Thinking types in the grip of inferior Extraverted Feeling may become passionately insistent on the application of logic, becoming quite emotional about their approach. As an extension of their loss of control over the Thinking function, the Introverted Thinking type begins to engage in excessively logical, unproductive thinking. There may be an obsessive quality to this thinking. One ISTP feels compelled to "prove" the accuracy of his perception of things. An INTP said, "If a problem comes up that I'm unable to resolve, I work at it anyway and can't let go of it, even if I know I can't solve it."

Other Introverted Thinking types report becoming less articulate, speaking rapidly and disjointedly, and using sharp, clear, but "paranoid" logic. They may find that they forget things, misplace objects, and engage in futile projects that don't accomplish anything and are marked by disorganization. One INTP described becoming rigidly stuck on a false belief that at the time seemed totally supported by logic. Later, he was able to reassess his conviction as an inferior "Feeling judgment masquerading as logic." "I am very impatient, demanding, and extremely logical," said another INTP. "I am obsessively analytical," said another.

Hypersensitivity to Relationships Effective dominant Extraverted Feeling types value their relationships with others. They carefully consider the well-being of others in making decisions and devote energy and enthusiasm to personal and social interactions. In the grip of inferior Extraverted Feeling, the Introverted Thinking type experiences increasing hypersensitivity to "Feeling" areas. And just as Extraverted Thinking types struggle to maintain controlled efficiency and competency when in the initial grip of the inferior function, so ISTPs and INTPs valiantly try to hide their formerly alien concerns with being liked and appreciated. In this unfamiliar state, they overinterpret or misinterpret others' innocent comments or body language. "I nail someone and babble forever about my feelings and all the terrible things 'they' are doing to me," said an ISTP. However, to the Introverted Thinking type, the perceived slights are accurate and authentic. Something as innocuous as someone failing to say hello upon entering a room, or briefly interrupting a conversation to greet a passerby, may be interpreted as an indicator of dislike and disapproval. ISTPs and INTPs tend to feel discounted when others do not listen to them attentively. "I tend to be emotionally hypersensitive when I'm 'not myself.' It's extraordinarily different from my usual state of logical 'emotional detachment,'" said an INTP.

Others are usually slow to catch on to the altered state of the Introverted Thinking type, as was noted earlier for Extraverted Thinking types. Distress, anxiety, and annoyance are typically expressed with minimal cues—a raised eyebrow, a distant look, or other subtle body language may be the only signal. Further, family, friends, and colleagues, who are in the habit of trusting the person's careful, objective analysis of people and events, are likely to take the ISTP's or INTP's conclusions as objectively true. They have little reason to doubt, for example, that the boss doesn't appreciate the INTP and won't let him do a particular project. They are therefore unlikely to inquire about the evidence used to reach this definitive-sounding judgment.

In its extreme form, the grip experience of Introverted Thinking types may manifest as a feeling of profound and infinite separateness from the whole of humanity. The ISTP or INTP is convinced that he or she is unloved and ultimately unlovable. Some relive childhood feelings of being extremely different from other children, marching to a different and unacceptable drummer, often with no clue about how others see things. The memory of childhood misery and helplessness may intensify the adult's inferior function experience.

Emotionalism Effective dominant Extraverted Feeling types readily share their values with others and are comfortable expressing their emotions. In the grip of inferior Extraverted Feeling, Introverted Thinking types may not differentiate between the expression of Feeling values and the expression of emotion. We may witness a confusion between Feeling as a judging function and emotion as a state of physiological arousal. Jung (1976b) was explicit in his differentiation of the two:

> What I mean by feeling in contrast to thinking is a judgment of value; agreeable or disagreeable, good or bad, and so on. Feeling so defined is not an emotion or affect, which is, as the words convey, an involuntary manifestation. Feeling as I mean it is a judgment without any of the obvious bodily reactions that characterize an emotion. Like thinking, it is a rational function. (p. 219)

Nevertheless, it appears true that dominant Thinking types, especially those who favor Introversion, do not have ready access to their emotions when they are operating in their habitual, dominant mode. Often they report not knowing or being able to describe a feeling at the time it is occurring. Some INTPs, however, report being able to infer the presence of a feeling by attending to intuitive cues; it may be recounted later in Thinking, analytical terms. They fear that once in the realm of intense emotion, they may become possessed by it and never be able to get out. That is why descending into "the depths" is rare and entered into against the will of the Introverted Thinking type.

Lack of familiarity with felt emotion is probably due to the fact that Thinking judgment typically excludes subjective values and affective data from the decision-making process. How the Thinking type or others feel about things may be judged irrelevant to the problem at hand and therefore as interfering with logical decision making. In contrast, Feeling types typically consider such data entirely relevant to their decisions. Their primary decision-making criteria include personal values, feelings, and consequences for important people and institutions.

Due to limited experience, therefore, Thinking types' emotional expression lacks the differentiation and subtlety of feeling seen in well-differentiated Feeling types. When positive feelings are involved, they may seem maudlin and sentimental. One INTP said she becomes "mushy, sentimental, very outwardly emotional, and unpredictably so." A young ISTP said, "At times I feel really emotional when I'm by myself thinking about things that normally wouldn't bother me." With greater intensity, inferior Feeling comes out as raw, extreme emotion. Feeling judgment seems to become increasingly exaggerated and obsessive, reaching a point where it no longer serves a judging purpose but becomes unbridled emotionalism. "I am 'hysterical.' I believe that nobody likes me and I am worthless . . . [and] have nothing to contribute to society. Whereas normally I am very happy to be alone, when I am 'not myself' I seek affirmation from everyone. I call all my friends until I feel better," related an INTP. An ISTP said, "I talk about inner feelings and show emotions. I don't usually do that; I also express criticism toward others—I usually keep it to myself."

When the contents of this normally unconscious, primitive function rise to the surface, they appear as a loss of control over emotional expression. There are reports of irritability and difficulty in holding back frustration and anger. In early phases, the Introverted Thinking type may become fidgety, trembling, and sarcastic, stomping around and making verbal attacks, exaggerating and accusing others. In more extreme cases, there may be physical outbursts that include breaking things and attacking people.

An INTP college student was deeply involved in a research paper when some of his friends invited him to go to a carnival with them. He refused, but they persisted anyway. When one grabbed his pen and paper and teasingly refused to return them, he began yelling at her and grabbed her arm. Both he and his friends were surprised and frightened by the swiftness and intensity of his reaction.

Although expression of anger is common, especially in younger ISTPs and INTPs, often there is increasing self-pity and a sense of feeling neglected, unappreciated, and even victimized. With greater loss of control, Introverted Thinking types can burst into tears with no warning. One wrong word can trigger an emotional outburst accompanied by rage, crying, and rising emotionality. Some describe feeling as if all their emotions are all mixed up, released with uncharacteristic spontaneity. "I start to notice my own feelings and become moody and impatient; I deny to others that anything is wrong, but all the while I feel like I am drowning in emotions," said one ISTP. Another described being "very emotional and unable to keep my reactions to situations under control."

Not only are their own emotions problematic, but so are the emotional reactions of others. Some Introverted Thinking types say they cannot truly understand something in the Feeling arena if they haven't actually experienced it. As a result, when they are in the grip of their inferior function, they find that emotions from others are upsetting and only intensify the magnitude of the situation. The three manifestations of the inferior function typically appear together. One INTP feels martyred and cannot help snapping, whining, and complaining to people. She reports becoming very emotional and a little irrational, unable to organize or problem-solve with her usual efficiency and competence. Another INTP describes feeling numb, frozen, or enraged, as well as exhausted and unable to concentrate.

Some describe an inability to keep their emotions to themselves, even though they wish to reveal little of their internal processes. In this state, said an ISTP, "I act out my displeasure rather than keeping it to myself as I am inclined to do. The actual acting out is usually brief, but feeling stressed out about it may last longer." An INTP described the shame she associates with experiencing extreme feelings; she also described blaming others for not appreciating or loving her enough. Paramount is a sense of being misunderstood, with no way to correct the misunderstanding. Other ISTPs and INTPs report similar reactions.

Lengthy Episodes in the Grip

The types of episodes described above are experienced by the ISTP or INTP as temporary states during which they are vulnerable to the three forms in which their inferior function is expressed. However, when an Introverted Thinking type is chronically in the grip of inferior Extraverted Feeling, inferior function behavior may become habitual. Both the individual and others are likely to believe that angry, emotional accusations, somewhat outlandish and complicated explanations of others' behavior, inefficiency, and poor use of logic are part of the natural makeup of the ISTP or INTP. Others may assume that the individual has always been hypersensitive, hypercritical, and overly emotional. Since the process of becoming chronically in the grip is often gradual, even people who have known the person in a nonstressed state are likely to be unaware of what, in retrospect, will be recognized as a radical alteration of personality. The Introverted Thinking type will appear to be a rather exaggerated, poorly developed Extraverted Feeling type, as illustrated in several of the stories in the next section. However, there are also occasions when a lengthy period in the grip of inferior Extraverted Feeling can stimulate new awareness and positive growth toward completion and individuation. The last story is an example of what Jung meant when he described the inferior function as the doorway to the unconscious and an important part of the self-regulating capacity of our psyches.

Grip Experiences

The stories included in this section illustrate one or more forms of inferior Extraverted Feeling as experienced by ISTPs and INTPs. Note the nature of Introverted Thinking that comes through in relating the episodes; they tend to be presented as a detailed, logical progression of events that are analyzed objectively. For this reason, some of the stories are longer than those for other types. Like their Extraverted Thinking counterparts, Introverted Thinking types report the inferior function experience as relatively rare but powerful.

"Who Was Sitting Beside Me?"

Andrea reported that her ISTP husband, Jim, was normally cool and controlled, rarely showing anger. But he was becoming increasingly frustrated over his failure to reach a compromise with his ex-wife over the education of their son. One afternoon, after a frustrating visit with Jim's ex-wife, Jim and Andrea were on their way home. Jim was driving. At a stoplight, the driver in the car beside them shouted at Jim that he was driving too close. Jim said nothing but got out and walked over to the other car, reached in, and punched the driver in the nose. Still silent, he returned to his own car and drove on. Andrea was shocked. She did not recognize the man beside her.

Jim made no mention of the incident and acted as though it had never happened. Days later, when Andrea asked him about it, he explained that his reaction had been completely spontaneous. He recalled that just before the incident occurred he had been feeling intense frustration and helplessness about the disagreement with his ex-wife. "That jerk in the car gave me a quick way to get rid of my anger," Jim said. "I felt better immediately. I stopped obsessing about that lousy visit right after that."

"I Can't Do My Job Because Nobody Likes Me!"

Eleanor, a CPA and professor of accounting at a small college, recalled a puzzling episode. She had recently undergone major surgery and had been very apprehensive about it. It was early March, the height of tax preparation time, when she typically works fifteen-hour days, seven days a week. Her children were involved in a lot of activities at school, and she was also responsible for running several training programs at her college. On the weekend preceding the "event," she had driven sixteen hours to get to a training session she was to run.

Orville, an administrator at her college, was fired on a Friday morning. Eleanor was aware of how upset everyone was as a result of the events precipitating the firing. On Monday, she was asked to replace Orville and reorganize his department. However, Orville's second-in-command, Ted—an ISTP who was also Orville's best friend—had thought he would be the one appointed to the position, and he verbally attacked Eleanor in an abusive, violent manner. Eleanor did not react emotionally. "I figured it was reasonable and logical that he would be upset, so I didn't take it personally."

Eleanor felt fine on Tuesday; but on Wednesday Ted repeated his abuse. She reminded herself of her logical analysis of the situation and thought about how stupid Ted was being. In fact, she phoned him that night and told him she was angry at him for his childish behavior.

On Thursday, Eleanor felt disconnected, couldn't concentrate, and was plagued with doubts about her judgment. On Friday, Ted resumed his attack on her, leaving Eleanor feeling confused and disliked:

I then began asking everyone in the organization whether they liked me. I made an appointment with the president of the college and told him I was resigning because no one liked me. I told a colleague I couldn't work in the department because no one liked me. I told my dean the same thing. I kind of took a survey of everyone to find out how they felt about me.

One colleague, knowing Eleanor's typical INTP values, told her it didn't matter if people didn't like her, as long as they respected her. "I just couldn't see the logic in that," said Eleanor. She felt she had to resign everything administrative and resume her teaching. This conviction lasted all day.

Eleanor went to bed very early that night and woke up the next day thinking, "My God, what have I done?" In analyzing what happened, Eleanor described herself as at first denying her own upset, excusing the behavior of her colleague, and disavowing her own humanness and vulnerability to being hurt. This new awareness led her to "try to recognize when I'm hurt and call people on it. But I have to give myself permission to take the time to get to my feelings."

Solving the Puzzle

Carl, an ISTP businessman, had for years kept an earlier life episode locked away as puzzling, unsettling, and unexplainable. Hearing a brief description of the effects of the inferior function provided him with instant understanding and relief from the unresolved but still disturbing memory of the event.

He had been divorced for several years when the incident occurred, some ten years before. It was close to the holidays, and he had just broken up with a woman he had been seeing for some time. He found that although he apparently functioned adequately at work, at the end of the day he could not remember what he had actually worked on. His work life was a blank. At night when he was alone, however, he was hypersensitive to any kind of stimulation, such as the sound of dogs barking or cars driving by.

Carl started reading various self-help and inspirational books. He recorded his feelings in the form of poetic yearnings for love and attention, and a need to be cared for. He became so immersed in this side of himself that he ate and slept little. When he discovered that he had lost thirty pounds in as many days, he visited his doctor, who recognized his need for a psychologist and referred him accordingly.

The doctor's confirmation that something was out of joint psychologically for Carl apparently pushed him out of his inferior Extraverted Feeling and back to himself. By the time he appeared for his appointment with the psychologist, he was back to equilibrium and handling things normally again.

In one of his late-night musings, Carl had written a lengthy essay that began with the words, "Am I a lost little boy in a grown-up world?" It went on to speak of his pain, loneliness, and desire for love and intimacy. He signed the essay, "By Author Unknown." After his insight into his grip experience, he revisited the earlier episode, reread his essay, and wrote a new conclusion: "Author Understands—ISTP," and signed it Carl Smith.

Descending into the Painful Depths

Elizabeth, an INTP, discovered that understanding her own inferior function and that of her son led her to valuable insights. She described "descending into the murky, confusing, painful depths and learning an important lesson." She wrote the following account of her experience:

> It had been a difficult year and a half. My fourteen-year-old INFP son, a handsome, loving, and smart child, had turned into an angry, surly teenager. I knew he was using drugs, shoplifting, even staying out all night. I was having my own problems—I was unemployed and dealing with a serious family illness. With the help of some wonderful people in social services, I found help for my son, which eventually resulted in his spending more than a year in a mental hospital treatment program.
>
> Now things were vastly better. I was working, the family illness problem had receded, and my son was able to come home from the hospital. Through family therapy, we had learned to deal with each other in a much more positive and cooperative way. I was cautiously optimistic.
>
> Almost immediately, a serious disagreement arose about what my son was to do in the long afternoons after he got out of school, before I returned home. My perspective was totally reasonable. He had been locked up for more than a year with every minute in his life structured. He needed structure and support as he made this big adjustment to freedom. The high school was full of drugs and the kind of people he had hung out with before his hospitalization. We needed to agree on a plan for his free time. But he was beginning to sound like he had before

the hospitalization: It's my life, I'm old enough to decide for myself, I can take care of myself, it's none of your business!

This discussion was repeated nightly for several days. I used my best calm and reasonable Thinking approach, while my son became more and more nasty and angry. Our new relationship seemed pretty fragile. After one of these evening discussions, I was suddenly swept by a feeling of total inability to deal effectively with my son and the fact that everything we had done had not worked—my daily visits to the hospital, the weekly meetings with his therapist, the agonizing learning I had done in the weekly family therapy, the thousands of dollars I'd spent were all for nothing. We were right back where we started. Worst of all, my son, my beautiful, intelligent son whom I loved and had tried to save, was back to his self-destructive behavior and completely lost to me.

I burst into tears and, fortunately, instead of recounting all the sacrifices I had made for him, what came out of my mouth was my deepest anguish—my love for my son. I sobbed, "Jim, I can't tell you how awful this is for me. At work, I can't concentrate. I'm distracted all the time. When I know it's almost time for you to get out of school, I start getting sick to my stomach. I can't eat lunch; I become ill. I'm so worried about what might be happening to you, that you might be hurt or in trouble and I wouldn't even know."

My disrespectful son was transformed into a loving boy again. "Oh, Mom, I'm so sorry. I didn't know you felt like that. I'm sorry, Mom, I'm so sorry!" By now, he was sobbing, too. "I don't want you to feel like that. Look, as soon as I'm out of school, I'll call you and tell you what I'm going to do. If I'm going to somebody's house, I'll give you their name and phone number. I'll call you when I'm going to leave. I'll call you every hour if you want," and on and on, with restrictions I would have never thought of suggesting to a fifteen-year-old boy. After a time of hugging and patting and wiping away tears, we were able to agree to an arrangement that worked for both of us.

What I now see is that my long, careful appeals to his reason—his inferior function—had not worked. They hadn't ever worked; I don't know why I thought they would then! In despair and helplessness, I fell into the grip of my inferior function and expressed spontaneous Feeling, something he had rarely, if ever, seen me do. This spoke to his dominant function and brought out his truest judgment—that he loved me and wanted me to be happy. Every other consideration fell by the wayside; all he wanted to do was relieve the genuine anguish he sensed in me.

The lesson I learned is that if I am willing and able to go into this alien part of myself—to experience and express what I spontaneously feel—I can make real contact with my son. It is so difficult to do, so uncomfortable for me, though, that I seldom do it. Only once can I remember doing it voluntarily. But it's good to know that when all my reason and logic and imagination and humor have failed, this other part of me is there.

The next story describes how a well-functioning INTP with a high stress tolerance became aware of her chronic inferior function state—and what she did about it.

Listening to an Inner Voice

I worked for a large nonprofit hospital before it went public. The culture of the organization revolved around a quality care mission, and this image was projected within both the hospital and the community.

As a senior-level manager, I was responsible for providing leadership for a hospitalwide quality improvement initiative. I was very committed to the initiative, which I believed would provide better health care for patients.

The administrator who had hired me for my position was promoted to national headquarters. The administrator who replaced him was not at all committed to our quality initiative. I was personally disappointed and frustrated by the new administrator's response. However, because I was in a leadership position, I tried to keep my feelings in check.

About six months after the new administrator arrived, the company merged with another health care system that was notorious for bottom-line thinking. The company went public, and increased profits became ever more important. Departmental budgets were cut and our high standards of patient care started to diminish. To make matters worse, my division now reported to someone five states away.

I love to work. When I'm in a leadership position, my mind is continually occupied, analyzing and looking for solutions to problems. When the administrative changes began, I found myself alternating between depression and anger. I couldn't bring myself to accomplish the kinds of tasks that had always energized me. I started to waste time, griping with other employees about problems we were no longer empowered to solve. For the first time in my working life, I wasn't proud of the work I was accomplishing.

One day, I had a sudden flash of insight. I realized that I had gone from a positive-minded and naturally good-natured person to a negative and often angry person. I recognized that I was not happy with myself. So, I made the decision to leave my secure and well-paying job. My friends and family thought I was making a bad financial decision

(I was one year away from vesting with the company's pension plan and I also lost the opportunity for stock options). In hindsight, I realize my sense of survival would not let practical considerations keep me from listening to my inner voice. I needed to let my positive faith in the future carry me through the decision.

With the way life works, my life's journey has taken many twists and turns, mostly positive but some not. Today I am very happy with my career and life. I look back and am glad that I had the courage to listen to my inner voice. I think my positive sense of self would have been diminished if I had not acted to change a situation that was inherently unhealthy.

Return of Equilibrium

As the preceding stories illustrate, equilibrium is often restored rather dramatically after an intense expression of emotion. However, when more short-lived experiences of the inferior are involved, Introverted Thinking types find that changing activities can aid the normalization process. What is most important for both ISTPs and INTPs is spending time alone, including exercising primarily alone. Introverted Thinking types need to be alone and physically separated from others, doing something they find enjoyable or relaxing. "I need alone time, to remove myself from the situation and to think about the problems, and then I need a close friend to help me analyze it," said a young ISTP woman. Trying to identify the problem and wrestling with its solution are typical approaches for Introverted Thinking types, who find that reframing the cause of the distress is often helpful. "I need time to think through the issues," said an INTP. "Others can help by affirming that my response is okay because the situation I'm in is unreasonable and stressful. They should *not* ask if I'm okay."

Light problem solving that engages but doesn't strain their Thinking, such as reading a mystery novel, can be helpful. Both types agree that they require time by themselves, that others need to leave them alone, and that it is most unhelpful for others to try to help them in any way, to ask how they feel, or to try to minimize their distress. Often there is little that others can do. Internal acceptance and calm are what is needed most. Others can help most by staying out of the way and forgiving the out-of-character behavior. A trusted person's physical presence is not intrusive, but psychological space should be respected. It is also helpful if someone close to them can gently encourage them to talk about their feelings after sufficient time has passed. However, many Introverted Thinking types report that the very worst thing someone can do is ask them how they feel about things.

ISTPs' auxiliary Sensing can be helpful in encouraging them to perform a reality check on the stressful situation. This occurred when Carl, the ISTP businessman, discovered that his doctor recognized his distress. This made his situation real and forced him to deal with it. Some INTPs can calm themselves down by playing unusual games of solitaire that don't depend on luck for success. Such games engage their auxiliary Intuition. The repetitive handling of the cards (tertiary Sensing) also has a calming effect. One INTP said that it helps to get engaged in a project he enjoys, and others describe engaging in distracting, absorbing forms of recreation.

Being excused from usual responsibilities and having someone else deal with the outer world helps Introverted Thinking types achieve equilibrium. Like many other types, ISTPs and INTPs find physical activity of some kind, especially hiking, to be a good way to detach themselves from a grip state.

Expressions in Midlife

Ideally, midlife is accompanied by a positive and progressive integration of inferior Extraverted Feeling, and along with it tertiary Intuition or Sensing. Some Introverted Thinking types, however, do not achieve such integration.

Older ISTPs and INTPs who have not succeeded in reaching their full developmental potential may become increasingly malicious in their criticism, seeming to take pleasure in others' distressed responses. Their sphere of interests and tolerance of others' differences narrow considerably. They may be seen as eccentric recluses to be feared and avoided. Others' responses then serve to confirm the Introverted Thinking type's conviction that he or she is unloved and unlovable. When this conclusion becomes immutable, there is little that can be done to alter beliefs on either side.

Midlife in well-differentiated Introverted Thinking types is accompanied by increasing sensitivity to the nuances of important relationships. There may be a corresponding decrease in the hypersensitivities that characterized their grip experiences when they were younger. Emotionalism is largely replaced by more readily expressed warmth and affection. An ISTP in his early forties discovered the pleasures of spending "unproductive" time with his wife and family. An INTP decided to marry her partner of twenty years, negating her previous view that "the piece of paper was irrelevant and illogical."

Notwithstanding the degree of adaptation of the individual, the right circumstances can still constellate a full-blown inferior function experience, with all its intensity. A 50-year-old INTP became increasingly depressed and despairing when her only son and his family left the country for three years. She became convinced that she had failed him emotionally and that his leaving was a result of that.

Some Introverted Thinking types become articulate about their Feeling values during the second half of life. A 54-year-old INTP said:

> When I am in the grip, it generally doesn't concern things that I know I am intellectually competent at doing, but rather relationship issues. Investments in relationships are made at the core of who I am. What sends me over the brink are incidents that significantly devalue the meaning I have attached to my part of the relationship. It is almost as if the other person has come along and erased the blackboard—first by indicating that the meaning I thought I had communicated no longer exists and second by indicating that the essence of myself that was invested in that meaning has no more significance than chalk marks on a blackboard.

Sometimes spending a lengthy period in the grip of inferior Extraverted Feeling can serve as an important stimulus to midlife development for Introverted Thinking types. The combination of the natural upheaval of midlife and the disruption and distress of a chronic grip experience may push an ISTP or INTP into serious soul searching and reconsideration of long-standing goals, which may lead to significant changes in the way the second half of life is lived.

Knowledge from Grip Experiences

In addition to recognizing and trying to avoid the stress and fatigue that may lead to a grip experience, Introverted Thinking types learn from their grip experiences to accept the fact of their emotions, to acknowledge that not everything can be explained by logic and that emotional reactions don't have to be based in logic. They learn that expressing their emotions can help them empathize with others and that others' expressions of emotion are natural and normal. With repeated grip experiences, ISTPs and INTPs also can come to appreciate their own natural style, accepting it as a valid way of being. As a result, they often become more willing to socialize in their own way and more comfortable and diplomatic in letting others know of their needs for physical and psychological space. When stress, either at work or at home, is extreme and persists over time, Introverted Thinking types are likely to suffer through as long as they are still able to devote sufficient time to activities that satisfy their dominant Introverted Thinking and there is some hope of eventual reduction in stress. When they have been in the grip for a lengthy period and finally become aware of their habitual out-of-character state, perhaps by becoming ill or seriously depressed, or by being confronted by others, they are likely to drastically change their work or home situation or simply leave.

Summary

In the grip of inferior Extraverted Feeling, Introverted Thinking types have difficulty functioning at their typical level of cognitive acuity, are hypersensitive to relationship issues, and can be touchy and emotional. Equilibrium is often reestablished via their auxiliary Sensing or Intuition. ISTPs acknowledge one or more important realities bearing on their situation; INTPs find a new idea or perspective that interrupts and modifies their exaggerated sensitivity or emotionalism.

As a result of important inferior function experiences, Introverted Thinking types can acknowledge the importance of the "illogical and unexplainable" and accept their vulnerability to their own and others' emotional states. They may then have access to and be able to express the depth of their feelings for others. Table 7, on the following page, provides an overview of the major features of their inferior function experience.

Table 7 Inferior Function of Introverted Thinking Types: ISTP and INTP

Triggers for the Inferior Function	Forms of the Grip Experience
• Strong emotional expressions	• Logic emphasized to an extreme
• Disconfirmations of Feeling values	• Hypersensitivity to relationships
• Insensitivity to Introversion needs	• Emotionalism

Ways of Returning to Equilibrium	New Knowledge
• Repect of their physical and psychological space by others	• Acceptance of the illogical
• Excusing them from responsibilities	• Acknowledgment of vulnerability
• Avoidance by others of asking them how they feel	• Ability to express depth of feeling

9

Extraverted Feeling Types
ESFJ and ENFJ

BASIC TYPE DYNAMICS

DOMINANT EXTRAVERTED FEELING

AUXILIARY INTROVERTED SENSING OR INTUITION

TERTIARY INTUITION OR SENSING

INFERIOR INTROVERTED THINKING

Extraverted Feeling Versus Introverted Thinking

THIS CHAPTER EXAMINES the way effective Extraverted Feeling types experience their inferior function and the temporary transformation they make into ineffective, inferior Introverted Thinking types when they are either briefly or chronically "in the grip." A review of the characteristics of Extraverted Feeling and Introverted Thinking will be helpful to our discussion.

Important Features of Dominant Extraverted Feeling

Extraverted Feeling types typically radiate goodwill and enthusiasm. They are optimistic about life in general, and human potential in particular. They prefer to focus on the positive, harmonious, and uplifting aspects of people and human relations, paying little attention to negative, pessimistic, limiting, and divisive messages, situations, and conclusions. Their primary goal is to create and maintain good feeling and harmony among people.

Although ESFJs and ENFJs may recognize judgments that rely heavily on logical analysis, cause-and-effect relationships, and statistical odds, they largely ignore such factors in making decisions. Others may therefore see these types as making decisions that "fly in the face of logic." Thinking types may be particularly puzzled and frustrated when an Extraverted Feeling type accurately describes the logical conclusions warranted by a situation but decides in favor of harmony and caring. From a Thinking point of view, using such a criterion in decision making is inappropriate.

Extraverted Feeling types are careful not to hurt others' feelings and try to take others' well-being into account. If they cannot avoid telling someone an unpleasant truth, they will carefully soften the message by putting it in an affirmative context. Unconditional positive regard is a strongly held value.

As a result of their natural pleasure in pleasing others, Extraverted Feeling types can mistakenly be seen as overly caring or even codependent. In reality, attending to others' needs is usually a satisfying, legitimate way of expressing their dominant Feeling preference.

In a crisis that does not activate their inferior function, ESFJs and ENFJs focus on alleviating the concerns and suffering of others. They are comfortable letting others manage the more technical aspects of a crisis so they can devote their energies to creating a cooperative, comfortable atmosphere for crisis victims. When a situation demands more forceful methods, however, they will take any action necessary for the benefit of others.

Extraverted Feeling Types at Work

A work environment that supports and encourages the enactment of important values is highly energizing and satisfying for Extraverted Feeling types. ESFJs and ENFJs welcome hard work and responsibility that enhance and contribute to the development and well-being of people. Both male and female ESFJs and ENFJs rank "helping people" as their first work priority. Interacting with other people at work is another source of great enjoyment.

Extraverted Feeling types also want to be acknowledged for their special contributions and valued as members of a team. "Seeing how my work affects people and their potential for working as a team; helping people accept and value themselves and each other" were cited as energizers by one ENFJ. An ESFJ described as most energizing "working on a team to carry out an activity or implement a design; getting recognition for a contribution I have made and having control over my time, schedule, and work." An ESFJ in his early twenties who is in a military training program is energized by "the positive effect I have on the American public. I love wearing my uniform and showing everyone what I am doing for my country." "Possibilities for people—personal development—is and always has been my greatest joy," said an ENFJ in her sixties.

Auxiliary Sensing is shown in an ESFJ preference for straightforward, simple tasks that can be accomplished in a stable and predictable environment. Auxiliary Intuition is reflected in ENFJs' preference for a broad range of activities that enable them to use their unique talents at work and their willingness to take risks in pursuit of professional advancement. They like having an opportunity for independent, aesthetic self-expression and place a high value on being able to use their own initiative in a flexible, varied environment.

Important Features of Dominant Introverted Thinking

The qualities associated with Introverted Thinking that are relevant to our discussion of its form as an inferior function are

- Impersonal criticism
- Logical analysis
- Search for accuracy and truth

For a detailed description of dominant Introverted Thinking, read the beginning of Chapter 8, "Introverted Thinking Types: ISTP and INTP," and the type descriptions for ISTP and INTP that appear in Appendix A. This will provide the background needed to explore the various ways in which inferior Introverted Thinking is expressed in ESFJs and ENFJs.

The Everyday Introverted Thinking of Extraverted Feeling Types

The inferior function affects Extraverted Feeling types in several different ways. These include their everyday sensitivities, projections, and ways of relaxing, as well as the dramatic manifestations that can be seen when the inferior erupts and a full-blown episode occurs, or when an ESFJ or ENFJ is chronically in the grip because of long-term stress.

Typical Sensitivities and Projections

Extraverted Feeling types can be particularly sensitive about others' assessment of their intellectual competence. Although they don't usually doubt their abilities, they may worry that they have not communicated their knowledge clearly. In comparing themselves to others, they may see themselves as slow to learn and lacking in analytical facility. Though many, especially ENFJs, are high achievers, some feel they are at a disadvantage in highly intellectual and technical endeavors.

This sensitivity about their intellectual competence makes Extraverted Feeling types particularly attuned to comments that could be interpreted as reflecting on their adequacy. In the early stages of an inferior function episode, this may manifest as a projection onto others of their own feared incompetence. They may notice and comment on others' inaccuracies and their failure to recognize reality and confront the truth.

Such projection can be seen in the intensity with which they criticize others' behavior, particularly in the area of control. An ESFJ became furious whenever her INTP supervisor barged into her office and interrupted her to talk about whatever was important to him at the time. In reflecting on her reaction, she realized that she herself needed to resist barging in on others and demanding their attention when she had a problem to solve or was upset about something.

Extraverted Feeling types may be quick to identify other people's illogical behavior, but they may apply a different set of criteria to their own equally nonlogical actions. An ENFJ complained that his INFP wife's art studio was not set up systematically. "You really should put things into some logical order so they'll be right there when you need them," he told her. She replied that her current system suited her way of working. "But it's just not rational," he responded. When his wife likened the "disorganization" he perceived in her studio to his illogical way of organizing his household chores—his inefficient way of ordering tasks and his tendency to leave tasks half done—he insisted that this was not the same thing. "The cleaning gets done, doesn't it?" he said heatedly. "My artwork gets done, too," she replied. He remained blind to the similarity.

Expressions Through Interests and Hobbies

Perhaps because the demands of their daily work and home lives require them to use their less-preferred processes, Extraverted Feeling types seem to choose recreational activities that engage their dominant and auxiliary functions rather than their tertiary or inferior ones. They enjoy such activities as entertaining, playing bridge, participating in group sports, and generally socializing. A hardworking, highly regarded ENFJ district attorney loved to organize large dinner parties that brought together people from different parts of her busy life. Extraverted Feeling types are often avid readers who enjoy discussing books with friends or becoming active members of book groups.

Home improvement hobbies are also quite satisfying to Extraverted Feeling types. Sewing, crafting, building, carpentry, decorating, and gardening are often mentioned as enjoyable activities. ESFJs and ENFJs may be great joiners of civic, political, or school-related groups and tend to willingly take on leadership roles. One ESFJ, who enjoys a demanding career, takes pleasure in cooking elaborate meals for others, working in her garden so it will look beautiful, and writing lengthy letters to old friends— all activities that give her special joy because she has so little time for them.

ESFJs and ENFJs may also enthusiastically support the work, interests, and hobbies of their spouses and/or children, taking great pleasure in developing at least some expertise in the relevant areas. One ENFJ learned all he could about his wife's research area and was as genuinely excited as she was when the results fit her hypotheses.

Eruptions of Inferior Introverted Thinking

When one or more of the preconditions for an eruption of the inferior function are present, Introverted Thinking appears in its more exaggerated, disruptive form. In addition to the general conditions described in Chapter 4, Extraverted Feeling types are vulnerable to the type-specific factors described below.

Typical Provocations or Triggers

Extraverted Feeling types respond with inferior Introverted Thinking when they perceive they are being misunderstood, not trusted, not taken seriously, or pressured to conform to some prevailing view with which they disagree. In fact, any situation in which conflict persists and remains unresolved can activate the inferior function of ESFJs and ENFJs. Being unable to use their natural preferences can also serve as a provocation since it arouses their sensitivity about their competence. An ESFJ mentioned as triggers "too many things to do all at once; short time frames, extra responsibilities and tasks that require me to think on my own and don't allow me to bounce ideas off of others."

When asked what provoked being "beside himself," an ENFJ responded, "too many demands and feeling that I'm not appreciated, that I'm being taken for granted, and that what I do doesn't matter to anyone." Another ENFJ cited "impersonal treatment, criticism, and not being appreciated for my contribution." An ESFJ said "when people disagree with my point of view and attack me personally." Another cited "if I can't get my point across no matter how hard I try; when I'm not allowed to talk something out to get it resolved."

ESFJs and ENFJs recognize that disagreements can arise and that criticism is a necessary aspect of working with people. However, the way in which critiquing and conflict are handled makes a difference. An ENFJ stated that what could provoke an inferior function response for her was "criticism that is delivered in an unfeeling way—or when I find out that I have done something that hurt another person and the person doesn't tell me until months later."

Triggers and Stressors at Work

Work environments that force conformity to values that are contrary to those of the Extraverted Feeling type, that place other concerns above the welfare of people, and that fail to recognize the individual contributions and value of employees are very stressful for ESFJs and ENFJs. For one ESFJ, the work demands that are most stressful are "high technology, strong competition between work peers, a lack of opportunity to show my strengths, and being placed in situations in which I am constantly using my inferior function." Conflict in the workplace is also upsetting for Extraverted Feeling types. Working with uncooperative or undermining people and dealing with an overwhelming workload are particularly stressful for ESFJs. Female ENFJs often mention dealing with details, general disorganization, and lack of recognition as quite stressful. One cited "details, proofreading—routine detail tasks," and another, "plowing through detail" as sources of work stress.

In work situations in which the particular stressors for Extraverted Feeling types continue over long periods, ESFJs and ENFJs may respond quickly and intensely to the triggers described here. This increases the likelihood that their subsequent demonstrations of "grip" behavior will be frequent and pervasive. When persistent stress causes them to be chronically in the grip of inferior Introverted Thinking, they are likely to lose touch with their natural optimism and trust in human potential and become negative, critical, and judgmental toward everything and everyone around them.

The Form of the Inferior Function

Some Extraverted Feeling types mention becoming uncharacteristically logical and analytical, with a tendency to think before they speak, when they are in the grip of their inferior function. Such experiences of Introverted Thinking are not generally seen as either positive or negative—merely as strangely different. Perhaps the prevailing societal favoring of Extraversion over Introversion makes Introverted forays into Extraversion (note the comments for Introverted Feeling types and Introverted Thinking types) more appealing to Introverts than the converse experience of Introversion for Extraverts.

For Extraverted Feeling types, the more obviously distressing aspects of "losing" their dominant Extraverted function seem more prominent. Falling into the grip for them is preceded by a diminution or an absence of characteristic Extraverted Feeling qualities. General optimism, enthusiasm, and interest in people give way to low energy, pessimism, and depression. Uncharacteristic withdrawal from usual activities and becoming highly critical of others are consistent responses for male and female ESFJs and ENFJs. "I'm different in being Introverted. I don't make contact, call friends, go to social events, meetings, the theater. I may accept an invitation, but only if someone urges me. I get concerned about my health. I have no plans, no vision, the future is bleak. I am numb, without feeling or zest for life," said an ESFJ. An ENFJ said, "I am quiet and withdrawn and want to be alone and reflect on what is happening." Commented another, "I feel phony and uncomfortable, like a fish out of water. I am unable to be my usual spontaneous self." Another ENFJ said, "I don't make eye contact. I can't share what is going on inside me. I feel tight and negative." An ESFJ said, "I want to be *alone*—I'm uninterested in anyone else."

Jung's (1976a) comment on the inferior function of Extraverted Feeling types touches on all three of these features:

> The unconscious of this type contains first and foremost a peculiar kind of thinking, a thinking that is infantile, archaic, negative. . . . The stronger the conscious feeling is and the more ego-less it becomes, the stronger grows the unconscious opposition. . . . The unconscious thinking reaches the surface in the form of obsessive ideas which are invariably of a negative and deprecatory character. (p. 359)

Tertiary Sensing and Intuition serve to support the negative judgments that are made. The tertiary Intuition of ESFJs generates vague, negative "hypotheses" that affirm their convoluted "logical" critical stance about themselves and others. ENFJs bring their tertiary Sensing to bear by coming up with negative past and present "facts" that support their complicated and largely illogical critical judgments.

As energy continues to be withdrawn from the dominant and auxiliary functions, inferior Introverted Thinking intrudes in the form of excessive criticism, convoluted logic, and a compulsive search for truth. The comparison between dominant and inferior Introverted Thinking is shown in Table 8.

Table 8 Dominant and Inferior Expressions of Introverted Thinking

As Dominant Function of ISTPs and INTPs	As Inferior Function of ESFJs and ENFJs
• Impersonal criticism	• Excessive criticism
• Logical analysis	• Convoluted logic
• Search for accuracy and truth	• Compulsive search for truth

Excessive Criticism   Effective dominant Introverted Thinking types critique ideas, products, systems, and methods. The inferior Introverted Thinking of Extraverted Feeling types appears in the form of a sweeping condemnation of people. In the grip of inferior Thinking, ESFJs and ENFJs may "dump" on other people, slam doors, yell, make biting comments, and say terse, blunt, or even cruel things to others. They often become physically tense, grit their teeth, clench their fists, and appear visibly agitated. Both Extraverted Feeling types frequently mention "laying a 'guilt trip'" on those closest to them as responses to being in the grip. An ESFJ said that her automatic response to anyone's "excuses" about his or her work is to state emphatically, "Well, it's not good enough!"

A hostile, negative atmosphere can elicit sharp, biting, even vicious comments from Extraverted Feeling types. They seem to dig in their heels, becoming impervious to either logical or feeling arguments. As one ENFJ described, "I become cranky, judgmental, and angry. I mistrust myself and others. Normally, I instinctively trust everyone. I am different when I am not acting from trust. Often this occurs when I feel I am not trusted or understood, or when there is conflict and tension around me."

An ESFJ reported becoming steely and caustic; another described herself as being coolly objective when her strongly held feelings were violated. One ESFJ was convinced that everyone took advantage of her good-natured, helpful ISFP husband. She persistently berated him for his weakness and loudly condemned his family and friends for their rude behavior.

"I am like Dr. Jekyll and Mr. Hyde," said an ENFJ, describing his reaction to extreme stress. "My humor becomes inappropriate, meant to shock people. I've even been known to throw things while in this frame of mind." An ESFJ said he becomes "angry, out of control, critical, responding too quickly to others with impatience, cutting a person off when they speak." "I'm critical rather than seeking harmony, self-protective rather than 'giving,'" said an ENFJ.

As their Extraverted energy further diminishes, their criticism is internalized, resulting in self-deprecatory judgments. Turning the criticism inward encourages depression, low self-esteem, and guilty embarrassment at revealing what they view as their alien and unacceptable side. An ENFJ related the following story, which illustrates a natural progression from using dominant Extraverted Feeling to projecting inferior Introverted

Thinking onto others, then to turning that judgment on herself, and finally returning to reasoned Extraverted Feeling judgment.

> When my father died, at first I thought I was okay. I was buoyed up by all the support I was getting from others. Also, he'd been sick a while. But then I had a delayed reaction. First, I started finding petty little faults with everything and everyone around me, like people on the subway. But then I became very self-critical. As an example, at the time, I was taking a facilitation workshop, in which I had to be videotaped. I was so sure I'd bombed that I cried in the bathroom after the taping. When I finally (reluctantly) watched the video, I saw that I actually had done pretty well.

Convoluted Logic   In the grip of inferior Thinking, the Extraverted Feeling types' attempts at logical analysis take the form of categorical, all-or-none judgments that are often based on irrelevant data. A highly idiosyncratic "logical" model may be developed internally, but the resulting conclusions may violate good logic.

In describing this quality, Von Franz (1971) stated that because Extraverted Feeling types' Thinking is neglected, "it tends to become negative and coarse. It consists of coarse, primitive Thinking judgments, without the slightest differentiation and very often with a negative tinge" (p. 45).

"My thinking becomes rigid and I insist on solving problems alone, with none of my typical sharing," said one ENFJ. "I maintain a front, even though I feel unworthy. I am verbally critical, organize more, and become rigid, perfectionistic, and angry. I want the world to go away." Another ENFJ described being "inside my head analyzing—adding two and two and getting five and knowing it's right."

Elaborate, logical "plots" may be developed by the Extraverted Feeling type in the grip of negative Introverted Thinking. These take the form of complicated and improbable scenarios for dealing with or eliminating the distress or disharmony in question. ESFJs and ENFJs frequently describe making up "stories," the goal of which is to explain some upsetting event or solve some nagging problem.

An ENFJ recalled that at the age of twelve, she was required to participate in a field day of sporting events. Convinced of her lack of skill in this area, she wanted to avoid embarrassing herself in front of her peers. She plotted various ways to break her leg or ankle, such as falling out of a tree or being run over by a car, but she abandoned her plans, reasoning that she would probably suffer more than minor injury. She also recognized that a lot of pain could be involved. Ironically, her forced participation resulted in her placing third in the broad jump.

Often the source of the problem stimulating the "story" is meanness or criticism directed at the Extraverted Feeling type or a close associate. An ESFJ with a long commute to work was frequently distressed by other drivers' rude, inconsiderate behavior. He found himself "making up a long and involved story about one particular rude driver, in which I imagined the kind of work he did, his family relationships, the daily events that affected him, and the possible mitigating circumstances that caused his meanness to me." The imaginary explanation served to restore harmony and allowed the ESFJ to retain his positive valuation of people.

Compulsive Search for Truth   Dominant Introverted Thinking types value truth as the criterion for judgments and decisions. They use logical analysis to arrive at the most objective truth possible. For Extraverted Feeling types in the grip of inferior Introverted Thinking, seeking absolute, ultimate truth can become an obsession. Many report turning to experts for advice but requiring them to have the "real truth," or at least the latest knowledge and thinking on the subject. When an expert is not immediately available, they may attempt an internal logical dialogue, often ending up recognizing that their logic is convoluted. This may make them feel frightened, out of control, and despairing of ever extricating themselves from their negative logical conclusions. An ENFJ said:

> I become stuck on an idea and don't have any perspective about it. The devastating truth of my conclusion is overwhelming. I try to think my way out of this tight box I'm in, but there is no escape from my conclusion. I feel compelled to find someone to tell me what to do.

Instead of searching for a specific person who might provide them with needed answers, many Extraverted Feeling types report turning to lectures or books relevant to their current problem; these types are often avid readers of self-help books. ESFJs and ENFJs agree that when stress occurs in some area of their lives, they search bookstore shelves for answers.

One ENFJ had a wall full of books in his office. His colleague wondered how he could possibly have read all of them. The ENFJ reported that when under pressure to solve a big problem, he virtually devours the books, having many of them open at once, searching for expert advice on the problem at hand.

When a stressful area is chronic or serious, Extraverted Feeling types tend to be attracted to support groups. In the company of others having similar experiences, they can find validation for their perceptions, as well as the latest expertise and thinking about the problem area.

Lengthy Episodes in the Grip

The types of episodes described above are experienced by ESFJs and ENFJs as temporary states during which they are vulnerable to the three forms in which their inferior function is expressed. However, when Extraverted Feeling types are chronically in the grip of inferior Introverted Thinking, inferior function behavior may become habitual. They will then be seen as having a sour, disapproving approach to people and to life in general. Instead of their upbeat and enthusiastic usual selves, others will experience them as gloomy, unhappy people who are reluctant to acknowledge and support optimism and good feeling in others. In this state of chronic, distorted Introverted Thinking, ESFJs and ENFJs become rigidly pedantic, expressing defensiveness and hostility when their often faulty judgment is questioned. Internally, the Extraverted Feeling person applies this same negative assessment to himself or herself. A sense of worthlessness and incompetence can become all-consuming, and the Extraverted Feeling type can project this onto others by being hypersensitive to imagined slights and negative assessments. Such a stance can lead to rifts in lifelong friendships that may never be healed.

The auxiliary Intuition of ENFJs may contribute to their reporting a greater variety of coping resources and options for dealing with stress than do ESFJs. ESFJs are particularly vulnerable in situations in which their experience level and self-confidence are already low, especially where they don't have others to help them. ENFJs report physical stress symptoms. Exercise is found to be helpful by both male and female ESFJs and ENFJs, as is talking to someone about issues (especially for female ESFJs). Extraverted Feeling types in general are also clear that they need time alone to reflect on what is happening, often before talking to others.

Chronic grip behavior may lead both the individual and others to believe that pessimism, negativity, and global disapproval are a part of the natural makeup of an ESFJ or ENFJ and that he or she has always been that way. Since the process of becoming chronically in the grip is often gradual, even people who have known the person in a nonstressed state are likely not to notice what, in retrospect, will be recognized as a radical alteration of personality. The person will appear to be a rather exaggerated, poorly developed Introverted Thinking type. For example, a woman had known an ENFJ many years ago but had lost contact with her. She was surprised when an acquaintance mentioned the ENFJ as a work colleague and described her as habitually negative, critical, and pessimistic. "But when I knew her, she was a happy, optimistic person who always saw the bright side of life!" the woman exclaimed. Apparently, the intervening years had been fraught with disappointment and loss for this ENFJ, leading to chronic grip behavior.

However, there are also occasions when a lengthy time in the grip of inferior Introverted Thinking can stimulate new awareness and positive growth toward completion and individuation. Remember that Jung saw the inferior function as the doorway to the unconscious and an important part of the self-regulating capacity of our psyches.

Grip Experiences

The stories included in this section illustrate one or more forms of inferior Introverted Thinking as experienced by ESFJs or ENFJs. Their dominant Extraverted Feeling emerges in their concern for and distress about the people they have hurt during their out-of-character episodes. Like their Introverted Feeling counterparts, they take responsibility for repairing damaged relationships when the episode is over.

The Experts Are in the Bag

Emma, an ESFJ, was seeing a psychologist because of ongoing problems with her marriage, her career, and her adolescent children. One afternoon after Emma's appointment, the psychologist discovered in her waiting room a large shopping bag filled with self-help books on topics dealing with marriage, family, children, and careers. On top of the pile was a note from Emma that read: "These are the experts I've been reading. I'd like to know what you think of them." Apparently, Emma wanted the newest expert, her psychologist, to evaluate the expertise of her predecessors.

"I Can, I Can, I Can, I Can't . . ."

When Extraverted Feeling types are vulnerable to an inferior function experience, they may decide that they absolutely must learn some new skill or accomplish some unfamiliar thinking task. This was the case for Sam, an ENFJ, who decided one March that he would no longer use an accountant to prepare his tax returns. His taxes that year were rather complicated, but he assured himself that any intelligent person could figure out how to fill out the forms.

Each time the instructions confused him, Sam laid the taxes aside, telling himself he could tackle the project successfully "tomorrow." As April 15 approached, he became increasingly agitated and angry at himself, but he continued to struggle compulsively with his tax problems. "I did not even consider asking for help. Conquering the tax code had become the essential criterion for my intellectual competence," he recalled.

"I couldn't let go of it. It became the symbol of my incompetence. I had to see it through, or forever acknowledge that I was intellectually inferior," he said several weeks later. He went on to explain:

> It was as if I had created a self-fulfilling prophecy. I still don't know why I picked that one thing. I tried to remind myself of all the things I was good at, but none of them counted. When I think about it now, I believe I had been undertaking too many things, both at work and at home, feeling like I had to be perfect at everything. This experience forced me to change my expectations of myself. I think that now I can be more reasonable about what I should be able to do.

"Or I Could Bribe the Doorman"

Angela, an ENFJ, was told that she would have to wait several weeks before learning whether she was to be hired for a coveted job. She felt anxious during that time, powerless to influence the decision in any way. She found herself developing complicated schemes to surreptitiously discover whether she had gotten the job: "I could put on a disguise and reapply for the job to find out if they'd filled it—or I could bribe the doorman of the building to look at my file!"

As time dragged on, she sought advice from others about which interventions to pursue. She reported feeling ungrounded and uncaring about people. Her single-mindedness about this one issue puzzled her friends, who were used to her sensitivity to others' needs and her wide-ranging interests. Her family accused her of not being herself, of being spacey, and of failing to take responsibility for the rest of the family. These accusations increased her sense of "otherness" and her feeling of being outside herself.

Receiving word that she would be hired for the job was a relief for Angela, but it was also anticlimactic. However, with the unaccustomed stress and her out-of-character reaction to it over, she recognized that she had allowed this one event to be the criterion for her competence:

> It forced me to think about my abilities and to recognize that I was indeed quite accomplished in my field. Since then I've been better able to deal with ambiguous situations and to put criticisms of my work in a positive perspective.

"What Kind of Father Would Raise Such a Son?"

Harold, an ESFJ single father, was helping his 21-year-old son, Dave, an ISFP, move into his first apartment. Dave had assured his father that he would have all the packing and organizing done ahead of time and would only need some help putting his things into the truck he was borrowing from a friend.

On the day of the move, however, Harold found that Dave's things were in general disarray, that little had been packed, and that he had forgotten to ask his friend for the pickup truck! From Harold's point of view, Dave did not know how to proceed and could not figure out how to ask for help—or even what kind of help he needed. Worse, his son seemed quite unconcerned about the whole thing. Harold then began to see his own fault in the matter:

> At first I felt frustrated and angry at Dave. But as the day went on and we got things under control, I felt more and more tired, depressed, and hopeless. I thought about how incompetent my son is about everyday life, recalled all the other examples of this same kind of inadequacy, how unprepared he was to live as an independent person. As a widower, I was responsible for Dave's upbringing. Clearly, I had failed in that task. It was due to my own incompetence as a parent that my son was unable to succeed in life. I sank deeper and deeper into despair.

But after a good night's sleep, things did not seem quite so bleak to Harold. Dave called to say he had gotten his phone hooked up and his utilities turned on and that he had done some grocery shopping. He seemed delighted with his apartment and was enthusiastic about being on his own.

"I started recalling all of Dave's many successes," remembered Harold, "how he could persevere and overcome situations that were difficult for him. I realized that being superorganized is my thing, not his, and that lives don't stand or fall on this one ability. My good humor and optimism about the future reappeared. I relaxed and was able to enjoy shopping with Dave for some household items."

Two Inferior Functions Meet in the Kitchen

Judy, an ENFJ, and her husband, Luis, an INTP, were doing the dinner dishes together after what had been an extremely stressful and tiring day at work for both of them. Judy let the dog out and he began to bark. Luis particularly disliked the sound of dogs barking and had previously asked Judy not to let the dog outside in the evening, as he often barked at the neighbor's dog. Without a word, Luis stopped drying the dishes, left the kitchen, entered his study, and slammed the door behind him.

Judy finished cleaning the kitchen, feeling increasingly despairing about her inability to meet Luis's need for quiet and solitude. She became angry with his habit of shutting her out and "sucking himself into his study."

> I knew he could avoid dealing with the hurt between us much longer than I could. But I couldn't imagine any way to alter the overwhelming fact of our incompatibility. Obviously, we were unable to meet each other's needs, so our marriage would have to end.

Judy sat down to write Luis a letter describing her conclusions. She wrote that she was incapable of creating a comfortable atmosphere for him, acknowledged his right to prefer being alone to being with her, and conveyed the logical conclusion that their relationship was therefore over.

Even while she was writing, Judy recognized that her thinking was off. At one point in the letter, she wrote, "This probably sounds out of bounds, even out of mind." She had an inkling that her logic was amiss but was unable to marshal the energy to remove herself from the logic-tight tunnel she was in. The larger and more potent issues in her marriage were thus unavailable to temper the relatively minor incident of Luis's irritable behavior.

Luis later described his irritation as brief and the result of his fatigue. It was unrelated to his commitment to their marriage. But in Judy's vulnerable state, the incident took on the importance of a defining event for their marriage and logically implied its termination. "Our discussion of this and other similar misunderstandings led us to a new appreciation for and interest in each other," explained Judy. "It brought us closer and made our relationship more intimate and satisfying."

Silence in the Face of Injustice

An ENFJ shared this detailed account of her lengthy grip experience.

A few years ago I was recruited to work in the public sector, I was very happy in my job and enjoyed my colleagues and manager very much. Then, due to a restructuring and interoffice conflicts, a new manager was hired, and soon the woman who had hired me was ousted. I had previously worked with the new manager as a colleague, and I hoped we could develop a good working relationship. This was not to be, however. The manager divided the staff, hired people who would "spy" on others, and tried to rule through intimidation and cruelty. It was not uncommon for her to refer to "my sources" when accusing people of ridiculous offenses and, when questioned, say she couldn't breach confidentiality.

Time after time, I challenged her cruelty. Once she demanded that a 42-year-old administrative assistant ask permission to use the restroom! I continued to speak up when I felt that she had humiliated others or tried to get me to speak against my colleagues. She apparently knew that I had been asked to apply for the manager position but had declined; having been on staff less than a year, I wanted more experience with the frontline work before climbing the administrative ladder. The manager kept telling me that "people on the outside wanted you to run this place, you know!" Our statistics were fabulous and our evaluations from the funding source and clients superb. She couldn't get rid of us. But she made it clear that anyone whom she hadn't personally hired was persona non grata, and she wanted us out!

As the weeks wore into months and incidents of irrationality became the norm, I definitely got "into the grip." This woman would accuse me of being "too positive" and "trying to hide something" because I didn't believe in saying negative things about my co-workers. She told me to "get real" and said "the sky isn't blue, you know" when I tried to explain my ways. She said I was "unrealistic" and that wasn't good for our clients, who were job seekers. She said being unemployed was nothing to cheer about and forbade me to get my resume work-shops rocking with cheers and laughter. (I had an almost 80 percent placement rate within ninety days of intervention with a client!)

As I rode the elevator up to the office each morning, I could phys-ically feel energy draining from my body. My face began to freeze and I could not even smile at the manager any more. Days would go by when I avoided her as much as possible and didn't speak to her (or the two other staff members who enjoyed her games). I refused all social gatherings where she might be present and remember fighting tears throughout the day. I became sullen, even maudlin, looked for oppor-tunities to complain about ridiculous things—like details that weren't important but might embarrass the powers that be.

Eventually, I began to enjoy watching my manager squirm as I pur-posely made her ill at ease. I laughed when someone did something that set her off and enjoyed her confusion. I attended public events and didn't show support when she spoke. (I really should have, considering her position.) That was so unlike me that my colleagues knew some-thing was up. Each day one of my team members would ask me how they could help. They took abuse from the manager and knew that if I saw it, I would speak out. It was awful because I didn't understand why they didn't speak out, too! I felt she would have no power if we didn't allow her to divide us, and I instinctively knew that the way things were going, she would destroy us one by one. My anger and frustration grew to encompass not only this horrible manager but my colleagues as well. Why didn't they *do* something?

I began to lose sleep and was short-tempered and critical at home, using snide comments with my family. My tears flowed readily. Nor-mally able to handle a hundred different tasks, now I was overwhelmed if the laundry built up or if something spilled on the floor. I felt that if this manager were to fall down in front of me, I would do only the min-imum to keep her breathing and would not really care whether any medical personnel showed up. For someone who worries about animals being hurt on the road, this was a huge departure from character. I felt like my heart was turning to stone.

Finally, after three others had quit, I knew that I couldn't go on any longer and handed in my resignation. I could not tolerate the person I was becoming. I had lost weight and become moody; I cried fre-quently and began to question my ability to work with people. The people I loved didn't like me anymore. It was time to move on.

That was the beginning of my road back to self-esteem and to get-ting out of the grip. It was also the impetus I needed to start my own business. So, in a strange and sad way, even though she was trying to hurt me and many others, the horrible manager actually helped me become a risk taker.

I now realize that silence in the face of injustice is never acceptable. I did the right thing in speaking up. The only thing I should have
done differently was leave earlier—before I became "in the grip"!

Return of Equilibrium

Normal access to dominant Feeling returns as Extraverted Feeling types
allow new information to enter their consciousness. This may occur
through either auxiliary Sensing or Intuition. Experiencing a change of
scenery, listening to a friend talk about something interesting or amusing,
spending time outdoors, and exercising can all aid the process of return to
equilibrium. (Although most of the types find that exercise alleviates stress,
Extraverted Feeling types, ENFJs in particular, consistently mention regular exercise as important in tempering both short-term and long-term
stress.) One ENFJ said he sometimes needs to take long breaks that allow
him to withdraw from his usual hectic schedule and spend time in more
solitary study and physical exercise. An ESFJ said that what helps is "humor
and laughing and light entertainment."

Extraverted Feeling types appreciate being encouraged to get involved
in projects. ENFJs find it helpful to embark on an ambitious new undertaking, even if they have to force themselves at first; ESFJs may prefer to
work on a smaller, detailed project that can be accomplished slowly and
methodically. An ENFJ said that returning to herself was aided by "talking
with a close friend who reminds me of my strengths and qualities, and
starting work on a task with possibilities." Talking things through with
someone who cares seems to be particularly helpful for ESFJ women, but
is also helpful for all Extraverted Feeling types. An ENFJ explained, "I need
to spend time with someone who gives me feedback and says I'm an
okay person—the conflict isn't because I've done something bad."

ESFJs and ENFJs frequently mention the need to be taken seriously
by friends and to be allowed to vent without being talked out of it. Like
other types when they are emerging from the grip, Extraverted Feeling
types do not appreciate being patronized or dismissed or told "It will be
okay; don't feel like that." They are being genuine when they say they want
to be left alone. An ESFJ said she returns to herself "by spending time
alone, working through things in my mind, often getting away from the
situation or environment physically." Writing in a journal can also help

them fulfill this function by allowing them to extravert auxiliary Sensing or Intuition on paper. They may get a handle on the problem without fearing external judgment or interference, and also get enough distance and perspective to recognize the tunnel vision with which they have been operating.

Expressions in Midlife

Many Extraverted Feeling types turn inward during midlife, pursuing more solitary activities. One ENFJ reported that when she was younger, she never spent her free time reading the way she does now. Often the desire to be alone also reflects an emerging attraction to activities that do not focus on having harmonious relationships with others.

Those ESFJs and ENFJs whose adult years were insufficiently fulfilling may become caricatures of their younger selves. Indeed, they may satisfy the criteria for codependency, demonstrating an inability to separate themselves from others. One ESFJ grandmother insisted on babysitting full-time for her three grandchildren. When her daughter later decided to enroll the children in preschool, she felt useless and rejected and needed to be treated for depression. In fact, the daughter's decision was in response to her mother's "smothering" care, which she feared was inhibiting her children's exploration and development of their independence.

An ENFJ minister in his sixties was advised by his physician to give up some of his many community activities, since the fatigue and stress that resulted were seriously affecting his health. He was unwilling to comply, however, fearing criticism for failing to fulfill his commitment to serve others. He became anxious and depressed when he was unable to fully devote himself to taking care of others.

Extraverted Feeling types whose adult development is more complete tend to temper the kinds of behaviors that earlier in their lives might have made them look overly attentive to the needs of others. Said one ENFJ:

> I am not the "ever-flowing breast" I was when I was younger. I don't give of myself indiscriminately as I once did. I can say no when a request doesn't appeal to me and not feel bad about it. I still enjoy being

helpful and seeing the people around me happy and fulfilled. But I've become very interested in going bird-watching by myself, and this often is more appealing than being with other people.

An ESFJ acknowledged her difficulty in taking care of herself because of her need to accomplish other necessary tasks first. So she has learned to include time for herself in her schedule. She may spend forty-five minutes reading a good book on a Saturday afternoon. This has proven so enjoyable that she no longer resents having to stay up late on Sunday night finishing her ironing.

Another ESFJ said:

I learned not to live through my children or be so concerned about controlling their happiness. I take one day at a time, enjoying the journey rather than the destination. Being liked is not as important to me as when I was younger. It's most important to be true to myself. I can say no a lot more easily and not try to fix everything.

In paying more attention to their own needs, many Extraverted Feeling types may also rediscover their earlier career interests that were not actualized. This sometimes results in a midlife career change. A 55-year-old ENFJ attorney gave up his successful law practice to attend divinity school and become a minister in the church he had been devoted to much of his life.

Both ESFJs and ENFJs report paying greater attention to their inner lives at midlife, often aided by formal meditation methods. They may feel and be seen as more calm and focused in their behavior. An ENFJ described the older ESFJs and ENFJs she knew as "having a gracious, warm Extraversion tempered with a calm wisdom. I experience it as containing a realistic objectivity that allows them to possess an acceptance of life's foibles with sad resignation and optimism."

Sometimes spending a lengthy period in the grip of inferior Introverted Thinking can serve as an important stimulus to midlife development for Extraverted Feeling types. The combination of the natural upheaval of midlife and the disruption and distress of a chronic grip experience may push an ESFJ or ENFJ into serious soul searching and reconsideration of long-standing goals, which may lead to significant changes in the way the second half of life is lived.

Knowledge from Grip Experiences

In addition to learning to recognize situations that are likely to lead to a grip experience, Extraverted Feeling types develop a greater ability to accept dissension and conflict, to stay with it and work through it. They also learn to delay making decisions until they are out of the grip—a useful learning for all types! Their devotion to helping others is tempered by accepting that sometimes it is appropriate to put themselves first. "I need others; I don't need to sort the world out," said one ESFJ. Recognition of their own intellectual competence is also a valuable learning, especially for ESFJs, who often feel at a disadvantage in this area. One said, "I need external affirmation of my strengths and intelligence. I am learning to affirm this for myself, also to tell myself not to panic when someone is talking 'N' (i.e., using Intuitive language), and to stay with it until I understand. And not to feel stupid if I have to ask for clarification."

When stress either at home or at work is extreme and persists over time, Extraverted Feeling types need frequent breaks from it and an opportunity to reflect on their essential values and goals. "I need to force myself to see the 'big picture' and try to make changes to improve my opportunities to use my strengths," said an ENFJ. If in a work situation such opportunities remain unavailable, Extraverted Feeling types may eventually leave.

Summary

In the grip of inferior Introverted Thinking, Extraverted Feeling types engage in excessive criticism of others as well as themselves, adopt a distorted and convoluted logic, and compulsively search for exacting truth. Auxiliary Sensing or Intuition may help them reestablish their equilibrium. ESFJs may work on a task requiring systematic attention to detail; ENFJs' return to equilibrium can be aided by planning new projects.

The new awareness Extraverted Feeling types gain as a result of an important bout with their inferior function often centers on achieving acceptance of the limitations reality imposes on their desire for peace and harmony. They may become better able to evaluate their own logical analyses and face adversity more dispassionately. Their auxiliary Sensing or Intuition can aid in this process. ESFJs may acknowledge previously rejected unpleasant facts, while ENFJs may permit their Intuition to flow into darker possibilities. Both are then able to increase their effectiveness in accomplishing goals important to their value structure. Table 9 gives an overview of the major features of the inferior function of Extraverted Feeling types.

Table 9 Inferior Function of Extraverted Feeling Types: ESFJ and ENFJ

Triggers for the Inferior Function	Forms of the Grip Experience
• Absence of trust	• Excessive criticism
• Pressure to conform	• Convoluted logic
• Interpersonal conflict	• Compulsive search for truth

Ways of Returning to Equilibrium	New Knowledge
• Solitude and journal writing	• Less need for harmony
• Taking on a new project	• Trust in own logical thinking
• Honoring by others of their need to be left alone	• Tempered response to adversity

Extraverted Sensing Types

ESTP and ESFP

Extraverted Sensing Versus Introverted Intuition

THIS CHAPTER EXAMINES the way effective Extraverted Sensing types experience their inferior function and the temporary transformation they make into ineffective, inferior Introverted Intuitive types when they are either briefly or chronically "in the grip." A review of the characteristics of Extraverted Sensing and Introverted Intuition will be helpful to our discussion.

Important Features of
Dominant Extraverted Sensing

Extraverted Sensing types are typically out "in the world." They experience sensory data from the environment purely and directly. At their best, they can cut to the heart of a situation and implement an effective solution. They are able to appropriately ignore hidden implications, hypotheses, past traditions, and future possibilities. This may underlie the economy of effort that characterizes their style. They tend not to dwell on problems that are outside their control, and they rarely focus for long on anything negative and thus are typically optimistic. In trusting the evidence of their senses, they do not attribute unseen motives to others; they take people and situations at face value and accept others as they are.

Unlike Introverted Sensing types, they do not organize their sensing data into preexisting categories or systems. Rather, data are accepted without discrimination and are only later subjected to sorting and selection through their auxiliary Thinking or Feeling function. This, in conjunction with the immediacy of their perceptual process, may underlie their natural affinity for sensual and aesthetic experience.

ESTPs and ESFPs are likely to be impatient with people who read between the lines and focus on the unseen and the unverified. They have little interest in theories, pure speculation, and imagination for its own sake. They tend to see people who prefer Intuition as living inside their heads while ignoring the realities and beauty of the world.

Extraverted Sensing types may be perceived by others as shallow in their pursuit of sensual pleasure and as lacking the goals and ambitions valued by society at large. However, others may also admire and envy the Extraverted Sensing type's carefree enjoyment of everyday living.

In a crisis that does not engage their inferior function, Extraverted Sensing types are likely to be calmly efficient and effective. Their knack for quickly identifying and attending to critical variables places them in a good position for emergency situations.

Extraverted Sensing Types at Work

Extraverted Sensing types are energized by work environments that not only encourage achievement in their areas of interest but accommodate their preferred ways of working. The freedom to control their time and work in their own way and at their own pace is important to both male and female ESTPs and ESFPs. One ESFP said she liked "being extremely busy and in control, having people notice, and hearing positive comments; knowing that I am not being watched at work and can do my job the way I want."

Extraverted Sensing types enjoy achieving and being recognized for their work, both as part of a team and independently, and they prefer working on projects with tangible outcomes. ESTPs enjoy leading and directing others and particularly want autonomy in their work, perhaps as an expression of their auxiliary Thinking function. Auxiliary Feeling for ESFPs emerges in their focus on friendly and compatible team relationships. In fact, ESFPs seem to enjoy their relationships with co-workers, and this may minimize their reported dissatisfaction with many aspects of the work environment, such as promotions and job security. They also put a high value on being able to interact with other people. ESFP women enjoy being busy at work, and a high activity level appears to energize ESTP men. An ESTP said he found it energizing "to be out and about talking with others, developing ideas, soliciting others' input, and socializing with friends and co-workers." Another likes "a lot of work that interests me that has to be done. It excites me."

Important Features of Dominant Introverted Intuition

The qualities associated with Introverted Intuition that are relevant to our discussion of its form as an inferior function are an emphasis on

- Intellectual clarity

- Accurate interpretation of perceptions

- Visionary insight

For a detailed description of dominant Introverted Intuition, read the beginning of Chapter 11, "Introverted Intuitive Types: INTJ and INFJ," and the type descriptions for INTJ and INFJ that appear in Appendix A. This will provide the background needed to explore the various ways in which inferior Introverted Intuition is expressed in ESTPs and ESFPs.

The Everyday Introverted Intuition of Extraverted Sensing Types

The inferior function affects Extraverted Sensing types in several different ways. These include everyday sensitivities, projections, and ways of relaxing, as well as the dramatic manifestations that can be seen when the inferior function erupts and a full-blown episode occurs, or when an ESTP or ESFP is chronically in the grip because of long-term stress.

Typical Sensitivities and Projections

Extraverted Sensing types may experience some uneasiness about their natural affinity for fun in the present moment, often picking up on others' disapproval of their carefree approach to life. One 49-year-old ESFP mother of three grown children confessed that she did not feel quite "grown up." Her peers had detailed plans for the future, including retirement, while she rarely planned beyond the next month. The 9-year-old son of another ESFP mother often tells her he would like her to "do more things the same way—like eat meals at the same time and know beforehand what we're going to do on Saturday." His mother's reaction is to feel (at least briefly) inadequate as a parent. "He told me I'm like the mother in that movie *Mermaids*—she was constantly moving the family around, and she fed them only snack foods instead of real meals."

An ESTP physician reported a recurring dream in which his medical degree was revoked because he had failed to keep current on the literature. An ESFP corporate executive felt he had to justify his managerial legitimacy since his function was to entertain important potential clients. He sensed that the other executives devalued his contribution to the firm. An ESFP sales representative worried that her supervisor would fire her for maintaining a very flexible work schedule, even though she continued to be the top salesperson in her district.

In the early stages of an inferior function episode, ESTPs and ESFPs may project their negative Intuition by attributing meaning to isolated minor occurrences. Because making inferences about meanings is not a natural, practiced activity for Extraverted Sensing types, it is to be expected that the conclusions they draw are often quite off the mark. A phone call from an old friend might lead to an inference about some impending event; a song popping into an ESTP's head might be taken to mean that her supervisor is angry; a "message" is read into a friend's request to borrow a car; or a wife coming home later than usual arouses suspicion in an ESFP that she is having an affair. One ESFP described seeking "divine intervention" when having to make decisions, especially about the future. He looks for signs that will tell him what to do (if three green cars pass in the next five minutes, it means yes; three blue cars means no). Although he never actually uses this strategy to make decisions, the thoughts come automatically and are quite compelling.

The everyday projection of inferior Introverted Intuition often emerges as intolerance of and disdain for the ideas, theories, and free-flowing musings of people who prefer Intuition. ESTPs and ESFPs are especially likely to disparage and even ridicule the complexity and perceived impracticality of their Introverted Intuitive opposites. An INTP recalled feeling hurt when, as a child, she wanted to buy a book of mathematical puzzles at the bookstore and her ESFP mother said, "Well, I don't understand why you would find that stuff interesting!" Extraverted Sensing types' own uneasiness with this and similar kinds of intellectual endeavors can also be observed in their belief (often an accurate perception) that Intuitive types judge the ESTP or ESFP as intellectually wanting, simpleminded, and shallow.

Expressions Through Interests and Hobbies

Extraverted Sensing types, like their Introverted Sensing counterparts, may be attracted to areas that address the mysteries of Intuition, especially Introverted Intuition. Systems that deal with inner forces, mysticism, and various forms of extrasensory perception may hold a particular allure. The pull is toward knowledge that depends on processes beyond the immediacy of the five senses. An ESFP-ESTP couple were active in a theosophical society in their city. Their other major recreational activity was the local ski club.

Extraverted Sensing types' ability to temporarily take on the qualities of their environment may contribute to their enjoyment of leisure activities. An ESFP is an avid reader of both nonfiction and fiction. She finds that she easily identifies with the characters in good books, "totally becoming them" while she is reading. An ESTP seeks out the company of happy people because it raises her spirits.

Extraverted Sensing types whose work lives require them to maintain strict schedules and focus on ideas and concepts often use their leisure time to satisfy their dominant and auxiliary functions. For example, an ESFP manager in a highly structured organization developed excellent calligraphy techniques to create unique greeting cards for friends and family.

Eruptions of Inferior Introverted Intuition

When one or more of the preconditions for eruption of the inferior function are present, Introverted Intuition appears in its more exaggerated, disruptive form. In addition to the general conditions described in Chapter 4, Extraverted Sensing types are vulnerable to the type-specific factors described below.

Typical Provocations or Triggers

Inferior Introverted Intuition can be triggered when Extraverted Sensing types spend a lot of time with people who are excessively serious or focused on future plans and goals. In fact, any situation that requires projection into the future and commitment to a distant goal may provoke an inferior function experience. For some, even committing to things in the near future can be unpleasant.

"I feel pinned down by commitments," said an ESFP. "What if I don't feel like seeing a movie tomorrow, or going out to lunch, or going on that vacation? Having to do something feels threatening and gives me a feeling of dread."

Extraverted Sensing types may experience even greater apprehension when they are forced to make decisions about distant possibilities. For them, the information needed for decision making won't be available until the future becomes the present! "How can I know now what major I'll want in college three years from now?" asked an ESFP high school senior. "What if I pick the wrong thing and have to stay with it?" An ESTP said, "If I decide to be a dental technician, I won't be able to be anything else."

Other Extraverted Sensing types agree that closing off options by making a choice makes them anxious and gloomy. "I'm filled with panic and dread when I am faced with 'have to's,'" said an ESFP. An ESFP was excited about her forthcoming wedding and looked forward to choosing silverware and fine china patterns, but she found herself quite distressed and unwilling to choose among the options. "I'll have to live with this for the rest of my life," she said. "What if after a few years I don't like what I'm choosing now?"

Triggers and Stressors at Work

Not surprisingly, Extraverted Sensing types find structure, routine, rigid time frames, and inhibiting rules to be stressful at work. Operating within a set structure that requires conformity to someone else's schedule may therefore prove debilitating to ESTPs and ESFPs. Lengthy periods in such an environment may lead to the inertia and despondence that often presage an inferior function experience.

Deadlines also raise the stress level of ESTPs and ESFPs, as does having to deal with interpersonal conflict and uncooperative people. "Structure and inflexible people" are stressful for one ESTP. Another cited as stressful "time—too many things to do in too little time; interpersonal conflict; deadlines; having to have everything (work, reports) organized and structured." An overwhelming workload and conflict in the workplace are especially stressful for female ESTPs and ESFPs. ESTP women in particular report trying to solve the stressful work problem. One said she typically reacts to work stress by "working through it. I blame myself for not being organized. I can become slightly paranoid; under high stress I talk my way out of it or pretend the work isn't there." The most prevalent way of dealing with work stress for ESFP women is to talk to others about it.

In a work situation in which the particular stressors for Extraverted Thinking types continue over long periods, ESTPs and ESFPs may respond quickly and intensely to the triggers described here. This increases the likelihood that their subsequent demonstrations of "grip" behavior will be frequent and pervasive. When persistent stress causes them to be chronically in the grip of inferior Introverted Intuition, they are likely to lose touch with their natural enjoyment of sensory data "in the moment" and become habitually worried, negative, indecisive, and deeply unhappy.

The Form of the Inferior Function

Both ESTPs and ESFPs typically become quieter and more thoughtful when they are in the grip, and this may either precede or alternate with becoming more emotional and/or easily angered. As was the case for

Extraverted Feeling types, no positive or negative value seems to be placed on this more introspective stance. Many Extraverted Sensing types who describe becoming "more introverted" convey a sense of wonder and surprise at this change from their usual way of being.

One early sign of an impending inferior function episode is a loss of the easygoing, agreeable character of the Extraverted Sensing type. Although becoming quiet and withdrawn is by far the most frequently mentioned effect, irritability and negativity are also frequently reported. No longer are sensory data accepted indiscriminately at face value. ESTPs and ESFPs often withdraw into themselves, appear to lose contact with their habitual optimism, and appear tired and worried. An ESFP remarked, "I gradually take on too much work and too many responsibilities, then I become overpowered with negative thoughts and become very quiet and sad."

An ESTP noted, "I start to feel that things are overwhelming, then I let them accumulate, and then I lose all motivation." Another ESTP said he becomes "quiet and reserved and withdraws from people." An ESFP said, "I become more contemplative, less talkative, and I'm seen by others as a serious, withdrawn person. This is not my usual self." "I feel like I have to get control of the situation," said an ESTP. "I avoid other people, feel guilty about it, and try to speed up everything I do."

As their hold on their dominant and auxiliary functions further diminishes, the qualities of inferior Introverted Intuition manifest in internal confusion, inappropriate attribution of meaning, and grandiose visions. For ESTPs, tertiary Feeling aids and abets inferior Intuition in the form of imagined personal slights that are incorporated into an elaborate "theory" that proves that others are rejecting them. ESFPs use their tertiary Thinking to come up with cold "logic" to support their theory that others see the ESFP as immature or incompetent.

The comparison between dominant and inferior Introverted Intuition is shown in Table 10.

Table 10 Dominant and Inferior Expressions of Introverted Intuition

As Dominant Function of INTJs and INFJs	As Inferior Function of ESTPs and ESFPs
• Intellectual clarity	• Internal confusion
• Accurate interpretation of perceptions	• Inappropriate attribution of meaning
• Visionary insight	• Grandiose vision

All three qualities of the negative, inferior forms of Introverted Intuition (internal confusion, inappropriate attribution of meaning, and grandiose vision) are reflected in Jung's (1976a) description of the inferior Introverted intuition of ESTPs and ESFPs:

> Above all, the repressed intuitions begin to assert themselves in the form of projections. The wildest suspicions arise. . . . More acute cases develop every sort of phobia, and, in particular, compulsion symptoms . . . contents have a markedly unreal character, with a frequent moral or religious streak. . . . The whole structure of thought and feeling seems, in this second personality, to be twisted into a pathological parody: reason turns into hair-splitting pedantry, morality into dreary moralizing . . . religion into ridiculous superstition, and intuition . . . into meddlesome officiousness. (p. 365)

Internal Confusion   Effective dominant Introverted Intuitive types are noted for their intellectual clarity—their ability to process and integrate complex information. In the grip of inferior Introverted Intuition, Extraverted Sensing types become confused by unfamiliar inner processes. An ESFP in her early twenties described being out of character when her mind starts wandering. An ESTP described herself as "flustered, haphazard, out of control, especially about details; I forget things." Because their negative Intuition is internalized, fantasies of impending disaster and dire possibilities are typically self-referential or limited to the people closest to them. They may have overwhelming fears about fatal illnesses, forebodings about losing an important relationship, and anxiety about harm coming to a loved one.

Fears of impending psychosis can also haunt ESTPs and ESFPs. The unfamiliar internal Intuitive information appears fraught with danger and impending doom. Extraverted Sensing types may feel overwhelmed by inner possibilities, disturbing images, unfamiliar self-doubt, and loss of connection to their environment. They may question their own abilities and fear subsequent exposure as incompetent in their most important endeavors.

"I feel like I am being enveloped in a whirling, swirling maelstrom," said one ESFP. "I get into a spiral filled with frightening possibilities," said another. A third ESFP said, "I cry! Everything is bad! I can be extremely creative (using my Introverted Intuition) about worrying about what could happen."

An ESTP describes feeling as though she is in a dark, endless tunnel. Another explains, "I become confused and paranoid. All possibilities are fearsome—any kind of change, anything in the future." When the trigger for the experience is being forced to think about future plans, the reaction can be devastating, as the following example illustrates:

> I am terrified that I won't be where I want to be. Not that my lack of accomplishment will be disastrous, but that it will be dreary. If I try to project myself to where I should be, it will cut off my ability to react to the moment. Instead of exciting possibilities, I can only think of disastrous ones. The thought of future change makes me feel lonely and gloomy and dreary. It all ends up with misery. So it's safer to stick with what is, but the possibilities in what is are also dreary.

For this ESTP, negative Introverted Intuition is accompanied by tertiary Feeling so that the negative possibilities appear as emotional states— loneliness, dreariness, and gloom.

Inappropriate Attribution of Meaning   Effective dominant Introverted Intuitive types are adept at interpreting their complex inner perceptions. They are highly selective in the environmental information they process. In the grip of inferior Introverted Intuition, an Extraverted Sensing type may, due to lack of experience, internalize random cues from the environment and interpret them as negative possibilities. If an intimate relationship is involved, there may be a foreboding that the ESTP or ESFP has done something to elicit a negative response from the other person. Or a simple request may be interpreted as a sign of disapproval or disappointment.

A young and newly married ESTP became overwhelmed by the thought that her husband, who had gone out with his friends, had left her and would never return—even though she knew that he visited his friends frequently and that the time at which he was expected to return had not yet arrived. She obsessed on the thought that she had been nasty to her husband earlier and became flooded with anxiety and apprehension. She thereupon drove over to his friend's house, only to find that he was just preparing to leave and return home.

Extraverted Sensing types in their vulnerable phase may start reading between the lines and attributing malevolent motives to people. A feeling of unreality or disconnection from others may occur, and this alien experience of isolation may in turn lead to terror. One ESFP was pleased to have free time while her children happily spent the weekend with her ex-husband and his new wife. But when the children were gone, she became consumed with the idea that they would prefer their new stepmother to her because she was not a good mother. They won't be my kids when they return, she told herself, so nothing is okay and it never will be again.

Grandiose Vision The visionary insight of effective dominant Introverted Intuitive types has often been noted. They have an uncanny ability to envision the distant future in an almost prophetic way. In its inferior form, this quality surfaces in Extraverted Sensing types as grandiose, often nebulous cosmic "visions." We saw hints of this quality in the "magical thinking" that was described earlier. Because dwelling on the past or future is unusual for Extraverted Sensing types, their inferior function episodes tend to be short-lived and magical ruminations are rarely acted on. However, when subjected to extended stress, Extraverted Sensing types may search for mystical meaning in the form of an obsessive interest in unseen forces of cosmic proportions.

The omnipresence of profound meaning may stimulate the ESTP or ESFP to search for or create a grand cosmology. Events typically given no more than a moment's thought are imbued with deep significance; unrelated chance occurrences are subjected to complex integrations and interpretations; theories about the ultimate purpose of life and humanity's place in nature are formulated. Such ruminations may engage the entire attention of the Extraverted Sensing type, and this interest may be seen by others as out of bounds and out of character.

An ESTP who lost his business during a recession became increasingly morose and distant. He tried reconnecting with the church of his childhood but was unable to find comfort there. By chance, he saw a notice in the newspaper advertising a lecture by an East Indian guru. He attended the lecture and felt instantly "transformed by the words of this wise man. I knew what my destiny must be," he explained. He abandoned his existing life and joined the guru's spiritual movement. During his year of spiritual exploration, he wrote lengthy mystical poems extolling the unseen forces that shape people's destinies. When he returned home, he started a new business with great enthusiasm and optimism and felt that he brought greater balance and breadth to his enterprise.

Although ESTPs tend to report that few aspects of life are very stressful for them (in comparison to ESFPs and most other types), when they do become vulnerable, both they and ESFPs are likely to lose their typical optimism, carefree enjoyment of the moment, and skill at solving immediate problems. ESTPs, especially women, may become emotional more readily. ESFPs can become angry and critical. "I'm less tolerant of other people, and I am just an angry person with a short fuse," said an ESFP in his early twenties. A young ESFP woman described becoming "sarcastic, oversensitive, negative, sad, worried, and cold." However, compared with other types, ESFPs report little work stress relative to the stress they experience in their personal relationships and responsibilities. They are likely to try to leave stressful situations if they can.

Lengthy Episodes in the Grip

The types of episodes described above are experienced by ESTPs and ESFPs as temporary states during which they are vulnerable to the three forms in which their inferior function is expressed. However, when Extraverted Sensing types are chronically in the grip of inferior Introverted Intuition, inferior function behavior may become habitual.

Chronic grip behavior may lead the individual and others to believe that he or she is typically negative, pessimistic, and worried about both the present and the future. Others will observe the ESTP or ESFP making inappropriate inferences or engaging in odd-seeming forays into mysticism. Since the process of becoming chronically in the grip is often gradual, even people who have known the person in a nonstressed state are likely not to notice what, in retrospect, will be recognized as a radical alteration of personality. The person will appear to be a rather exaggerated, poorly developed Introverted Intuitive type.

However, there are also occasions when a lengthy time in the grip of inferior Introverted Intuition can stimulate new awareness and positive growth toward completion and individuation. Remember that Jung saw the inferior function as the doorway to the unconscious and an important part of the self-regulating capacity of our psyches. The last story in this section shows how a lengthy, painful, and seemingly devastating midlife experience in the grip resulted in a wonderfully fulfilling second half of life.

Grip Experiences

The stories included in this section illustrate one or more forms of inferior Introverted Intuition as experienced by ESTPs or ESFPs. Note that their dominant Extraverted Sensing comes through in the evocative sense impressions and the rich detail described.

The Cloud of Unknown

Christine, an ESTP, recalled a time when she was so out of character that her friends became frightened for her. Knowing that her friends were concerned added to her own fear; it meant that she was out of touch with reality (her dominant Sensing function). She related the following story:

> At the end of my first Ph.D. year, I realized that I was not very happy. My specialty area was complex and theoretical, and I was unsure about whether to go on. So I made an appointment with my supervisor and told him my doubts.
>
> I remember that it was a sunny afternoon. I anticipated that he would say, "Of course you should go on. You've come this far!" He in fact said, "Well, perhaps you should reconsider."
>
> This put me into a swirling spiral of doom. Every possibility I came up with ended with me as a bag lady. I saw myself constantly feeling like a failure for giving up on the program, and I was sure I would fail at everything else because I would lack confidence. I had this sinking feeling that I was burning a bridge behind me; where I stepped off was a cloud of unknown. But then I realized that I had not burned any bridges and didn't have to go into all this unknown because I hadn't left the program. But this wasn't a happy thought. It was dreary. I thus saw that my only choice was between dreariness and terror.

Finally, Christine decided to stay in the haven of security of school, and she subsequently completed the Ph.D. program. In retrospect, she related her reaction to the prospect of change. She felt terrified of losing her security and everything tangible she could grasp. If she lost these real things, she'd become an outcast. Her school grant was a secure base. If she left school, she would be penniless.

Christine explained that the experience taught her about her need for security and the "limits of my venturousness." Perhaps this need tempers or compensates her dominant Extraverted Sensing.

The Telltale Greeting Card

Linda, an ESFP, found her work as a labor relations negotiator exciting and satisfying. She was successful and highly regarded. At one point, she was involved in a particularly demanding and stressful negotiation situation that went on for several months. She was often tired and distracted because of the long hours she had to put in at work. Nonetheless, she and Don, her boyfriend of several years, decided to go forward with their plans to live together. So they rented a house, moved their belongings in, and set about unpacking and organizing their things.

Linda was unpacking a box of Don's books when a greeting card envelope fell out of a book. She glanced at the return address, noticed that it was from a woman who lived in Don's hometown, which he frequently visited on business, and handed it to him. Don quickly took the card without looking at it and went into the kitchen, saying nothing. Linda recounted her response in this way:

> I was suddenly overwhelmed with anxiety, convinced that Don had been carrying on an affair with someone in his hometown, that our living together was a terrible mistake. I thought about all the times he'd been out of town on business, phone calls he had made and received when I was at his apartment, things in his past he wouldn't talk about. It all added up. At the same time I was convinced of this, I also knew it was irrational and really didn't add up to anything. But I couldn't stop myself from being flooded with these dark ideas and the frightening conclusion they led to. I wrestled with this for several hours, gradually becoming calm enough to look rationally at all the consistently loving things in my relationship with Don. I was reminded that Don becomes particularly uncommunicative when he's busy with details and decided that telling him about the card would be merely an unwelcome interruption. My distress went away and I was back to normal.

Looking for Escape Routes

Steve, an ESTP sports journalist, was excited and happy about the impending birth of his and his wife's first child. Although it was the height of football season, he was confident that he would be able to get someone to cover for him on a moment's notice should Cindy go into labor earlier than expected. He figured that his uncharacteristic distractibility at work and at home were the result of anticipation and his heavier-than-usual workload.

Cindy had the baby a week after her official due date. Steve comforted her during her long and difficult labor. Both parents were thrilled with their new baby girl and, though they were quite exhausted, were happy to bring her home. That first night home with her, however, Steve awoke suddenly and was overwhelmed with the thought that a fire might break out in the house. He recalled:

> I was in a panic. I got up and roamed all over the house trying to identify possible escape routes. After satisfying myself that we could escape, I went back to sleep. But the next night and every night for a week, the same thing happened. I awoke, roamed the house confirming escape routes, and finally went back to sleep. I knew my concerns were unusual for me, but at the time the chances of a fire, the danger to our baby, and my need to protect her were all-consuming.

Steve recalls that some time after this episode of terror, he realized that his overly happy-go-lucky demeanor prior to his daughter's birth was perhaps a denial of his anxiety about becoming a father and being responsible for a helpless baby. It occurred to him that this new role in life forced him to explore and become more comfortable with a previously unfamiliar area—a long-term vision of the future.

The Minister's Ordeal

A pastoral ministry of thirty-seven years ended with an ESFP minister's forced resignation. With only five years until his retirement, he had become burned out. He also had been dealing for several years with his wife's debilitating chronic illness. He was seen by parishioners as rigid, controlling, pessimistic, and ineffectual. In retrospect, he recognized that he had been in the grip of inferior Introverted Intuition for several years prior to his resignation.

The added humiliation and loss of identity associated with his resignation resulted in a profound feeling of isolation from the world and a fear of being overwhelmed by mysterious, malevolent forces: "I felt totally abandoned by the God who had been my protector and guide throughout my life."

In this state of hypersensitivity to signs and portents, he found new meaning in phone calls from colleagues, chance encounters, and books friends sent him. He experienced "flashbacks as clear as videos" and pictures and metaphors that gave meaning to his issues. He began paying close attention to dreams and spontaneous images.

Gradually, he emerged from his state of otherness and alienation, profoundly changed by his lengthy grip experience. He found that this extended period in the throes of abstract meaning gave him an appreciation for his "other side" and thus gave him renewed energy for his work. He learned to value things that had previously been of little interest to him, and people whom he had judged "foolish dreamers."

With the renewal of his relationship to himself, his tertiary Thinking and auxiliary Feeling helped him recognize that he needed to be gainfully employed. He was then able to use his dominant Sensing to search for and get a job.

Later, with his expanded understanding of himself and of the value and meaning of abstractions, he sought out and counseled other ministers experiencing burnout in their work and personal lives. Eventually, he established a new ministry that incorporated his thirty-seven years of experience with his newfound expanded consciousness.

Return of Equilibrium

Extraverted Sensing types report that inferior function episodes occur moderately frequently but are typically quite brief. Perhaps their relative frequency is due to the fact that society's demands for regularity, predictability, and security conflict with the natural predilections of their type. The brevity of the episodes is likely influenced by Extraverted Sensing types' distaste for dwelling on things and their tendency to be open to seeing the positive in any situation.

As with other types, the influence of the auxiliary function in the process of reestablishing equilibrium is evident. An ESFP's need to get back in control is quickly aided by the tendency to come up with contingency plans to deal with the anxiety-provoking situation—"if I lose my job, I'll move in with my mother; if she won't have me, I'll get a job as an apartment manager." Just having a plan can be calming, even if it later changes. Auxiliary Introverted Feeling thus focuses on what is important and finds solutions to ground out-of-control negative Intuitions. Others can help ESFPs set priorities and "give gentle suggestions, but not push," said one ESFP. Another ESFP finds it helpful to talk to others who tell her what she is doing well, so she can retain her focus.

In the case of the disaffected ESFP minister, needing to get a job to support his family (Feeling judgment) encouraged his extrication from the nonfunctional state he was engulfed in. Tertiary Thinking was probably also involved—it was logical for him to get a job to help him care for the family he loved. Both kinds of reasoning helped ground him in the real world and reconnect him with his dominant Extraverted Sensing.

Other Extraverted Sensing types mention needing others to help them set priorities and provide insight and perspective. One ESTP recognized that he needed others "to understand that I have feelings, too. It helps if they can listen and be less critical and judgmental." Being reassured that dire consequences won't happen can be helpful. One ESFP relies on her sister for reassurance:

> When I can't decide what to do, I let her decide for me. She never judges me, but she's very direct in telling me when something I do is wrong. But she won't dwell on it. She says, "That was stupid. Let's go out to lunch." Pretty soon I put it behind me and am back to my normal, happy self.

ESTPs and ESFPs of both genders find that talking to someone is a helpful way to gain perspective on their grip experiences. ESTPs are more likely than ESFPs to value spending time alone, and ESTP women are oriented to devoting energy to solving the problem or completing whatever task is causing the stress. "I establish a work pattern and stick to it. I consciously focus, try to ignore distractions, and am realistic about my limitations. I say no." Solitary activities such as exercising or gardening can help both types reestablish control over themselves, and exercising as a stress reducer is frequently mentioned. "I do something physically engaging and mentally distracting," said an ESTP. The solitude allows them to regain confidence in their inner auxiliary Thinking or Feeling judgment. Security here then permits them to reconnect with their familiar and reliable comfort in the outer world.

As with most experiences of being in the grip of an inferior function, humor does not provide a good way to help Extraverted Sensing types return to normal. Most report that they lose their sense of humor when in their altered state. However, one ESTP was aware of the somewhat perverse humor she uses to deal with her infrequent depressions. At those times, she reflects on the fact that eventually she will die anyway, so she might as well enjoy life now and not get too upset about things!

Expressions in Midlife

Ideally, midlife for Extraverted Sensing types is accompanied by a positive, progressive integration of inferior Introverted Intuition, and along with it tertiary Thinking or Feeling. For some ESFPs and ESTPs, however, this may not be the case.

Older ESFPs and ESTPs who instead become stuck in their dominant Sensing and auxiliary Feeling or Thinking often resemble adolescents who never grew up. They may bore family and friends by retelling tales of their youthful exploits, buy the clothing and pursue the activities associated with much younger people, and in general appear to deny and resist the aging process. A successful ESTP insurance agent often entertained his clients with tales of his youthful exploits as a semiprofessional baseball player. When he reached age 50 and continued to wear his baseball cap and carry his "lucky glove" to appointments with customers, he was seen as inappropriately adolescent and an embarrassment to his colleagues in the insurance agency.

Others may find their natural development inhibited by their rigid adherence to outdated formulas that once worked but are no longer appropriate, resulting in the loss of their spontaneous relationship to the environment. This may have been the case with the ESFP minister who was seen as rigid and restrictive by his parishioners.

The more adaptive route to integration of inferior Intuition and tertiary Thinking or Feeling is aided by Extraverted Sensing types' increasing attraction to quiet contemplation. Some Extraverted Sensing types find themselves drawn to literature and television programs involving hypotheses and theories. One 55-year-old ESTP thoroughly enjoyed reading books on chaos theory and astronomy, areas that had been of little interest to him in his youth.

Others notice an unfamiliar interest in their own internal mental processes. A 52-year-old ESFP elementary teacher entered individual psychotherapy to explore some of her psychological reactions, which in the past had only mildly puzzled her. She felt a growing need to understand these strange responses in order to feel comfortable with herself now and in the future.

Sometimes spending a lengthy period in the grip of inferior Introverted Intuition can serve as an important stimulus to midlife development for Extraverted Sensing types. The combination of the natural upheaval of midlife and the disruption and distress of a chronic grip experience can push an ESTP or ESFP into serious soul searching and reconsideration of long-standing goals, which may lead to significant changes in the way the second half of life is lived.

Knowledge from Grip Experiences

In addition to learning to recognize and avoid the stress and fatigue that may lead to a grip experience, Extraverted Sensing types report a greater tolerance of and respect for knowledge that cannot be acquired directly though the senses. They are less apprehensive about anticipating the future and more willing to make binding commitments without feeling controlled by them.

ESTPs and ESFPs become more comfortable with their own intuitions and free-floating ideas, learning to observe and enjoy them with no need to verify their sensory accuracy. When stress either at work or at home is extreme and persists over time, Extraverted Sensing types tend to weigh the benefits of tolerating the stress against the daily discomfort they are experiencing. One ESFP became aware that her habitual out-of-character state was caused by the inherent stressfulness of her job. She resolved to deal with the present stress as well as she could by looking forward to a financially comfortable retirement. She imagined the joy of then being able to do whatever she wanted using her own spontaneous style.

Summary

In the grip of inferior Introverted Intuition, Extraverted Sensing types experience internal confusion that often results in uncharacteristically strange fantasies. They find meaning and significance in everyday, benign events and may have insights of cosmic proportions. Auxiliary Thinking or Feeling often aids their return to equilibrium. ESTPs may analyze an overwhelming situation and use logic to extricate from it, or they may seek the advice of a Thinking type as a reality check on the problem. This helps to delimit the disturbing issue and encourages a more balanced view. ESFPs may regain control of a situation when they recognize their own and others' Feeling values. Both ESTPs and ESFPs find contingency plans helpful in reestablishing their groundedness in external reality.

As a result of important inferior function experiences, Extraverted Sensing types become more comfortable with and less fearful of possibilities. This enables them to make difficult decisions in ambiguous situations, accept the reality of their decisions, and avoid looking back. They also become more appreciative of the unknown and mysterious and gain respect for Intuitive approaches. Extraverted Sensing types report seeking out the company of Intuitive colleagues and acquaintances and finding new pleasure in these relationships. Table 11 provides a brief overview of the major features of inferior Introverted Intuition.

Table 11   Inferior Function of Extraverted Sensing Types: ESTP and ESFP

Triggers for the Inferior Function	Forms of the Grip Experience
• Excessive focus on the future	• Internal confusion
• Closing off of options	• Inappropriate attribution of meaning
• Excessive structured activity	• Grandiose vision
Ways of Returning to Equilibrium	New Knowledge
• Making contingency plans	• Less fear of possibilities
• Resassurance by others regarding "dire" consequences	• Appreciation of the unknown
	• Access to their own intuition
• Helping by others in setting priorities	

11

Introverted Intuitive Types

INTJ and INFJ

BASIC TYPE DYNAMICS

DOMINANT INTROVERTED INTUITION

AUXILIARY EXTRAVERTED THINKING OR FEELING

TERTIARY FEELING OR THINKING

INFERIOR EXTRAVERTED SENSING

Introverted Intuition Versus Extraverted Sensing

THIS CHAPTER EXAMINES the way effective Introverted Intuitive types experience their inferior function and the temporary transformation they make into ineffective, inferior Extraverted Sensing types when they are either briefly or chronically "in the grip." A review of the characteristics of Introverted Intuition and Extraverted Sensing will be helpful to our discussion.

Important Features of Dominant Introverted Intuition

Introverted Intuitive types are the most intellectually independent of the types. They have a theory to explain everything, prefer innovative solutions to established ones, and are adept at seeing situations from an unusual perspective. Their skill at taking a very broad, long-range view of things contributes to their reputation as visionaries. Regardless of whether their auxiliary judging preference is Thinking or Feeling, their dominant Intuition tends to be sharp, quick, and often uncannily correct. It is as if they have antennae that enable them to detect things long before other people do.

People often count on INTJs and INFJs for insightful analyses and forthright judgments. They are adept at appropriately discounting distracting details and homing in on the essential meaning of complex, confusing situations.

Introverted Intuitive types report being puzzled by others' perception of them as rigid and intractable. This perception may result from their tendency to express their views directly and forcefully. This is especially true for INTJs. Misinterpretation of their forthright communication style as inflexibility may make others reluctant to present alternatives or argue their own point of view. But, as described in Chapter 3, dominant Perceiving types are unlikely to be wedded to their decisions, since they give greater weight to data (perceptions) than to conclusions (judgments). Experience bears this out for the most part. INTJs and INFJs readily modify their incorrect conclusions when they receive convincing contradictory new information.

The spiritual, sometimes mystical, bent of Introverted Intuitive types has been frequently noted. At the very least, they seem to be aware of subtle cues or nuances long before others notice them. INFJs are especially sensitive to unexpressed anger and conflict, whose presence is usually denied by others. This contributes to the sense of separateness from others that many Introverted Intuitive types report, which may lead them to doubt their own mental stability.

Introverted Intuitive types, especially INTJs, readily see the big picture in crisis situations and know how to direct others to take the most effective action.

Introverted Intuitive Types at Work

Work can provide INTJs and INFJs with the ideal opportunity to fulfill their typological nature. They are highly energized when they are able to use their creativity and independence of thought and action to achieve important goals. They enjoy variety in the projects they work on and prefer complex problems to simple ones. "Planning and strategizing that will help fulfill a vision—in silence or with a small group, and *after* I've had some time to reflect and gather information" is how one INTJ described what is most energizing for her. Another INTJ stated that he liked "an opportunity to put all my facilitation in place to solve a problem, reorganize a section, and then run it—some autonomy and complexity." An INFJ described as most energizing "creativity, variety, people, time alone, helping people grow and develop."

Introverted Intuitive types want to see their vision of the future enacted at work. This desire for completion contributes to the intensity and single-mindedness that others observe. One INTJ described as energizing "working on projects that have a beginning and an end, which I can work on autonomously, especially those that have a visible, tangible, beneficial impact on the organization and individuals. Finishing tasks and multitasking, making improvements, getting recognition, and keeping people happy." An INFJ in her early twenties said, "I place all of my heart and soul and expectations into my work, so I like to see these expectations fulfilled or exceeded." Another INFJ is energized by "thinking up the best process and ways to work with my staff to accomplish tasks. To be able to juggle tasks and complete them."

INTJs and INFJs very much want to be recognized and appreciated for their contributions at work, but they may not receive such appreciation. Co-workers may misperceive their desire for autonomy and their single-minded concentration as arrogant and controlling. They may be seen as overly critical and hard to please. Their typical long-range vision can also be an obstacle if others at work do not trust the Introverted Intuitive type's ability to accomplish his or her often complex and interconnected objectives. However, in environments that support the needs and talents of Introverted Intuitive types, others readily recognize, appreciate, and encourage their devotion to excellence and accomplishment.

Important Features of Dominant Extraverted Sensing

The qualities associated with Extraverted Sensing that are relevant to our discussion of its form as an inferior function are

- Focus on external data
- Seeking sensual/aesthetic pleasure
- Delight in the outer world

For a detailed description of dominant Extraverted Sensing, read the beginning of Chapter 10, "Extraverted Sensing Types: ESTP and ESFP," and the type descriptions for ESTP and ESFP that appear in Appendix A. This will provide the background needed to explore the various ways in which inferior Extraverted Sensing is expressed in INTJs and INFJs.

The Everyday Extraverted Sensing of Introverted Intuitive Types

The inferior function affects Introverted Intuitive types in several different ways. These include everyday sensitivities, projections, and ways of relaxing, as well as the dramatic manifestations that can be seen when the inferior erupts and a full-blown episode occurs, or when an INTJ or INFJ is chronically in the grip because of long-term stress.

Typical Sensitivities and Projections

Introverted Intuitive types easily gloss over facts and details in their everyday behavior but can be hypersensitive about this. When they become aware that they have made a "Sensing" mistake, or an error of fact is pointed out to them, they are likely to become annoyed and defensive. Like their Extraverted Intuitive counterparts, they may compensate for their uneasiness in this area by becoming expert in some highly specific area. This can sometimes resemble a fetish. An INFJ who had little interest in most aspects of housekeeping knew all the ingredients of different household detergents; an INTJ was pleased with his ability to identify any kind of cloud formation.

INTJs and INFJs sometimes assert as "fact" information that may have no basis in reality but that strengthens a conclusion they have arrived at using Introverted Intuition alone. When the validity of such facts is challenged, they may become defensive or simply change the subject.

In the next chapter, we will discuss how Introverted Sensing types worry about dire possibilities occurring in the future. In contrast, Introverted Intuitive types focus on relentless realities in the present. They have a readiness to distrust the outer world and to assume that the environment, things, or people will fail them. An INFJ dreaded an impending vacation trip because she was sure the highway signs would be inadequate or confusing. An INTJ father prepared to teach his daughter long division because he was convinced that her teacher would not instruct her correctly. Another INTJ questioned whether the electrician installing new wiring at his office had used the proper grounding. To deal with these kinds of concerns, INTJs and INFJs may acquire detailed knowledge about the issue at hand—carefully studying highway routes, modern arithmetic teaching methods, electrical wiring, and so on.

Discomfort with the environment can also be seen in an overconcern with keeping track of things. One INTJ reported having to check his pocket two or three times to be sure his keys were there. Introverted Intuitive types try very hard to avoid losing things or getting lost in unfamiliar surroundings. They can become disproportionately upset when their efforts fail, frequently blaming others for their own carelessness.

INTJs and INFJs readily project their own distrust of the environment onto others. They may comment on other people's failure to notice details or assume that everyone experiences the anxieties they experience when dealing with an unfamiliar environment. They may therefore be overly cautious in giving people directions and provide too many—often irrelevant—details. One INFJ instructed his 28-year-old son as he was about to head out on a long trip in the car, "And when you smoke, you use the ashtray."

In giving a friend directions to her new house, an INTJ detailed the following:

> Take Central Avenue to Fifth Street and turn right. Go two blocks to Smith Street and make a left at the next corner, Avenue M. Go three blocks and turn right into Mulberry. That's my street. About halfway down the block you'll see a blue house with a two-car garage and a "For Sale" sign on the lawn. Next door to that house is a small cottage with a peaked roof. My house has no address number on it, but it's diagonally across from the blue house. . . . Oh, and did I mention that my house is the only two-story house on the block?

Expressions Through Interests and Hobbies

For Introverted Intuitive types, relaxing their dominant and auxiliary functions may occur through such sensual pleasures as eating, exercising, and gardening. One INTJ especially enjoys and appreciates sunshine in spring, autumn, and winter. Another likes to "go somewhere beautiful— mountains, ocean, water." INFJs often mention the pleasant luxury of taking an afternoon nap. Other Introverted Intuitive types describe craving very hot curries, or escaping by becoming totally absorbed in a mystery or adventure novel. "Escape literature" seems to be a particularly effective way for Introverted Intuitive types to suspend their intense inner focus and vicariously enjoy adventures in the external environment.

An INTJ reports that at times she feels exceptionally relaxed and able to focus totally on observing her environment. At these times she is able to step away from her usual goal-oriented approach and does not feel she must immediately do something with her observations. Often doing aerobic exercise precedes and stimulates this relaxed state. An INTJ who is a passionate bird-watcher tries to arrange his worldwide consulting work to take advantage of bird-watching opportunities. Other Introverted Intuitive types take up hobbies that require careful attention to details and memory for facts, such as photography, woodworking, furniture refinishing, or cooking.

Introverted Intuitive types mention going for walks or drives and noticing interesting details, such as the shapes of houses, the designs on garage doors, the arrangements of trees and flower beds in parks. One INFJ described taking walks by himself and noticing how many different shades of green he could identify on a nature trail, or closing his eyes and trying to identify as many different sounds as he could.

Using Sensing for relaxation seems to be particularly enjoyable because there is no pressure to achieve any particular goal. "Gardening is an activity I love. I don't worry about performance or doing it perfectly," said an INFJ. "I like pulling weeds, smelling flowers, removing dead flower heads, admiring the colors. All of this nurtures me." Another INFJ enjoys the aesthetic aspects of gardening, the shapes and colors of the flowers, as opposed to the straightness of the planting rows. And an INTJ's hobby is making flower arrangements. She tries to achieve an overall look with the colors of the flowers, rarely wanting to learn the names of the various blossoms.

Eruptions of Inferior Extraverted Sensing

When one or more of the preconditions for eruption of the inferior function are present, Extraverted Sensing appears in its more exaggerated, disruptive form. In addition to the general conditions described in Chapter 4, Introverted Intuitive types are vulnerable to the type-specific factors described below.

Typical Provocations or Triggers

Dealing with details, especially in an unfamiliar environment, can trigger inferior Extraverted Sensing in Introverted Intuitive types. In fact, these types frequently mention that feeling overwhelmed by details often provokes characteristic inferior function reactions. Unexpected events that interrupt planned activities can also unsettle INTJs and INFJs enough to arouse their inferior function. One INFJ said that "sometimes it can be something like having to get from the airport to a hotel. It can happen if I'm driving a rental car in a foreign city, and even if I'm in my own country."

Another INFJ reports having the following response when she has to deal with unfamiliar details like taxes and finances:

> I feel like I become instantly stupid. I truly don't seem to be able to take in explanations and process them. I have such anxiety I can't get through it. I feel panicky inside and desperately look for help from someone who can talk to me on my level so that I can slowly begin to understand.

An INTJ finally turned the accounting for his small business over to an accountant when he found himself becoming tense, irritable, and depressed whenever he had to work on the books.

Of the four dominant Introverted types, it is Introverted Intuitive types who most frequently mention "too much extraverting" as a common trigger for inferior function responses. They describe being provoked by such things as crowds; people overload; noisy, busy environments; feeling that their personal space is being invaded; and frequent interruptions. When faced with such provocations, they retreat inside themselves and become intolerant of intrusions by others. They either express irritation at people's questions or do not respond at all to attempts to communicate with them.

An INTJ described having been raised in a large family with no private, personal space for anyone. All family members were expected to behave in the same way, as prescribed by a narrow set of acceptable behaviors. "Even though we had separate rooms," he said, "we had no freedom to decorate them in our own way or use them for anything but sleeping. I had a sense of frustration and rage at the absence of private territory. In hindsight, I was too often 'in the grip.'"

Triggers and Stressors at Work

Work settings that do not permit sufficient autonomy or that offer few opportunities to work alone and intensively, and that do not provide the opportunity to be creative, think independently, and accomplish goals, are extremely stressful and undesirable for Introverted Intuitive types. INTJs and INFJs hold very high standards of excellence for themselves and others, so issues of competence at work are quite important.

INTJs in particular are intolerant of and impatient with inefficiency and with others' avoidance of problems. They like to get to the heart of an issue immediately, which sometimes makes others uncomfortable. An INTJ finds it stressful "when there are multiple 'agendas' at play so that there is no sense of purpose or direction about an issue that may be a legitimate problem." She added, "I don't suffer fools or foolishness well. I like to focus on real issues." Other INTJs mention as stressful "noise, confusion, lack of order and direction," "working with others and not being able to get alone," "being led by the nose, not having a degree of autonomy."

INFJs are distressed by similar work characteristics, often focusing on the inability to achieve their vision of growth and development for people. Being unable to work at their own pace and within their own structure is also stressful. An INFJ cited as work stressors "lack of organization and vision by management." And another INFJ is stressed by "unclear goals and expectations and others' unwillingness to fit into my flexible time line." Both INTJs and INFJs find that dealing with details (often seen by them as irrelevant to the task at hand) is extremely stressful.

In a work situation in which the particular stressors for Introverted Intuitive types continue over long periods, INTJs and INFJs may respond quickly and intensely to the triggers described here. This increases the likelihood that their subsequent demonstrations of "grip" behavior will be frequent and pervasive. When persistent stress causes them to be chronically in the grip of inferior Extraverted Sensing, they are likely to lose touch with their natural confidence and pleasure in their Intuition and come across as picky, fault-finding, narrow-minded, and unimaginative.

The Form of the Inferior Function

INTJs and INFJs appear less likely than other Introverted types to get much pleasure from a lessening of introverted "inhibitions," although some INTJ males describe becoming more extraverted in a positive, sociable way. An INFJ said he is "surprisingly more extraverted, especially in the company of strangers; more expressive and less contained." Female Introverted Intuitive types mention increased sociability less frequently, possibly because they, like other women who are Introverts, are encouraged (or required) to develop social skills. However, for the most part, the obsessiveness and discomfort that accompany extraverting their Sensing function is experienced as overwhelmingly distressing for both male and female INTJs and INFJs.

As dominant Introverted Intuition loses its position of primacy, INTJs and INFJs start to lose their characteristic wide-ranging, global perspective. Their field of operation narrows considerably, and their range of acknowledged possibilities becomes limited and idiosyncratic. They may make more factual mistakes and become careless with spelling and grammar. "I am unable to cope with simple decisions and problems," said an INTJ woman. "I'm frustrated by the physical world—I lose things, drop them, hate them. I don't know what to wear or what to eat. I'm impatient with people and can't read or concentrate." An INTJ said she obsessively looks for the "right" factual piece of information that will solve the problem. "I notice things not put away around the house—things that are broken or things to do." As their hold on their dominant and auxiliary functions further diminishes, the qualities of inferior Extraverted Sensing manifest in an obsessive focus on external data, overindulgence in sensual pleasures, and an adversarial attitude toward the outer world. For INTJs, tertiary Feeling may abet the process in that the "facts" (real or invented) on which the INTJ obsesses are often used as "proof" that others discount, devalue, or dislike the INTJ. Similar "facts" may be used by the INFJ's tertiary Thinking to prove that the INFJ is inadequate or a failure. The comparison between dominant and inferior Extraverted Sensing is shown in Table 12.

Table 12 Dominant and Inferior Expressions of Extraverted Sensing

As Dominant Function of ESTPs and ESFPs	As Inferior Function of INTJs and INFJs
• Focus on external data	• Obsessive focus on external data
• Seeking sensual/aesthetic pleasure	• Overindulgence in sensual pleasure
• Delight in the outer world	• Adversarial attitude toward the outer world

Jung (1976a) incorporates the three qualities of inferior Extraverted Sensing (obsessive focus on external data, overindulgence in sensual pleasures, and an adversarial attitude toward the outer world) in the following comment:

> What the introverted intuitive represses most of all is the sensation of the object, and this colours his whole unconscious. It gives rise to a compensatory extraverted sensation function of an archaic character. The unconscious personality can best be described as an extraverted sensation type of a rather low and primitive order. Instinctuality and intemperance are the hallmarks of this sensation, combined with an extraordinary dependence on sense-impressions. This compensates the rarefied air of the intuitive's conscious attitude. (p. 402)

Obsessive Focus on External Data Effective dominant Extraverted Sensing types are open to the widest variety of information from the environment—the more the better for them. Fully experiencing the outside world is their greatest pleasure. For an INTJ or INFJ in the grip of inferior Extraverted Sensing, data from the outside world can seem overwhelming. Facts and details in the world demand the attention of the Introverted Intuitive type in the grip, so he or she obsesses about them. This may be experienced by both INTJs and INFJs as a state of intensity and drivenness. Their attempts to control the details in their environment are often expressed in such activities as feverishly cleaning the house, moving furniture, and organizing records and other materials. They may show an adamant concern about minute details and an unrelenting effort to control everything in their immediate vicinity.

An INFJ described her obsessiveness and withdrawal from her usual interests this way: "I stew about what's going on. I can't sit still and am restless. I am mentally fatigued and find myself compulsively putting things in order and trying to control everything around me." An INTJ said that when he is in this state, he feels like a top spinning faster and faster. If he is working with tools and getting frustrated and angry, he has learned that it is best for him to stop or he will get hurt or break something. An INFJ described "obsessing about details." He gave as an example:

> When I'm using power tools that can cause injury, I will spend an inordinate amount of energy making sure that I'm not going to inadvertently hurt myself when I turn the thing on. I will triple-check to make sure my fingers are out of the way, etc. Usually I take in the world more globally and have less concern about details until I need them.

"I'm more likely to have accidents," said an INTJ. "I'm robotic, forget things, say things backwards; I'm obsessed with a thought and can't get it out of my mind. I try to control situations and people and engage in strange behavior, like checking on things," said an INTJ woman. And another INTJ woman said, "I can become obsessed by detail. I'm less able to function and make decisions—sort of paralyzed."

An INFJ said, "I alphabetize my compact discs; or suddenly it's time to do that thing I thought about doing two months ago. I drop everything and do it; or I fixate on smells and sounds." "I organize or clean. I feel pressured and can't think clearly," reported another INFJ. "I nitpick about things in the environment. I bombard people verbally and obsess out loud."

An INTJ recalled the following from his childhood and adolescence:

> When my studies were not going too well I would start to develop detailed tables of data, or drawings to support technical/science answers. These were frequently in too great detail, taking a lot of time and usually out of all proportion to the task and the length of the answers sought—or even irrelevant to the original questions.

Often the external input that becomes the object of obsession is something someone said or even failed to say. When the last client on an unusually busy day left without saying her usual "See you next week," an INTJ therapist became convinced she had made a mistake during the psychotherapy session. She spent many hours going over the content of the session. She felt the only reason the client had not terminated therapy that day was politeness, so as not to hurt the therapist's feelings.

A common focus, particularly for INTJ and INFJ women, can be an aspect of their physical appearance. They may become convinced that they have prominent skin blemishes, that others are noticing that they don't dress very well, or that they look fat. In combination with the "overindul-gence" manifestation described below, a powerful effect can occur.

Overindulgence in Sensual Pleasures In effective dominant Extraverted Sensing types, the enjoyment of sensual pleasures is natural, spontaneous, and quite consistent with their focus on the reality of the immediate environment. In Introverted Intuitive types in the grip of inferior Extraverted Sensing, this quality takes the form of sensual excess rather than sensual pleasure. It is interesting that a number of INTJs and INFJs described themselves as becoming "self-centered" and "self-indulgent" when they are in the grip—a descriptor often projected onto well-functioning Extraverted Sensing types by INTJs and INFJs (and by other types as well).

Overdoing gratification of the senses is a commonly mentioned behavior for INTJs and INFJs in the grip of their inferior function. They may overeat or binge. They see themselves as obsessively doing harm to their bodies. A typical "tactic" is to overindulge compulsively and imme-diately thereafter—if not during the episode—berate themselves for their uncontrolled, shallow, destructive behavior.

An INTJ described the experience this way:

> There is a clear preliminary state where I am totally apart from the real world. I am not even an observer, and I can completely ignore anything real. It's a nice fantasy, that's all—just absorbing. But later I become excessively indulgent, getting totally immersed in physical experi-ences—eating, exercise, pulp fiction, TV. But I don't enjoy it. It feels like a dangerous roller coaster, but I'm immobilized and can't get off.

An INFJ said, "I have to get away from reality. I do too much of some-thing—one thing. I eat more or stop eating; I shop for useless things." Another said, "I eat too much, spend too much, watch TV or read exces-sively to escape. I'm late for everything." An INTJ said her pattern is to overeat, feel guilty about it, wake up in the night and feel worse, get too little sleep, causing her to feel more vulnerable, and then eat more. Another INTJ feels bad about her overeating but not guilty: "I hate it when peo-ple brag about how much they exercise!" she said.

Adversarial Attitude Toward the Outer World Effective dominant Extraverted Sensing types approach the outer world with eager anticipa-tion of all the wonderful experiences awaiting them. For Introverted

Intuitive types in the grip of inferior Extraverted Sensing, the immediate reality of the outer world spells difficulty and danger. They expect obstacles and problems to plague them as they move through a strange and potentially hostile environment.

Their hypersensitivity to potentially dangerous surroundings can promote uneasiness about people as well. "I can have negative forebodings and feel that people are against me," said an INTJ. An INFJ said she "becomes suspicious. Usually I'm tolerant, curious, and compassionate, so 'out of character' for me means I'm unaccepting and frustrated with the world."

An INTJ said, "I start tripping over things and feel out of control in the external world. I feel like I'm under a dark cloud. I get hung up on some false fact and distort it. I get stressed out about time—too many things and not enough time. I attack others with words and then feel guilty." An INFJ described herself as "shutting down, communicating very little. I misplace things, especially keys and watches. I'm very harsh, critical, not diplomatic. I lose my temper, obsess about details, organize, reorganize, yet nothing gets done."

Anticipating the worst can often elicit anger and blame in INTJs and INFJs. "I'm moody and gloomy, with sudden deep anger," said an INTJ. An INFJ also describes experiencing deep anger: "I am emotionally aroused and am terribly critical of others. I accuse people of never helping me. I become dogmatic and blast people with facts. If no one is around to attack, I write a scathing letter to someone." Another said, "I internally check off all the events that happened leading up to the 'conflict' and then I verbalize this list with a sense that the impeccable logic of it will convince others I am right and I will be vindicated."

The altered state of any inferior function is typically accompanied by a lessening of social controls and therefore more frequent expressions of anger. However, the character of the anger may be different for different types. For INTJs and INFJs, the "cause" of distress is often one or more "objects" in the environment. The anger directed at either things or people may therefore be more focused, intense, and extreme than with other inferior functions. Introverted Intuitive types may be unable to recognize alternative possibilities so that their perspective becomes extremely narrow. This tunnel vision and externalization of blame can produce ruthless results.

One INTJ said, "I get into verbal raving and am out of control. I regress emotionally and act childish. I feel anxious, exposed, childlike."

Another INTJ said, "If I bump my head on a cupboard, I get mad at the world for putting a cupboard there. Others think I'm cursing at myself—but it's really at the inconsideration or stupidity of the cupboard being there." An INFJ observed, "I am angry, unreasonable, totally irrational, closed-minded, and impatient. I feel vulnerable and then become angry at others for it. I can't communicate with anyone. I am hard, callous, unfeeling, and I have no energy to be bothered with anyone else."

Lengthy Episodes in the Grip

The types of episodes described above are experienced by INTJs and INFJs as temporary states during which they are vulnerable to the three forms in which their inferior function is expressed. However, when an Introverted Intuitive type is chronically in the grip of inferior Extraverted Sensing, inferior function behavior may become habitual.

Obsessiveness about details in the form of micromanaging others both at work and at home may cause great distress to other people in these environments. "Irrational" accusations by the INTJ or INFJ can alienate others, causing them to avoid the person or attempt to remove him or her from a position of authority. Family members of an Introverted Intuitive type in a chronic grip state may be unable to find ways to sidestep the ready anger and criticism expressed by their loved one. Co-workers are likely to be similarly at a loss.

If and when INTJs recognize the extremeness and persistence of their out-of-character behavior, they are likely to try to confront and solve the problems that beset them, especially in a work situation. INFJs, who report a high level of stress in many areas of life, tend to rely on their spiritual and religious beliefs to help them cope and rise above persistent stress.

Chronic grip behavior may lead the individual and others to believe that fierce anger, excessive control of others and the immediate world, and distrust that approaches paranoia are a part of the natural makeup of the INTJ or INFJ, and that the person has always been that way. Since the process of becoming chronically in the grip is often gradual, even people who have known the person in a nonstressed state are likely not to notice what, in retrospect, will be recognized as a radical alteration of personality. The person will appear to be a rather exaggerated, poorly developed, and distorted version of an Extraverted Sensing type.

This can sometimes lead to a productive, valuable outcome, however, as illustrated in the last story in the next section. There are also occasions when a lengthy time in the grip of inferior Extraverted Sensing can stimulate new awareness and positive growth toward completion and individuation. Remember that Jung saw the inferior function as the doorway to the unconscious and an important part of the self-regulating capacity of our psyches.

Grip Experiences

The stories included in this section illustrate one or more forms of inferior Extraverted Sensing as experienced by INTJs and INFJs. It is interesting to notice that these Introverted Intuitive types, whose dominant focus is typically global, diffuse, and complex, relate their experiences of the inferior in that same style. The two examples that appear in the form of specific "stories" were actually contributed by the spouses of the Introverted Intuitive types involved.

"Help, I Can't Change the Channel!"

Gretchen is an INTJ whose work requires intense, uninterrupted extraversion not only of her auxiliary Thinking function but also of her dominant Intuition and tertiary Feeling functions. Although she excels at her job and very much enjoys it, it tends to "unbalance" her. When she experiences a lack of sleep and increased stress, her inferior Extraverted Sensing manifests in the following ways:

> I seem to get stuck on one sensory channel, often a visual one, like watching TV. I watch but am unable to extract any meaning from it, and because it lacks meaning, it is unacceptable to my usual criteria. I think, What kind of person engages in this meaningless pap? I must be careful to keep my worthless behavior from other people because it reveals my lack of competence. If other people knew about it, they would not like me.
>
> Sometimes I get stuck on something auditory, like listening to one audiotape over and over again. The tapes are often those with a sentimental twist. My judgment then is, Who with any brains would listen to this garbage?

Sometimes Gretchen makes good use of the Extraverted Sensing that takes over her personality. "Even though I do some task obsessively, I actually accomplish something," she explains. "I'm less upset with myself then, even though I know I haven't made the best use of my time and my method was inefficient." She may be aware that she is doing something inefficiently or in a harder way than is necessary, but she feels compelled to continue in spite of this: "If my inefficient obsessiveness doesn't accomplish something, I become self-critical and really angry at myself."

Because so much extraverting is a continuing aspect of her work, Gretchen has found some ways to use Extraverted Sensing in relaxing, nonthreatening ways. She believes her efforts have resulted in a decrease in the intensity and length of her grip experiences.

"The Harder I Work, the More You Criticize Me!"

In Chapter 4 we noted that skill in one's least-preferred process does not prevent its eruption as an inferior function. This can be particularly baffling to other people, especially those closest to the person.

Jane, an ENFP, manages her husband's repair business. She takes care of the bookkeeping, makes appointments, and does all the many other tasks associated with running a successful repair shop. She is satisfied with her work and especially enjoys her warm relationships with customers. Her INTJ husband, John, appreciates her skills and the fact that her enjoyment of people relieves him of having to make small talk.

But Jane finds one thing about John quite puzzling and difficult to cope with. She described it this way:

> John is a skilled repairman by life circumstances rather than by choice. He is incredibly good at his work. He discovers the source of a repair problem by visualizing it, but he cannot describe what he visualizes. He is also excellent with the meticulous detail his repairs require. He is therefore much sought out by people who have experienced his very exceptional repairs.
>
> The problem is that he is supersensitive about his work. He is touchy and readily interprets comments as criticism. In short, one cannot talk to him about his work. He says, "The harder I work and the better I do, the more you criticize me." I have to walk on eggshells on the topic of John's work. It's not even okay to compliment him, since he manages to find something negative even in this. He dismisses expressions of appreciation from his clients as insincere politeness.

In most other things, John is objective and good humored. He enjoys politics and philosophy, and his hobby is Civil War history. In these areas he welcomes discussion and is not overly sensitive when people disagree with him or criticize his conclusions.

Jane got a glimmer of understanding when she discovered the form in which inferior Extraverted Sensing is expressed. She recognized that John spends most of his waking hours using his least-preferred process, Extraverted Sensing. His innovative use of dominant Intuition in detecting repair problems is certainly an asset. However, contrary to what is more common and desirable, his dominant Intuition is being used in the service of his inferior Sensing, rather than his inferior Sensing being used in the service of his dominant Introverted Intuition.

John consciously uses his least-preferred process. He is usually not in the grip when he works; however, his inferior function comes out when things are not going well or when he is stressed, fatigued, or otherwise vulnerable. A comparably vulnerable ESFP technician would probably respond to stress in a quite different way.

"Being Autistic or Catatonic Sounds Good to Me!"

Polly, an INFJ, has given a lot of thought to her reactions when she is off-center. As with many other Introverted Intuitive types, her description of her reactions is not oriented to specific incidents. Rather, she provides an integrated, global analysis. She related the following:

> If I have too much contact with people in one day, especially if I am doing the kind of reality-based crisis management that used to be a large part of my job, it can be extremely draining for me. I just want to withdraw—being autistic or catatonic sounds good to me at that point! I lose my focus and my energy center when I have to extravert too much, especially around facts and people.
>
> When I am fully "in the grip," I don't get anything done. I try to obsessively control every detail, I notice everything that is disorganized or needs cleaning in my outer world, and I want to fix it all perfectly and immediately. I eat too much, don't enjoy it, and feel guilty about losing control. I feel like nobody helps me; I have to do it all myself and nobody appreciates me. I can't see any possibilities or alternatives around negative facts. I really focus on negative facts. I feel immobilized and unproductive and have trouble concentrating.
>
> I think this side of me comes out in my dreams in both pleasant and unpleasant ways. My dreams tend to be in color with a lot of

emotion, feeling, action, and detail in them. It is almost like all the sensory details I overlook or don't even recognize in my conscious life exist in my unconscious. I have very beautiful and very horrible images in my dreams.

"Let Me Help You Diagnose My Illness"

Angie, an INFJ who had always been plagued with allergies and frequent infections, became ill one winter with some new symptoms. Numerous specialists and clinicians were unable to diagnose her condition. They agreed that she was ill and growing worse, and many had theories about the possible causes, but what she eventually heard from each one was something along the lines of, "I don't know what's wrong with you. And I don't know what to suggest."

Though often ill and discouraged about her situation, Angie began a systematic study of all the medical literature relevant to each of her puzzling symptoms, singly and in combination. She pored over volumes in the medical library, sent for all of her own medical records from childhood on, and racked her memory for even remotely relevant past symptoms or events that might have triggered or influenced her current condition. She explained the nature of her search:

> My dining room table was piled high with neatly arranged insurance forms, physicians' reports, synopses of medical articles, and a chronological accounting of my medical history—all the facts I could find. Before each appointment with yet another specialist, I summarized the relevant facts and brought them along. But all save a few doctors didn't welcome my help. They seemed overwhelmed by it. Most seemed to believe that because I was so knowledgeable about my condition, I must be a hypochondriac. Of course I was an expert on my symptoms. After three years of seeing doctors who didn't have a clue, I figured they needed all the help I could give them!

Angie's way of coping with her illness by collecting facts was consistent with inferior Extraverted Sensing as a response to stress. In this case, however, the data she so meticulously collected constituted an adaptive approach to her situation. But most of her doctors treated her behavior as excessive and pathological. No doubt this judgment was abetted by her single-minded intensity in trying to help her physicians arrive at a diagnosis.

Return of Equilibrium

Introverted Intuitive types need space and a low-pressure environment to regain their dominant Intuition and auxiliary Thinking or Feeling function. Like Extraverted Intuitive types, they are not amenable to suggestions and deny the possibility of alternatives. Stuck in a negative, omnipresent "reality," they are unable to process contradictory information. They may respond to those who offer it with anger and rejection, adamantly insisting that no alternatives exist. In fact, INTJs and INFJs agree that the worst thing others can do when they are in this state is to give them advice or try to fix the problem for them.

INTJs and INFJs agree that a period of solitude and silent, nonintrusive acceptance from others is important in their return to equilibrium. INFJs may welcome more direct support, empathy, affirmation, and acceptance, but they are unlikely to let others know what they need when they need it. INTJs typically just want to be left alone. They need to give themselves the time to recover, often finding that accomplishing a simple, nonthreatening Sensing task is beneficial. Sometimes removing all stimulation helps the most. One INTJ said that after too much sensory stimulation and too much people-dealing what she does is "lie in bed with earplugs and a pillow over my head—remove all stimuli—often even fifteen minutes of this is enough." An INFJ said that when stressed, she wants the room to be dark to eliminate external sensory stimulation.

All types engage in self-criticism at some point during or after an episode of the inferior function. However, the focus of that criticism varies according to type. Introverted Intuitive types are especially hard on themselves, later viewing their obsessive concerns or angry intensity as a sign of unacceptable personal imperfections. One INFJ said that when she is in this state, she needs others to remind her that she is as human as the next person and that she should not be so hard on herself.

A change of scenery or activity can help break the negative, obsessive focus. This may entail getting outside, exercising, walking in the woods, or seeing a movie. As with other types, often a good night's sleep helps. And exercising, particularly alone, is consistently mentioned as helpful by INTJs and INFJs.

Some examples of methods Introverted Intuitive types use for returning to normal include submerging themselves in peaceful, quiet, natural surroundings, being outdoors and looking at nature, canceling activities, lightening their schedules, making more space for being alone, and taking time out to "recharge" and sort things out. One INTJ said:

> A Sunday afternoon nap is a wonderful escape. I make an obsessive list of all the things I'm thinking about, do some light reading or reading I "should" do, and go right to sleep. If I write in a journal just before I go to sleep, I will often dream, and that calms me and helps me find a solution to my troubles. In addition, my cat purring and sleeping next to me is a great way to put life in perspective. I know my equilibrium has returned when I can't find my list of things to do and I don't care!

INTJs may call upon auxiliary Thinking by strategizing to help extricate from obsessiveness. One described forcing himself to get control of at least one situation. This calms him down enough so that he can start to regain a broader perspective. Another INTJ is able to focus on details that are actually productive. "I normally can't proofread well since I fill in the blanks and errors myself, but when I'm in the grip, I can find the smallest error," she said. Gretchen's story in the preceding section also illustrates productive use of inferior Extraverted Sensing. Similarly, another INTJ said that what helps her is "to stop and sort things—think the situation through logically and make some decisions. I usually decide to drop one whole task or responsibility, or ask for help of a practical nature."

Auxiliary Feeling helps INFJs by encouraging acceptance of their less serious side. They can then give in to the urge to cry during "trashy" movies. Or they can read bad novels and recognize that doing so is normal and acceptable. Recognizing that others are hurt and distressed by their out-of-character actions often signals to INTJs and INFJs that the process of extricating from the inferior is occurring. Both types report that they know they are coming out of it when they become bored and frustrated with themselves.

Expressions of understanding, sympathy, and empathy aid the return of equilibrium for some, but usually not for all Introverted Intuitive types. INTJs may find it embarrassing to have others recognize their "weaknesses," or may find such expressions condescending. Gentle humor can be helpful, especially for INFJs. An INFJ said she found it helped to remind herself to be as kind to and accepting of herself as she would be for another person in the same situation.

Expressions in Midlife

Ideally, midlife for Introverted Intuitive types is accompanied by a positive, progressive integration of inferior Extraverted Sensing, and along with it tertiary Thinking or Feeling. This unfortunately does not occur for all aging Introverted Intuitive types.

Some Introverted Intuitive types retreat into themselves in midlife. Attention to their inferior Sensing and tertiary Thinking or Feeling may be limited to idiosyncrasies. They may devote a lot of energy to an ill-conceived project and get lost in its details. They then become frustrated and despairing when they find that others are less and less understanding and appreciative of their efforts. This creates a sense of isolation and alienation.

After retirement, an INTJ political scientist devoted all her time to working out the details of an obscure social interaction theory. Her attempts to publish her work failed, and she became more and more focused on it, until it became her main topic of conversation with family and friends. They began to avoid her or "tune her out." Sensing this, she became bitter and withdrawn.

Other Introverted Intuitive types are more successful in incorporating previously neglected aspects of themselves. They are likely to find new pleasures in the environment and with people. They may take up a new form of exercise, like hiking or fishing, or enjoy a hobby like model building, gardening, or photography. They may also cultivate more moderate and therefore enjoyable ways of gratifying their sensual desires. One INFJ found that she enjoyed watching pro football:

> I am amazed at how physical a sport it is and how crazy the fans get. I don't understand a lot of the rules, but I get a kick out of following the antics and fortunes of my team. When I was a teenager and young adult I hated sports and thought jocks were stupid. In midlife, this is an unexpected source of enjoyment for me.

Another INFJ became very absorbed in the stock market, which had been of little interest to her before. She pored over information, made Internet stock purchases, and thoroughly enjoyed studying the details and using them in a logical way to select promising stocks. An INTJ and her

ENTJ husband, both in their mid-forties, took ballroom dancing lessons together. Though learning the intricate and detailed dance step sequences was difficult for them, they very much enjoyed getting to the point where a new step became skilled and automatic. Until they got to that point, however, they engaged in heated but enjoyable arguments about who was making the most mistakes.

Sometimes spending a lengthy period in the grip of inferior Extraverted Sensing can serve as an important stimulus to midlife development for Introverted Intuitive types. The combination of the natural upheaval of midlife and the disruption and distress of a chronic grip experience may push an INTJ or INFJ into serious examination of goals and values, which may lead to significant changes in the way the second half of life is lived.

Knowledge from Grip Experiences

In addition to learning to recognize and avoid the stress and fatigue that may lead to a grip experience, Extraverted Thinking types report being better able to appreciate the value of their inferior function as an "antidote" to being overloaded by their dominant Introverted Intuition. They can thus accept the legitimacy of Extraverted Sensing in its own right. INTJs and INFJs also recognize and honor their need for solitude and their right to set limits on how much others may intrude on them. This is especially true for INFJs, who tend to be hard on themselves when they can't meet others' expectations. INTJs also learn not to feel guilty for nurturing themselves—it is not a flaw in their sense of competence.

After repeated experiences in the grip, Introverted Intuitive types learn to recognize some of their recurring unrealistic themes, which often stem from the INTJ's or INFJ's lack of understanding or acceptance of the way other types are. They thus find themselves able to be more tolerant of others and to accept and appreciate people who are quite different from them. When stress either at work or at home is extreme and persists over time, Introverted Intuitive types may develop physical stress symptoms such as muscle tension and headaches. If their available ways of reducing ongoing stress fail to help, they are likely to leave the stressful situation, especially if the primary arena is the workplace.

Summary

In the grip of inferior Extraverted Sensing, Introverted Intuitive types obsess about details in the outside world, overindulge in sensual pleasures, and externalize blame to outside objects. Their auxiliary Thinking or Feeling can be the vehicle through which they regain equilibrium. INTJs develop a strategy for analyzing what they are experiencing, achieving distance and objectivity from it, while INFJs examine the important meanings and feeling connections involved and are therefore able to regain their normal wide-ranging perspective.

As a result of important inferior function experiences, Introverted Intuitive types may become better able to adapt to changing surroundings, incorporate sensual experience into their lives in a satisfying way, and moderate a perhaps overly ambitious, visionary stance into one that is more realistic and possible. Table 13 summarizes the major features of their inferior Extraverted Sensing experience.

Table 13 Inferior Function of Introverted Intuitive Types: INTJ and INFJ

Triggers for the Inferior Function	Forms of the Grip Experience
• Dealing with details	• Obsessive focus on external data
• Unexpected events	• Overindulgence in sensual pleasure
• Excessive extraverting	• Adversarial attitude toward the outer world

Ways of Returning to Equilibrium	New Knowledge
• Time alone to recharge	• Adaptability to outer details
• Lightening of usual schedule	• Pleasure in temperate sensuality
• Avoidance by others of giving advice or suggestions	• More realistic goals

12

Introverted Sensing Types
ISTJ and ISFJ

BASIC TYPE DYNAMICS

DOMINANT INTROVERTED SENSING

AUXILIARY EXTRAVERTED THINKING OR FEELING

TERTIARY FEELING OR THINKING

INFERIOR EXTRAVERTED INTUITION

Introverted Sensing Versus Extraverted Intuition

THIS CHAPTER EXAMINES the way effective Introverted Sensing types experience their inferior function and the temporary transformation they make into ineffective, inferior Extraverted Intuitive types when they are either briefly or chronically "in the grip." A review of the characteristics of Introverted Sensing and Extraverted Intuition will be helpful to our discussion.

Important Features of Dominant Introverted Sensing

Introverted Sensing types are careful and orderly in their attention to facts and details. They are thorough and conscientious in fulfilling their responsibilities. They may sometimes even do the work of others rather than leave important tasks undone. They are typically seen as well grounded in reality, trustworthy, and dedicated to preserving traditional values and time-honored institutions. With their focus on the reality of the present, they trust the evidence of their senses, relying on carefully accumulated past and present evidence to support their conclusions and planned courses of action. They derive great pleasure from perfecting existing techniques with the goal of maximizing efficiency and cost-effectiveness.

Introverted Sensing types tend to have a skeptical, critical attitude toward information that has not been verified by the senses and are likely to distrust people who are careless about facts, sloppy about details, and apt to favor imagination and novelty over accuracy and solid substantiation. Both ISTJs and ISFJs are uncomfortable moving beyond sensory experience until they have thoroughly absorbed and understood it. They want to review and assimilate the facts and events of a movie or book before discussing its meaning with others.

In a crisis that does not constellate their inferior function, Introverted Sensing types typically appear calm and unruffled, efficient and pragmatic. Others may marvel at their serene demeanor, but the Introverted Sensing types themselves may report that they are actually feeling quite anxious and distressed and their visible behavior does not accurately reflect their inner state.

Introverted Sensing Types at Work

An ideal, energizing work environment for Introverted Sensing types is one in which they can achieve goals and reach closure on tasks in an efficient, timely manner in quiet, organized surroundings. They prefer minimal conflict and competition among co-workers and want to be recognized for their knowledge and contributions to the organization—a desire that may remain unfulfilled because they often work in the background of organizations.

ISTJs and ISFJs value and support organizational change that is based on solid information and careful reasoning, but they see little sense in change for its own sake, or for brainstorming with no attention to realistic limitations. They want what they do at work to make a difference. One ISTJ said that what energized her was "accomplishing tasks and improving processes in some way." An ISFJ teacher described as energizing "relating to the children on a personal level—figuring out what approach to learning works best for them; having a child feel successful because I utilized a strategy." An ISTJ woman described an energizing environment as having "a combination of people interactions and reading and writing; a serene office and busy hallways; good light and lots of filing space."

Important Features of Dominant Extraverted Intuition

The qualities associated with Extraverted Intuition that are relevant to our discussion of its form as an inferior function are

- Comfortable inattention to sense data
- Flexibility, adaptability, risk taking
- Optimism about future possibilities

For a detailed description of dominant Extraverted Intuition, read the beginning of Chapter 13, "Extraverted Intuitive Types: ENTP and ENFP," and the type descriptions for ENTP and ENFP that appear in Appendix A. This will provide the background needed to explore the various ways in which inferior Extraverted Intuition is expressed in ISTJs and ISFJs.

The Everyday Extraverted Intuition
of Introverted Sensing Types

The inferior function affects Introverted Sensing types in several different ways. These include everyday sensitivities, projections, and ways of relaxing, as well as the dramatic manifestations that can be seen when the inferior function erupts and a full-blown episode occurs, or when an ISTJ or ISFJ is chronically in the grip because of long-term stress.

Typical Sensitivities and Projections

Inferior Extraverted Intuition seems to color the everyday personality of Introverted Sensing types. They see themselves and are seen by others as worriers. They are ready to notice and comment on negative possibilities even in everyday, nonstressful situations. A new plan, a previously unexpe-rienced event—anything new—is likely to elicit a list of all the many neg-ative possibilities or all the many things that might go wrong. Anything that is not grounded in past or present experience is suspect. In a work sit-uation, Introverted Sensing types' focus on the negative may prove frus-trating to their Intuitive colleagues, who may see them as impossibly rigid and stodgy. They may, however, merely need time to reflect and recognize the connections between anticipated new experiences and the known past. Once that connection is made, the ISTJ or ISFJ can be comfortable pursuing actions that initially may have seemed potentially dangerous. Colleagues who can be helpful in providing such connections will likely find the effort quite successful.

As parents, Introverted Sensing types may appear unreasonably over-protective, especially in situations in which the child wants to do some-thing new, test his or her independence, or take any degree of risk. The untried and untested may automatically raise the specter of disaster, de-spite the parents' awareness that they may be overreacting to a reasonable request.

A 10-year-old boy asked his ISFJ mother if he could spend the night at his friend's house. "Where will you sleep?" his mother asked. "He has bunk beds," the child replied. "You can't go, then. You'll convince him to let you sleep in the top bunk, and you're not used to sleeping on the top. You'll fall off and break your leg. No!"

Although this is often the initial parental response to minor risk tak-ing, children of Introverted Sensing parents report that when their parents receive additional factual information and reassurance about precautions, they often amend their original decisions.

In projecting their inferior Extraverted Intuition onto others, ISTJs and ISFJs are likely to see Intuitive types as totally ungrounded, unrealis-tic, and irresponsible in their focus on possibilities and theories. Introverted Sensing types' own inexperienced Intuition is thus attributed to those in whom Intuition is developed and practiced. Their unease with the un-known may also manifest in suspiciousness about others' motives and fears that the environment will somehow betray them. They may thus see Extraverted Intuitive types' natural comfort with the outer world as fool-ish risk taking, judging them to be irresponsible, immature show-offs.

ISTJs and ISFJs may engage in self-pity, blaming the outer environ-ment and other people for whatever difficulties they are experiencing.

This is in marked contrast to their typical willingness to accept responsibility and solve problems calmly and methodically.

Expressions Through Interests and Hobbies

Poetry, music, and art may provide a way for Introverted Sensing types to engage their "other side." Their choice of artists and styles within the arts may tend toward the expressive and dramatic, and they often prefer romantic musicians and artists. The favorite opera of one rather austere and conventional ISTJ is *La Boheme*.

Some Introverted Sensing types are attracted to astrology and the more occult spiritual movements. The evidence presented for such systems often involves detailed eyewitness testimony collected over long periods. Perhaps this Sensing method lends the data legitimacy, thus providing a comfortable, acceptable way to develop familiarity with the vagaries of Intuition. In some ISTJs and ISFJs, interest in such areas can become excessive and obsessive and may be an attempt to control unruly, disorganized, and frightening eruptions of Intuition. However, as long as it does not take too much energy away from the person's dominant Introverted Sensing, even such interest may prove adaptive.

Introverted Sensing types may enjoy relaxing their use of Sensing by reading fantasy fiction, watching science fiction movies, or entertaining themselves with idle speculation and daydreams. One ISTJ described his hobbies as astronomy, painting, and gardening. He identified his fascination with Hubble telescope photos as engaging his Intuition is a very satisfying way: "It opens a whole new dynamic, evolving universe." He wondered what would come of this. Another ISTJ very much enjoys reading adventure stories with animal characters, such as *The Wind in the Willows*.

Eruptions of Inferior Extraverted Intuition

When one or more of the preconditions for eruption of the inferior function are present, Extraverted Intuition appears in its more exaggerated, disruptive form. In addition to the general conditions described in Chapter 4, Introverted Intuitive types are vulnerable to the type-specific factors described below.

Typical Provocations or Triggers

Issues of reality are likely to push the inferior "button" of Introverted Sensing types. Dealing with people whose approach denies facts and actualities (often identified as Extraverted Intuitive types) serves as a trigger for eruptions of harsh, negative, extreme reactions to whatever is being proposed. With the usual preconditions in operation, even slight deviations from present reality or minor suggestions for future change will provoke Introverted Sensing types to intractable anger and stubborn immovability.

One ISFJ said, "If I'm watching the devastating effects of an ongoing crisis and someone says to me, 'Don't worry, everything is going to be fine,' I come unglued. I steamroll over the person and mow them down!" An ISTJ reported that her usual calm demeanor is replaced by cold fury and biting sarcasm when someone tries to contradict the evidence of her senses: "I'm seeing and smelling the ash from this guy's cigar and smelling the smoke on his breath and he's telling me he doesn't smoke cigars!"

The prospect of unknown, previously unexperienced activities and situations is a common trigger for Introverted Sensing types. The anxiety associated with the unfamiliar and unimaginable future acts directly on their most unconscious arena. Making careful contingency plans and giving attention to details normally tempers such an unconscious reaction. But when the new possibility comes up suddenly, an inferior function response is likely. An ISTJ described this provocation:

> When I have to do something that is a completely new experience—for example, fly to a city I've never been to, move to a different city, attend a workshop on a topic I know nothing about. Any situation in which I don't have a clear picture of what I can expect and what is expected of me. The before and waiting period is always worse. Once I'm doing it, I'm fine.

"Overdoing" their own type may also provoke an inferior "grip" response in ISTJs and ISFJs. When this takes the form of doing other people's assigned duties, working long and hard, and feeling unappreciated or taken for granted, the stage is set for an extreme, spontaneous eruption of inferior Extraverted Intuition. "I get to feeling used and abused," said an ISFJ. "Then I explode and say awful things that I'm embarrassed about later."

Triggers and Stressors at Work

Stressful work environments for Introverted Sensing types are those that are chaotic, noisy, and disorganized; where the rules and procedures frequently change, their work is often interrupted, they are criticized for "lacking vision" or "resisting change," and they are not recognized for their substantial and consistent work for the organization. ISTJs and ISFJs are quite uncomfortable with unsubstantiated, sweeping statements that lead to decisions at work. ISTJs tend to be more distressed when a system is involved and ISFJs when people will be affected. However, both types find it stressful to do tasks that require Intuition, especially when they have insufficient time to think things through. The teacher quoted earlier in this chapter described as stressful "writing narrative reports, constant interruptions, figuring out what to do with unplanned time."

Introverted Sensing types find an overwhelming workload to be the most important stressor in their work environment. Having too much to do inevitably affects their ability to live up to their own high standards of performance. One ISTJ said that his strong work ethic forced him to complete his work, but, as a result, he had no time for other things. For other Introverted Sensing types, not having sufficient information to do a good job is equally stressful. One ISFJ teacher cited the following as work stressors: "working with students when I'm not clear on who they are and the new material I'm supposed to teach them."

A source of stress mentioned frequently by ISTJ women is dealing with incompetence at work. Having too much to do appears to be secondary to this stressor for them. One ISTJ woman provided the following very detailed description of work stress, which incorporates many of the issues mentioned by other Introverted Sensing types:

> Back-to-back meetings. Having to deal with meeting or workshop details while also having to lead a discussion that is hypothesis-like or strategic in nature. Having to check sloppy work of others or deal with another department that maintains low standards. I have to watch myself because I tend to "fix" others' incompetencies.

Too much interacting with people can also be stressful for ISTJs and ISFJs, especially if a great deal of talking occurs. They are likely to view too much talking and too many meetings as wasting time they could be devoting to accomplishing things. The same impatience relates to being interrupted when they are concentrating on tasks, and to lack of follow-through by co-workers. In fact, anything that prevents or slows achieving closure in their areas of responsibility creates stress for Introverted Sensing types.

In a work situation in which the particular stressors for Introverted Sensing types continue over long periods, ISTJs and ISFJs may respond quickly and intensely to the triggers described here. This increases the likelihood that their subsequent demonstrations of "grip" behavior will be frequent and pervasive. When persistent stress causes them to be chronically in the grip of inferior Extraverted Intuition, they are likely to lose touch with their natural talent for assessing reality and their practical grasp of problems. They may become habitual "naysayers," spreading doom and gloom throughout the workplace.

The Form of the Inferior Function

Younger Introverted Sensing types, like other Introverted types, report becoming more sociable, outgoing, or outspoken as part of their grip experience. This is especially true for young men, and to a lesser extent for young women. "I'm more outspoken and friendly," said a 21-year-old male ISTJ about his grip experiences. "I'm also more into people's needs and how they feel. I guess I'm more of a 'people person.'" An ISTJ young woman said, "I'm more sensitive and understanding, more outspoken and outgoing." Introverted Sensing types often report that their increased sociability occurs in social situations in which they feel comfortable. An ISTJ is his mid-thirties said he becomes "outgoing, daring, dancing the gorilla dance, whereas I'm usually reserved and calculated." This is stimulated by festive, comfortable occasions with family and friends. Some young Introverted Sensing types, however, report going too far, becoming loud and obnoxious in social situations.

ISTJs and ISFJs of all ages also report a high frequency of becoming more withdrawn, angry, irritable, and pessimistic when in the grip. However, there are some notable differences by auxiliary function and gender. ISTJ and ISFJ men tend to report becoming angry, while women report withdrawing from others. ISTJ women report becoming both pessimistic and scattered, while ISFJ women mention becoming more irritable, emotional, and worried.

Table 14 Dominant and Inferior Expressions of Extraverted Intuition

As Dominant Function of ENTPs and ENFPs	As Inferior Function of ISTJs and ISFJs
• Comfortable inattention to sense data	• Loss of contol over facts and details
• Flexibility, adaptability, risk taking	• Impulsiveness
• Optimism about future possibilities	• Catastrophizing

Introverted Sensing types' characteristic task orientation and calm attention to responsibilities begin to disappear as they move further into the grip. "I feel like I'm in a fog of sand and can't absorb details around me," said an ISTJ. As their hold on their dominant and auxiliary further diminishes, command over dominant Introverted Sensing is lost. If this state persists, the qualities of inferior Extraverted Intuition manifest in a loss of control over facts and details, impulsiveness, and catastrophizing. For ISTJs, tertiary Feeling combines with inferior Intuition so that the negative possibilities are focused on important relationships with loved ones. The tertiary Thinking of ISFJs contributes the "logic" used to support negative possibilities regarding career, money, natural disasters, and so on. The comparison between dominant and inferior Extraverted Intuition is shown in Table 14.

Two qualities of the negative, inferior forms of Extraverted Intuition (loss of control over facts and details, and catastrophizing) are reflected in Jung's (1976a) description of the inferior function of ISTJs and ISFJs:

> Whereas true extraverted intuition is possessed of singular resourcefulness, a "good nose" for objectively real possibilities, this archaisized intuition has an amazing flair for all the ambiguous, shadowy, sordid, dangerous possibilities lurking in the background. (p. 398)

Loss of Control over Facts and Details Effective dominant Extraverted Intuitive types are comfortable glossing over facts and details as they focus on the complexities of an engaging new idea. Their strength lies in emphasizing generalities; the particulars can be dealt with later. In the grip of inferior Extraverted Intuition, however, Introverted Sensing types' relationship to details becomes problematic. As they begin to lose trust in dominant Sensing and auxiliary Thinking or Feeling, ISTJs and ISFJs have difficulty attending to relevant factual information and arriving at rational conclusions.

On the last afternoon of a difficult training session, an ISTJ imagined that a small-group exercise in which trainees practiced their presentation skills was preparation for each class member to give a presentation to the entire class. He became anxious and agitated as the time to return to the workshop room approached. He later admitted that he did not feel adequately prepared to present the material publicly and feared he would be humiliated. What he failed to recognize was that no such activity was listed on the schedule (Sensing data) and that with only sixty minutes left in the workshop, thirty-five people could not possibly make presentations (Thinking judgment). His general anxiety and fatigue at the end of a stressful day contributed to his abandonment of his Sensing and Thinking functions.

Impulsiveness Flexibility and adaptability are assets to effective dominant Extraverted Intuitive types. These qualities permit them to manage the multiple activities and interests characteristic of their operating style. As expressions of inferior Extraverted Intuition, however, these same qualities take on an aspect of thoughtlessness and impulsiveness, not unlike the qualities ISTJs and ISFJs project onto dominant Extraverted Intuitive types. When they experience a gradual slide into their inferior function, Introverted Sensing types may become uncharacteristically spontaneous, sometimes to the point of later judging themselves irresponsible and reckless.

One ISFJ reported giving in to the urge to leave work in the middle of the day and go to the movies. An ISTJ made a spur-of-the-moment decision to buy a new computer before thoroughly researching the options. He returned the computer later, assessing the purchase as rash and foolish.

Introverted Sensing types may experience increasing lack of focus, confusion, anxiety, and even panic, even though their demeanor remains calm and seemingly unperturbed. Their uncharacteristic spontaneity, however, may come out in snappishness and terse, hurtful comments to others, or in out-of-character behavior. After being divorced by his wife of twenty years, an ISTJ dated forty different women in six months. It was as if his inexperienced Intuition went haywire and his tertiary Feeling judgment was unequal to the task of deciding among the overwhelming relationship possibilities available.

Catastrophizing Whereas effective dominant Extraverted Intuitive types thrive on the exciting possibilities the future will bring, Introverted Sensing types in the grip of inferior Extraverted Intuition anticipate the future with fear and trembling. As their descent into the grip proceeds, they become ever more negative, less willing to tolerate the unfamiliar, and more wildly imaginative about disastrous outcomes. One ISFJ described this as "awfulizing."

In its full-blown state, inferior Extraverted Intuition anticipates all the catastrophes that might happen in an unsafe, threatening world and focuses on dire possibilities in the future. (Remember that the other Introverted perceiving types, the Introverted Intuitive types, focus on negative realities in the present.) ISTJs and ISFJs imagine that anything not previously experienced—any unfamiliar place, any new activity—will provoke horrifying consequences. In the full grip of their inferior function, even familiar, previously safe areas may be reassessed as fraught with danger. This level of catastrophizing is the hallmark of inferior Extraverted Intuition.

"I start imagining a lot of terrible things that could happen," said an ISTJ. "If I tell anybody what I'm thinking, the usual response is, 'you worry too much,' or 'don't think about that.' I appear emotional, not my usual controlled self. I am not being realistic, which I always pride myself on being, but borderline ridiculous," she concluded. An ISFJ school choir director is usually in a good mood when she awakens—except when a choir performance is scheduled for that day. On such occasions, she experiences a general feeling of dread and impending disaster, even though there is no specific content associated with her forebodings.

After having knee surgery, which resulted in a good deal of pain and immobility, an ISTJ was convinced that he would never feel any better: "I couldn't stop expressing my pessimism and was a real pain to one and all. Before that I'd always been a pretty optimistic person." In fact, research evidence supports this ISTJ's experience. ISTJs and ISFJs are among the types most frequently treated for chronic pain.

An increase in fatigue and stress often lowers Introverted Sensing types' tolerance and patience in the face of others' inattention to or denial of important facts and details. A full-blown exhibition of negative possibilities is likely to ensue. One ISFJ said, "I am given to very sarcastic humor, slashing and unpredictable explosions of cold, hard statements about here-and-now reality. I get stubborn and let loose a negative barrage covering all the bad consequences of what is being proposed."

When her work situation becomes particularly stressful, another ISFJ's recurrent fear is that her most recent promotion will be rescinded, or that she will receive a letter from her college informing her that her degree was granted by mistake and they are going to have to take it back.

One evening in May, an ISTJ returned home tired after a long day of hiking in the mountains. Distressed to discover that his garage door would not open, he immediately imagined all the possible negative effects—he would have trouble getting to work on time, he wouldn't be able to go on vacation in the summer, and he certainly could not make it to his niece's wedding in August!

Introverted Sensing types report having strange or paranoid thoughts when they are in this state, feeling overwhelmed and irritable and imagining that a current stressful situation will go on forever, as will their inability to handle both the stress and the situation. Alternatively, they may come up with off-the-wall, unrealistic positive possibilities when faced with unfamiliar situations. They then must deal with the extreme disappointment that results when the positive possibilities don't materialize. For example, an ISTJ was quite attracted to a young woman he met and talked with briefly at a party one evening. He planned to get her phone number from his friend so he could ask her out. He imagined where they would go, what they would talk about, and how pleasant their date would be. On calling his friend, therefore, he was upset to learn that the young woman was engaged to be married and had left town that morning to return home to plan her wedding.

One ISFJ's description of not being herself includes all three forms of inferior Extraverted Intuition:

> I ignore facts and details—create monstrous, horrible outcomes that have far-reaching impacts (for instance, in my lifetime and my daughter's lifetime). I dwell exclusively on these "realities." I believe that I need to act right now, this moment (for instance, leave my husband or quit my job). Generally, I am very loyal and steadfast, however.

Lengthy Episodes in the Grip

The types of episodes described above are experienced by ISTJs and ISFJs as temporary states during which they are vulnerable to the three forms in which their inferior function is expressed. However, when Introverted Sensing types are chronically in the grip of inferior Extraverted Intuition, inferior function behavior may become habitual. Their typical hesitation to accept change and their desire for data to back up decisions may become extreme and take the form of angry accusations about the disasters others are perpetrating at work or at home. Their work output is likely to suffer because their judgment about what to pursue is distorted by being in the grip. Even their typical calm demeanor in the face of stress is gone, and others are likely to see their worry, negativity, and catastrophizing most of the time.

Continued stress takes its toll on ISTJs and ISFJs, who are likelier than other types to report having hypertension or heart disease. Chronic stress may be more prevalent for these two types because of the increasingly rapid change that characterizes the workplace and the world at large. Leaving a stressful work or home environment may be quite difficult for Introverted Sensing types because of their natural loyalty, persistence in spite of adversity, and devotion to duty and responsibility. If they do recognize the unreasonableness of the demands made on them and manage to leave bad situations, they may discover a newfound freedom and a greater ability to accurately assess bad work and home situations.

Chronic grip behavior may lead the individual and others to believe that he or she is typically sloppy and forgetful of details, impulsive, and habitually focused on negative possibilities. This was the case in the last story in the next section, where a supervisor new to a company clashed with a longtime ISFJ employee who had been in the grip for some time. Since the process of becoming chronically in the grip is often gradual, even people who have known the person in a nonstressed state are likely not to notice what, in retrospect, will be recognized as a radical alteration of personality. The person will appear to be a rather exaggerated, poorly developed Extraverted Intuitive type.

Bear in mind, however, that there are occasions when a lengthy time in the grip of inferior Extraverted Intuition can stimulate new awareness and positive growth toward completion and individuation. Remember that Jung saw the inferior function as the doorway to the unconscious and an important part of the self-regulating capacity of our psyches.

Grip Experiences

The stories included in this section illustrate one or more forms of inferior Extraverted Intuition as experienced by ISTJs or ISFJs. Although the next-to-last example demonstrates evidence of all three forms of the inferior function, most of the Introverted Sensing experiences reported are relatively brief and to the point, often focusing on only one aspect of inferior Extraverted Intuition. This is consistent with the pragmatic, singular focus of Introverted Sensing types.

From Anxiety to Indignation

Deborah, an ISTJ, recalled an incident that occurred early in her marriage as she was waiting for her husband to pick her up from work:

> It was pouring rain and I was standing at a transfer point of a bus stop. Even though I was under an awning, I was getting really wet. He was late. At first I worried that he had gotten into an accident. But that soon switched to anger at my own plight. As I told him later—"I buried you; then I dug you up and divorced you!"

The Worrywart

An ISTJ army chaplain in his early sixties recognized the influence of his inferior function in the following facts about himself:

- He has always been interested in apocalyptic literature.
- He and others believe he is overconcerned about his retirement options.
- An important prayer in his personal devotions is "Lord, remind me, 'Don't worry about the future.'"
- He recalls that his mother's earliest admonition to him was "Quit being a worrywart!"

Explained the chaplain: "I felt quite liberated by discovering that this familiar but distressing part of me is natural and adaptive. It hasn't stopped my habitual worrying, but I'm relieved to know that my reactions make sense and are predictable, normal parts of my personality."

Is a Better Job Worth It?

A career counselor had a young ISFJ client who was contemplating a career change. The career that most interested him, however, might have involved moving to another state. There were few external impediments to such a move, since he was unmarried and had no romantic involvements. However, he expressed great concern that if he got married before he changed his work, then changed careers, and then met a more compatible woman in his new work and living environment, his happy home would be broken up and he would have to get a divorce! The counselor's attempts to point out the unreality of his concerns were ignored.

In a somewhat similar scenario, an ISTJ man was moving to a new city because he had received a coveted work promotion. He became increasingly anxious, imagining all kinds of terrible things that would happen: His car would break down on the freeway and no one would stop to help him; he would get mugged on the street; no one would ever talk to him; or he would become ill and die alone in his apartment.

ESFP's New Experience or ISFJ's Worst Nightmare?

Annette, an ISFJ, and Dan, an ESFP, were having a drink before dinner in a revolving cocktail lounge at the top of a twenty-story hotel in Texas. The clear glass walls on all sides of the lounge gave customers a full view of the city. It was an early August evening. As they talked, the skies darkened, heavy clouds appeared, and the wind started blowing very hard.

Dan, leaning against the glass outer wall, said, "Hey, this is great. I can feel the glass vibrating from the wind!"

"Let's go inside the main part of the restaurant," said Annette.

"Why would you want to do that? We won't have the beautiful view," said Dan.

"I want to move away from all this glass and go into the central part where the restaurant is," insisted Annette.

Dan was puzzled. "But I don't understand why," he said.

"Because it's August—we're in Texas, the wind is blowing hard, those clouds look ominous, and it's tornado season!" she declared vehemently.

Replied Dan, "But if there's a tornado, this is a wonderful place to watch it from!"

"Let's Be Realistic!"

Steve, an ISFJ, was managing director of a major division in a large international company. During a routine audit it was discovered that his assistant, a trusted employee of fifteen years' tenure, had been systematically embezzling funds for five years. This was devastating to everyone in the company, especially Steve, who felt the credibility of his department had been dealt a mortal blow. He held himself responsible for not seeing his assistant's criminal behavior.

As the police handcuffed the embezzler and hauled him off to jail, John, an ENFJ company vice president, said to Steve, "This really isn't a bad situation, Steve. Look at everything we've learned from this and how much better we'll be for the experience."

Replied Steve heatedly, "Let's be realistic, John. We're not having a developmental opportunity here. We're having a crisis!"

"Stop! Don't Think About Anything!"

Alice, an ISTJ, was having her dream house built. After a two-month delay, it was close to completion. Alice was looking forward to moving out of her temporary accommodations and into her long-awaited new house. The following is an example she provided of her reactions when her inferior Extraverted Intuition was engaged during this time:

> The stress of building the house was ongoing. The delay made the closing date uncertain, and I was working within a contract deadline. There was high stress at work as well: My department was being downsized and I would have to lay people off; I was behind in reviewing proposals; and I was put in charge of a new program that I disapproved of but would have to implement anyway.
>
> I was concerned because there were still construction tasks to be done. I had fleeting thoughts that Curtis, my contractor, was purposely slowing down work on the house, but I couldn't imagine why. Early one evening, Dick, a friend who was in the construction business and knew Curtis, told me he had heard that Curtis was delaying completing my house until after the contract had expired so he could charge me more money. He told me Curtis had failed to meet previous promised completion dates on three other houses.
>
> I knew in an instant that this must be true. I recalled that Curtis was known for taking his time on finishing touches. He would play on my desperation to leave my temporary housing, and I would give in and agree to a higher price, which I couldn't afford. I would lose the house. After waiting all this time and designing just what I wanted, someone else was going to live in my house. I would have to find another, inadequate, house. And then interest rates would rise and I would never be able to afford a house I really wanted. Besides, I would have to sue Curtis to get back the money I had already paid other contractors to do the landscaping and fireplace, so I would have much less money available to invest in a house I wanted.

Throughout the evening I tried desperately to fight off my anxiety by focusing on other tasks, but those thoughts kept creeping back in and I would find myself on the verge of tears. I calmed myself down enough to get to sleep but woke up at 2:30 A.M. and couldn't go back to sleep. I spent the night tossing and turning as I thought about how I would be moving out of my temporary housing but wouldn't have a house to move into. Plus my furniture was going to be delivered on Tuesday, but they would have to leave it on the side of the road because the house wouldn't be mine. But then there was always the possibility that the moving company had lost my furniture and wouldn't be able to deliver it anyway. And then I'd be too upset to implement the new program and we wouldn't get it done by the deadline, so my boss would get in trouble, and then I'd get in trouble, too.

I was finally able to calm myself down enough to get some rest, though not sleep. To do that, I had to think through contingency plans [auxiliary Thinking] for how I would handle various scenarios should they occur, just to convince myself that I wasn't totally at the mercy of others' whims. I also convinced myself that I had to be willing to walk away from the contract in order to maintain any bargaining power in the situation and to withhold some of the contract funds in escrow until all items were finished to my satisfaction.

On the other side of this grip experience, I think of these contingency plans as appropriate and necessary, though I feel a little silly about my anxiety attack. I must say it helped to talk to two people in the construction business the next day who were able to confirm that my negative fantasy about Curtis's deviousness was just that—a negative fantasy. But this morning as I prepared to sign the contract with my landscaper, I had to consciously fight off the inclination to cancel the appointment, though I knew this would further impede closing on the house.

This was an awful experience. I rarely have a sense of panic like that, and it seemed that any direction I turned to counter my negativity, there were more frightening fantasies lurking to increase my panic. I was in a negative spiral and it was moving faster and faster. At one point I remember telling myself, "Stop! Don't think about anything!" It wasn't until later that I realized I had been in the grip.

Why Joyce "Lost It" at Work

Joyce, an ISFJ in her mid-fifties, was a hardworking, skilled, and experienced manager who had been working for the same male-dominated company for twenty years. Everyone marveled at her efficiency, consistent attention to the complex details and procedures involved in her work, and unswerving commitment to meeting deadlines. In spite of having to prove herself several times as new supervisors were assigned to her division, she generally managed to maintain her professionalism, spirit of cooperation, and good humor. Eventually, even the most difficult of bosses came to respect and value her.

But her newest boss, Garth, proved a hard nut to crack: He was persistently critical of everything Joyce did, double-checked and redid much of her work even though it was correct to begin with, and generally made her life miserable. Joyce was relieved to discover that a number of her co-workers were getting the same kind of treatment from Garth. But despite this validation, she admitted that for the past several months, she had in fact been making a lot of mistakes, losing some important paperwork, and even missing a filing deadline—something that had never happened before.

Things finally came to a head with Garth at a staff meeting. Joyce glared at Garth and shouted, "I've tried every which way to please you and nothing works. You're suspicious and critical and I can't do anything to get your approval. Why, if I set myself on fire because you asked me to, you'd criticize me for using the wrong kind of gasoline!"

Everyone who knew Joyce was shocked at her "losing it" in front of the whole staff. Garth was startled. He acknowledged that he was hard to please and assured Joyce he thought she was doing a great job. This made Joyce even madder. "Empty, meaningless compliments won't make up for your attitude!" she said.

"You're the one with the attitude," replied Garth. "And I can't believe this is just about me," he said. "There must be something else going on."

"Okay," said Joyce. "I'll tell you what's going on! A year ago my father died. Last summer my mother was deathly ill and almost died and I nursed her back to health at my house until she was well enough to go back home. Right after that my granddaughter was sexually molested by a family friend and everyone's making believe it didn't happen. And two months ago, my mother, who was doing really well, had a stroke and died a week later. So that's what's been going on in my life! And I think I need to see a counselor because I can't stop crying and you'd better give me time off to do it!"

Garth immediately agreed to give Joyce whatever time she needed. He apologized for his attitude, and he and Joyce agreed to put their relationship on a better footing. Joyce's counselor assured her that her feelings of grief and intense loss were normal and legitimate, especially because she and her mother had enjoyed a very close and satisfying relationship. Joyce was further reassured when she learned that her atypical mistakes at work and her "loss of control over facts and details" were natural and predictable expressions of her inferior function—a consequence of the severe and persistent stress she was experiencing. Her fears that her present poor performance would continue forever (catastrophizing) were thus allayed. She began to feel calmer, more optimistic, and able to look forward with pleasure to spending time with her family and renewing her interest in work.

Return of Equilibrium

Introverted Sensing types tend to make excellent use of their knowledge about their inferior function reactions. This was well demonstrated by Joyce's experience. She knew about type and the inferior function from previous sessions with her counselor. Over the preceding years she had sought help on several occasions when she was having difficulty coping with other stressful episodes in her life.

Both male and female ISTJs and ISFJs consistently report that they need time alone in order to regain their equilibrium, but how they use that time may differ by auxiliary function and gender. For example, female ISTJs report wanting to reflect on, reframe, and solve the problem (auxiliary Thinking) that caused their stress. An ISTJ woman said, "I think logically—or decide what the possibilities might be. Once I've accepted them, I'm prepared, even for the negative ones." Another ISTJ said she needs "some quiet time, and then for someone to slowly ask me questions and slowly play back what they're hearing from me. I also need acknowledgment that I'm struggling—someone else who can label my plight."

For one ISFJ woman, the helpful "alone" time is spent "rehashing how I would have handled the situation (in my mind), relive it a better way. Analyze why I was reacting the way I did." Both auxiliary Feeling and tertiary Thinking are called upon to aid her in this process. Another ISFJ perhaps uses both auxiliary Feeling and tertiary Thinking to "figure out how I got to not being myself in the first place." Yet another ISFJ engages auxiliary Feeling when she "reads materials that are personally moving—that is, spiritual things to get back in touch with my feelings."

It is interesting to note that female ISFJs (in contrast with male ISFJs and male and female ISTJs) want the support and reassurance of others (auxiliary Feeling) after they spend some time alone. It is also interesting that male and female ISTJs and male ISFJs typically cite physical exercise as important in aiding their return to normal, but female ISFJs rarely mention it —although some describe using deep breathing to calm themselves down. The natural pathway out of the inferior function for Introverted Sensing types seems to be through their auxiliary Extraverted Thinking or Feeling. This may take the general form of engaging in physical activity with others or perhaps changing their environment. ISTJs report using their Thinking to remind them of what is real—that they can take control and that things always work out. ISFJs find it helpful when they (with great difficulty) talk to someone and reveal their irrational fears, and then receive quiet reassurance.

As with other types, ISTJs and ISFJs report needing to "hit bottom" before they can extricate themselves comfortably from a grip experience. One ISFJ used the metaphor of being sucked into a whirlpool. "The worst thing to do is fight it," he said. "That will guarantee you'll drown. Instead, you have to let yourself be drawn into it and pulled all the way down to the bottom. Then you will emerge alive."

Introverted Sensing types also report needing others to take them seriously, not to patronize them or judge them as irrational. Being allowed to vent with an active listener who resists offering solutions is useful. Unobtrusive help with some of the overwhelming details contributing to the Introverted Sensing type's fatigue and stress is also welcome.

Expressions in Midlife

During the first half of life, many Introverted Sensing types come across as workaholics, demonstrating their devotion to family by providing financial security and setting and meeting realistic goals. In their relationships with their children, they may emphasize duty, accountability, and rules as the best ways to fulfill their parental responsibility to raise independent, successful future members of society. Because of this, they may be seen as disinterested and distant, in the case of ISTJs; or as demanding, overprotective, and guilt inducing in the case of ISFJs. Others can experience both Introverted Sensing types as controlling and rigid, when in fact such characteristics are merely by-products of the natural style of these types.

Ideally, midlife for Introverted Sensing types is accompanied by a positive, progressive integration of inferior Extraverted Intuition, along with tertiary Thinking or Feeling. For some ISTJs and ISFJs, however, this may not be the case.

Some Introverted Sensing types become more exaggerated versions of themselves in their older years. They may develop rigid rules and unvarying routines, insisting that everyone conform to their way of doing things. This can prove quite painful for family members and others, often leading relatives and friends to avoid dealing with an aging Introverted Sensing person. The older ISTJ or ISFJ may experience this avoidance as confirmation of his or her real or imagined failures in the first half of life, furthering a sense of despair and isolation.

Introverted Sensing types who are able to add Intuition to their resources seem to "mellow" in the second half of life. They appear more flexible and open to new experiences, more accepting of alternative viewpoints and lifestyles, and more interested in exploring previously rejected or ignored aspects of themselves and of the world in general. Things that they were likely to ignore in their earlier years may now intrigue them.

One ISTJ reported that in her early efforts at cooking she followed recipes exactly. In her mid-thirties she began deviating from written instructions in minor ways and doing some mild experimenting. Now in her fifties, she makes up her own recipes, using published ones only to get ideas. When guests rave about her creations, she feels especially pleased and affirmed.

An ISFJ recalled that in his younger years he gave little thought to what he now recognizes were eruptions of his inferior function. They were too disruptive and unlike him to be explainable. However, in middle age he became curious about these episodes and gave them a good deal of thought. Even before becoming aware of the concept of the inferior function, he learned to predict when episodes would occur and what triggered them: "I had a really terrible fall season last year. And then for several days in a row I woke up and told my wife I'd better not go to work because I would lose control. I felt like a coffeepot that percolates and then boils over all of a sudden."

Older Introverted Sensing types also seem more tolerant of others' "failings." The daughter of one 78-year-old ISTJ woman noted that her mother had become quite relaxed and philosophical about people not coming to her house on time and not keeping their promises—events that would have greatly annoyed her in her earlier years. This same ISTJ re-called her own mother (probably also an ISTJ or an ESTJ) criticizing her mother (another likely STJ) for moderating her views and loosening her standards as she aged!

Many "mellowing" ISTJs and ISFJs devote more attention to per-sonal interactions with family members and friends, become more flexi-ble and accepting of lifestyle and value differences, and often form the kind of close, warm relationships with their grandchildren that their own children would have welcomed.

Sometimes spending a lengthy period in the grip of inferior Ex-traverted Intuition can serve as an important stimulus to midlife develop-ment for Introverted Sensing types. The combination of the natural upheaval of midlife and the disruption and distress of a chronic grip expe-rience can push an ISTJ or ISFJ into serious soul searching and reconsid-eration of long-standing goals, which may lead to significant changes in the way the second half of life is lived.

Knowledge from Grip Experiences

In addition to learning to recognize and avoid the stress and fatigue that may lead to a grip experience, Introverted Sensing types, even prior to their midlife development, are able to broaden their perspective and be-come more accepting of others' different approaches to life tasks. They report a greater willingness to consider what is important to themselves as well as to others in deciding what goals to pursue and how to use their time. This inclusion of a range of possibilities and other ways of doing things enables them to benefit from their Intuition, as well as to accept and use theories and hypotheses they might otherwise reject as unrealistic.

When stress either at work or at home is extreme and persists over time, Introverted Sensing types may persevere longer than some other types before they consider leaving the stressful situation. They are likely to believe that the stress they are experiencing is uniquely theirs and that others in the same situation are handling things much better. They may see that their opposite types at work (ENTPs and ENFPs) seem to thrive on stress, change, and upheaval and thus may view themselves as weak and inadequate. It may take a crisis situation such as becoming physically ill, having an emotional breakdown, or being confronted by family members for them to recognize that they are in a habitually out-of-character state. Only then might they realistically assess the role of their environment in their plight and consider a drastic change.

Summary

In the grip of inferior Extraverted Intuition, Introverted Sensing types lose control over facts and details, become impulsive, and catastrophize about the unknown, especially the future. Auxiliary Thinking or Feeling aids their return to equilibrium. ISTJs use objective analysis to begin to control their anxious imaginings, while ISFJs solicit the reassurance of trusted companions and friends to modify their perceptions.

As a result of important bouts with inferior Extraverted Intuition, Introverted Sensing types recognize and incorporate a broader, more flexible perspective into their lives. They are better able to stand back from the absorbing tasks and responsibilities of daily living and consider what is most important to them. Often the awareness involves a renewed appreciation of family and other close relationships. Table 15 highlights the main features of the inferior function experience of Introverted Sensing types.

Table 15 Inferior Function of Introverted Sensing Types: ISTJ and ISFJ

Triggers for the Inferior Function	Forms of the Grip Experience
• Issues of reality	• Loss of control over facts and details
• Anything unknown	• Impulsiveness
• Overdoing their own type	• Catastrophizing

Ways of Returning to Equilibrium	New Knowledge
• Need to hit bottom	• Broadened perspective
• Being taken seriously by others	• Clarified values
• Being helped with overwhelming details	• Flexibility in relationships

13

Extraverted Intuitive Types

ENTP and ENFP

BASIC TYPE DYNAMICS

DOMINANT EXTRAVERTED INTUITION

AUXILIARY INTROVERTED THINKING OR FEELING

TERTIARY FEELING OR THINKING

INFERIOR INTROVERTED SENSING

Extraverted Intuition Versus Introverted Sensing

THIS CHAPTER EXAMINES the way effective Extraverted Intuitive types experience their inferior function and the temporary transformation they make into ineffective, inferior Introverted Sensing types when they are either briefly or chronically "in the grip." A review of the characteristics of Extraverted Intuition and Introverted Sensing will be helpful to our discussion.

Important Features of Dominant Extraverted Intuition

ENTPs and ENFPs have a passion for new ideas and especially enjoy the pursuit of possibilities in the world. They prefer what might be to what is, approach the outer world with trust and optimism, and see the environment as welcoming, safe, and exhilarating. They are bored by facts, details, and repetitive activities, especially those that are irrelevant to their current interests. However, an incoming fact may stimulate their intuition and lead to new theories or models.

Extraverted Intuitive types seem to have a natural trust in the environment as supportive of all things possible. They may therefore ignore sensory data that might portend danger or take risks that others might avoid. As a rule, new challenges are more appealing to them than what is known and verified. They have an uncanny instinct for spotting trends and future developments, often before others are even mildly aware of them. Some may, in fact, predict future programs or outcomes and be told they are really "out in left field." Months, sometimes years, later they may see those ideas come into their own.

Their enthusiasm for a current project can be so compelling that they may be oblivious to time and energy limitations, often ignoring their own and others' needs to take breaks from the activity for food and rest. At an extreme, they may become so physically run down that they are forced to stop their work or risk serious illness.

ENTPs and ENFPs tend to enjoy the company of like-minded Intuitive types and may be somewhat disdainful of their opposite types, finding them drab, predictable, and conventional. They may see Introverted Sensing types as overconcerned with health, safety, and comfort.

Their noninferior mode of responding to mild or moderate crises can verge on the dramatic, sometimes accompanied by a wealth of either affect or critical intensity that may seem excessive to others.

Extraverted Intuitive Types at Work

Interacting with other people and having opportunities to use their creativity in a flexible, open, exciting environment form the basis of what energizes Extraverted Intuitive types in the workplace. Whereas their Introverted Intuitive colleagues (INTJs and INFJs) want the highest degree of freedom to use their creativity in working independently, ENTPs and ENFPs want that same freedom to use their creativity in interaction with or as applied to other people. An ENTP described what energized her as "new projects, researching a new subject, meeting new people, interactive events, and enthusiasm from others." An ENFP said he was most energized by "interacting with people in training and creating new material for training." Another cited "social contact, working out difficulties and challenges regarding human nature and relationships."

Teamwork is very important to female ENTPs and ENFPs, and ENFP women often mention "helping others" as energizing. An ENFP woman said she is energized by "empowering and enlightening others— contributing to the growth, development, and self-awareness of others; making a positive difference or impact." Another ENFP woman cited "exciting new projects, high-quality work with interesting people, interacting with my team, helping people develop, and getting others enthused."

Excitement, enthusiasm, and a spirit of fun in the workplace are highly desirable for Extraverted Intuitive types. An ENTP said he is energized by "working on new projects, developing new courses and ways of doing things, finding time to relax or play while I am working." An ENTP woman mentioned "creativity, working in a group setting, competent people, adventure, and nonstructured work." Two other ENTP women listed between them the following energizers: "talking to people, connecting, new problems, brainstorming, freedom, autonomy, open space, people thinking, respect for ability, visioning, fun, big picture, new challenges, competence acknowledged, winging it, interaction, stimulating, debate with no set outcome."

Important Features of Dominant Introverted Sensing

The qualities associated with Introverted Sensing that are relevant to our discussion of its form as an inferior function are

- Solitude and reflection
- Attention to facts and details
- Awareness of internal experience

For a detailed description of dominant Introverted Sensing, read the beginning of Chapter 12, "Introverted Sensing Types: ISTJ and ISFJ," and the type descriptions for ISTJ and ISFJ that appear in Appendix A. This will provide the background needed to explore the various ways in which inferior Introverted Sensing is expressed in ENTPs and ENFPs.

The Everyday Introverted Sensing of Extraverted Intuitive Types

The inferior function affects Extraverted Intuitive types in several different ways. These include everyday sensitivities, projections, and ways of relaxing, as well as the dramatic manifestations that can be seen when the inferior erupts and a full-blown episode occurs, or when an ENTP or ENFP is chronically in the grip because of long-term stress.

Typical Sensitivities and Projections

Extraverted Intuitive types report varying degrees of concern about whether others see them as having substance, stability, and depth. They can therefore overdo attention to facts or be somewhat defensive about their knowledge and use of facts and details.

One ENFP becomes so deeply involved in the details of a new project that she obsessively searches out supporting evidence in the form of ever more facts, which are often irrelevant to the goals of the project. An ENTP lawyer acknowledged that she often feels unprepared with data to support her legal arguments, so she makes sure she has at least a few facts she can bring forth at appropriate moments to convince others of her thoroughness. An ENFP teacher says she always overprepares for lectures, bringing enough material to fill twice the amount of time she actually has to present.

When a strongly held value or principle is involved, ENTPs and ENFPs will carefully collect important facts and details. However, people who disagree with their viewpoints may accuse them of overvaluing certain facts, which in turn may lead the ENTPs or ENFPs to doubt their own perceptions and judgments. As a general rule, it is relatively easy to shake people's confidence in the area of their inferior function. When put in this position, Extraverted Intuitive types seek confirmation of their factual basis from others. For example, an ENFP whose company was planning a major move became increasingly concerned because critical financial facts were being ignored by management. When her expressed concerns were discounted, she began to doubt her perceptions, even though a few of her colleagues shared them. Only after the move actually resulted in a financial crisis did she (and others) accept the validity of her fact-based perceptions.

Less mature Extraverted Intuitive types may sometimes present themselves as "experts" about some factual area, eager to educate others about it. This can prove embarrassing if they try to impress a true authority in a particular field. An ENTP at a basic training session for volunteer firefighters complained that the level of information being presented was "too elementary for someone of my level of knowledge and experience. After all," he explained, "I've already witnessed a forest fire and helped put out a couple of brush fires!"

Some Extraverted Intuitive types recall being sensitive about their factual knowledge even as children. An ENFP described an incident when he was about 9 years old. "My school class was doing a project on ponds and streams and the indigenous wildlife. I stated that a creature known as the great crested newt could be found in this habitat. My teacher denied the creature's existence, and then I felt belittled in front of the class. I returned to school a few days later armed with reference books from the town library and copious notes and photographs to prove the creature's existence. I felt vindicated and seldom went to the library to borrow similar books again."

Overconcern with selected areas that involve facts or sensory data can also occur. One ENFP was characteristically picky about making selections from a restaurant menu. He invariably requested some alteration in the standard fare, adding or deleting a vegetable, grilling rather than broiling, and so on. His companions at these events would be subjected to a lengthy explanation of his finely discriminating gourmet tastes.

In mildly stressful or fatiguing situations, an uneasiness about facts comes out in projected form as a pickiness and obsessiveness about what would otherwise be judged by the Extraverted Intuitive type to be irrelevant detail. Often there are irritated complaints about others' failure to attend to "important" details like typos, misplaced footnotes, motel beds that are too soft or too hard, or fussiness about food. One ENTP was surprised to learn from his wife that every time they discussed household finances, he would ask the same questions about their insurance policies—using exactly the same tone of voice.

Expressions Through Interests and Hobbies

For many Extraverted Intuitive types, the least-preferred function may be expressed through the development of expertise in one or two specific areas that require the use of Sensing. One ENFP who doesn't care much for cooking is known for her superb pie crusts; another takes great pride and pleasure in doing all her own business accounting; and one ENTP has a passion for meticulous gardening and landscaping.

An ENFP described her interest in horse shows, especially turnout classes, as an adaptation of her inferior Introverted Sensing: "It involves a lot of preparation of the horse in the very early hours of the morning. I am alone and have to spend a large amount of time paying attention to very specific details to make sure everything is perfectly in order to be competitive." Another ENTP described his lifelong hobby of model railroading:

> It connects me to facts and reality. I literally create a world in a very direct way, and I run that world. I operate it and manipulate it. It is also pure relaxation of my usual intense cognitive activity. When I stop working on my railroad, I can't remember a single thought, only what I actually did.

Another appeal of his hobby is its connection to his grandfather, who was an acclaimed master woodcarver. The hobby thus provides a strong sense of connection to his past.

Some ENTPs and ENFPs whose work lives involve primary use of their inferior and tertiary functions may welcome the opportunity to use their dominant and auxiliary functions in their hobbies. An ENFP listed his hobbies as "sports/exercise (especially team sports), travel, and going to clubs and concerts to listen to music and chat with friends." He sees these hobbies as primarily addressing Extraverted Intuition and auxiliary Feeling. "I believe this is because I work in a highly ISTJ environment as an engineer and thus I work in my tertiary and inferior functions a lot. It can be exhausting."

Eruptions of Inferior Introverted Sensing

When one or more of the preconditions for eruption of the inferior function are present, Introverted Sensing emerges in its more exaggerated, disruptive form. In addition to the general conditions described in Chapter 4, Extraverted Intuitive types are vulnerable to the type-specific factors described below.

Typical Provocations or Triggers

Fatigue and pressure from overcommitment often trigger inferior function reactions in ENTPs and ENFPs. Not surprisingly, given the typical expressions of their type, they mention physical exhaustion as an inferior function trigger more frequently than other types. Often the enthusiasm of Extraverted Intuitive types encourages them to overextend themselves and neglect their physical needs for food and rest. The result may be a physical illness that forces them to stop overdoing things and also may serve as a trigger for an inferior function experience.

An ENFP aptly described this when he said, "I think of myself as a high-stimulus person, and I enjoy having many things on the go at once. My 'issue' is knowing where to draw the line between so much to do that it becomes impossible and 'just enough' to keep the challenges interesting and attainable." Both ENFPs and ENTPs mention taking on too much, but ENFPs seem particularly distressed by this tendency, often attributing it to their poor time management. Said one ENFP, "Too often, it is me not allowing enough time to finish a task or not leaving early enough to be on time."

An important and frequent trigger for inferior Introverted Sensing is having to deal with a lot of details or attend to practical matters for long periods with no breaks. This is an especially effective provocation if the Extraverted Intuitive type's efforts meet with failure. Dealing with bureaucratic red tape can be particularly noxious for Extraverted Intuitive types, who are likely to dig in their heels and refuse to capitulate to "ridiculous rules."

For some ENTPs and ENFPs, violation of important values can constellate a reaction. Explained one ENFP, "It happens when I feel the pain of others who are the victims of someone's extreme aggressiveness." An ENTP economist's severe inferior function reaction was triggered by working on a theoretical model that had negative social implications.

Triggers and Stressors at Work

Not surprisingly, the very opposite of what makes Extraverted Intuitive types excited about work is cited by them as very stressful. One major stressor is dealing with an overwhelming workload. This stressor may be particularly problematic for ENTPs and ENFPs because of their difficulty in distinguishing between the challenge and excitement of multiple demands and a totally unreasonable workload. Other stressors consistently mentioned by both male and female Extraverted Intuitive types include the following: too much structure, routine, rigidity, planning, specifics, being watched, being forced to work alone, staying in the same environment, no change, repetition, being unable to deviate from an agenda, being overcontrolled by others, a prescriptive approach. Dealing with details is particularly stressful for female ENTPs and ENFPs. An ENTP woman cited as stressors "doing planning and detail and not having the right equipment, although I can adapt very quickly to crisis situations." An ENFP woman listed the following: "details, managing my schedule, boundaries, rules, judgmental attitudes, too much paper, problems that don't go away."

Lack of stimulation and a constraining atmosphere can quickly cause Extraverted Intuitive types to lose energy and become demotivated at work. An ENTP said that what he finds stressful is "lack of space, routine and mundane activities, people looking over my shoulder, unproductive meetings, unnecessary reports." Another ENTP added "boundaries, a judgmental atmosphere, constraints, negativity or apathy from others." An ENFP described as stressful "long hours of work (more than fifty-five per week), a bad organizational climate, having to work for long periods by myself."

Detailed work, deadlines, and excessive structure can all sap energy for these types, and the longer they operate in such an environment, the more likely it is to take its toll on their productivity and well-being. An ENFP described "spending an extended period of time on systematic, procedural, detail-oriented data and working with chronic, argumentative, antagonistic individuals" as quite debilitating.

In a work situation in which the particular stressors for Extraverted Intuitive types continue over long periods, ENTPs and ENFPs may respond quickly and intensely to the triggers described here. This increases the likelihood that their subsequent demonstrations of "grip" behavior will be frequent and pervasive. When persistent stress causes them to be chronically in the grip of inferior Introverted Sensing, they are likely to lose touch with their natural enthusiasm for future possibilities and their trust in their ability to successfully overcome obstacles. They may doggedly focus on minor facts and details and habitually complain about others' factual and detail errors.

The Form of the Inferior Function

Many young male and female ENTPs and ENFPs report becoming uncharacteristically quiet and reserved when they are out of character and find this in marked contrast to their usual openness and sociability. Like other young Extraverted types, they do not seem to find anything positive in moving to this Introverted approach, but are rather puzzled and surprised by it. "I become very quiet and reserved," said an ENTP young man, "and I don't talk to people like I normally do." An ENFP young woman said, "Sometimes I withdraw from everyone, sit alone for hours, and just think. Let stuff stew in my head alone." Older Extraverted Intuitive types also do not report much pleasure in being withdrawn, quiet, and reserved, and in losing their natural Extraverted Intuitive qualities. Said an ENFP, "I become very quiet, unsure about my thoughts and expressing them. I think a whole lot."

As the connection with dominant Intuition diminishes, so do Extraverted Intuitive types' characteristic enthusiasm, optimism, and energetic approach to life. When their hold on their dominant and auxiliary functions continues to taper off, the qualities of inferior Introverted Sensing manifest in withdrawal and depression, obsessiveness, and a focus on the body. For ENTPs, tertiary Feeling emerges as strong, uncontrollable, and emotional criticism that accompanies the obsessive "facts" that overwhelm them. The tertiary Thinking of ENFPs contributes to their obsessive "facts" the sarcastic, legalistic "logic" that proves others' failings. The comparison between dominant and inferior Introverted Sensing is shown in Table 16.

Table 16 Dominant and Inferior Expressions of Introverted Sensing

As Dominant Function of ISTJs and ISFJs	As Inferior Function of ENTPs and ENFPs
• Solitude and reflection	• Withdrawal and depression
• Attention to facts and details	• Obsessiveness
• Awareness of internal experience	• Focus on the body

Two qualities of the negative, inferior forms of Introverted Sensing (obsessiveness and a focus on the body) are reflected in Jung's (1976a) description of the inferior Introverted Sensing of ENTPs and ENFPs:

> They take the form of intense projections which are . . . chiefly concerned with quasi-realities, such as sexual suspicions, financial hazards, forebodings of illness, etc. . . . [The Extraverted Intuitive may] fall victim to neurotic compulsions in the form of oversubtle ratiocinations, hair-splitting dialectics, and a compulsive tie to the sensation aroused by the object. . . . But sooner or later the object takes revenge in the form of compulsive hypochondriacal ideas, phobias, and every imaginable kind of absurd bodily sensation. (p. 370)

Withdrawal and Depression   Effective dominant Introverted Sensing types are in their element when they spend time alone in reflection. Processing their stored information is familiar and pleasurable, and they are energized by their Introverted Sensing activities. For ENTPs and ENFPs in the grip of inferior Introverted Sensing, the inward focus of energy is unfamiliar and disturbing. The diminution of Extraverted energy results in feelings of sadness and despair. Tertiary Thinking or Feeling may emerge as well. For ENTPs this comes out in a conviction that no one understands them or cares about them; they may become emotional and vulnerable in this state. ENFPs may demonstrate perverse logic and accuse others of not being rational, insisting that logic is the only acceptable criterion for making a decision.

In this condition, one ENTP describes feeling isolated, convinced that no one loves her or ever has. Another reports feeling hollow, turned off, "fixated on a narrow linear trap." Another ENTP is plagued by an uncharacteristic emotionalism. "When things don't go well, I resort to emotion to get my point across," he explained. "There is a sense of feeling numb and frozen with no way out," said an ENFP. "I have tunnel vision and lose my sense of time." Another noted that when he is under too much pressure, his verbal skills deteriorate until "I become almost mute."

Many ENFPs describe turning inward, eventually becoming grumpy and depressed and putting people off. Their Feeling side seems to disappear. One ENFP said, "I realized I had become numb and frozen inside—there was no light, no energy—just a wasteland of a landscape, and I was plodding through it." Another ENFP described "deep depression and hopelessness. The most extreme unrealistic scenarios become real and factual. I will be broke, I will die of some dread disease, I will lose all respect among professional colleagues."

Both ENTPs and ENFPs report a loss of enthusiasm and motivation accompanied by low energy. They are prone to an uncharacteristic, un-comfortable pensiveness and are unable to find pleasure in the things they normally enjoy. This may lead to self-neglect and, ultimately, illness. This kind of approach to life is particularly alien to them, for they are usually enthusiastic, fun-loving, and full of energy. An ENFP said, "There is a lot more going on inside my head. I want to be alone to think and it becomes one-track thinking. Everything else is clouded by this one issue—I can't stop thinking about it. I lose confidence in myself and doubt myself in every realm of my life."

One ENFP noted that twice a year, in winter and summer, she regu-larly experiences ten days to three weeks during which she retreats into herself and broods. Others describe periods of becoming withdrawn, crit-ical, unfriendly, and cold. Isolation can exacerbate this reaction. An ENFP who was forced to spend a lot of time alone while recuperating from a badly broken leg was put on antidepressant medication after a month of increasingly lengthy periods of sobbing and despair.

Obsessiveness Effective dominant Introverted Sensing types are adept at dealing with many facts and details and at putting their knowledge to practical use. In the psyche of ENTPs and ENFPs in the grip of inferior Introverted Sensing, this appears as an obsessive focus on one or two facts or details. This is in marked contrast to their typical perspective, which includes the broadest range of possibilities in the world.

The tunnel vision that accompanies the expression of all the inferior functions is particularly dramatic for ENTPs and ENFPs because they no longer have the Extraverted Intuitive energy necessary to envision a future that differs from their present obsession. All sense of possibilities is elimi-nated. An ENTP said that sometimes the details involved in a major proj-ect overwhelm her so much that she slips into an obsessive focus on how much time is left to work on the project: "I get it down to minutes and keep repeating the time frame over and over."

An ENFP said, "I can become compulsive when I begin to bring order into my kitchen or when I'm balancing the bank statement. I'm generally pretty relaxed about order and usually have piles of books and stuff that needs to be returned to file cabinets." Another ENFP said, "I examine, analyze, question stupid things. I also get overly organized, planning and cleaning things rather than getting to the task appropriately. I work overtime to create organization for myself. I count things (like sides on a piece of furniture) over and over. I remember and get obsessed with facts and details, remember dates, memories of being bombarded with 'unwanted greatness.' I have an overwhelming need for all data to make every 'little' fact relevant."

When their Intuition is not working, sensory data become the all-encompassing objects of perception for Extraverted Intuitive types. But as their statements indicate, their lack of expertise in this area usually leads to an inappropriate selection of sensory data. And because "the future is now" in a very distorted way, they take the data at hand and project it into a vague, oppressive future. They may focus on a thought, such as "I'm alone now and will always be alone," rather than the dominant Intuitive type's more typical response of "I'm alone now; I wonder what interesting things I can find to do, and what exciting people I'll find in the world." In this state, the depression and hopelessness described earlier readily occur.

It seems that when inferior Sensing focuses on a single fact, dormant dominant Extraverted Intuition intrudes and generalizes it. Because their Extraverted Intuition is not functioning in its usual well-developed way, ENTPs and ENFPs cannot recognize the fact in question as one possibility among many. No perspective exists for the person beyond the one fact. Extraverted Intuitive types in this state report being unable to respond to alternatives presented to them by others. The present fact—be it pain, depression, or whatever occupies the central focus at that moment—is projected into forever.

Extraverted Intuitive types report one or more of the following ways of obsessing: being overly picky, getting upset about little things, becoming irritable, escalating small irritations into major issues, getting finicky over unimportant things, being nervous and jumpy with people, and becoming fussy, crabby, short-tempered, and rigid. "I am usually a very happy and relaxed person," said one ENFP. "Sometimes I want people to just get to the bottom line, and then I want to analyze for them where they went wrong and just get on with it. This is quite out of character for me and I feel bad when I've been like this. People tell me that when I'm in my negative mode I become terse and clipped in my interactions with others. I give orders and delegate in a very autocratic manner." An ENTP described becoming outraged by minor errors, irritated by detail, intolerant of interruptions and people—"the very things I usually welcome." Another told of feeling overwhelmed and out of control, being unable to sort out priorities, and thus becoming inflexible.

An ENFP described becoming curt with people, insensitive, literal, logical, and critical, and being especially insensitive and pedantic about language and vocabulary. Other ENFPs report doing obsessive record keeping, organizing data from their checkbooks, making endless lists of things to do, and putting minute details in order. "I become incredibly organized; everything is step by step when I'm under stress. I also act to get things done, not worrying as much about the impact," said an ENFP.

Many ENFPs report fanatically mowing the lawn or cleaning house and being unable to stop themselves, even though they typically view these activities as relatively unimportant and avoid them. The ISTJ husband of one ENFP reluctantly admitted that he rather liked it when his wife was highly stressed because it was the only time the house ever got thoroughly cleaned! An ENFP described the following reaction as very distressing:

> I cannot respond to another's conversation. I pace, the traffic is loud, the clock is loud, sounds I never noticed before are deafening and very slow. It's almost as though time is standing still. My usual self is calm, patient, and friendly. I would classify not responding to the conversation of another as exceedingly rude behavior. And I'm generally oblivious to noise.

Another ENFP becomes picky and critical of himself and others. Usually, he sees the bigger picture, is flexible, and allows others to be who they are without trying to control or change their behavior.

On the day before the final examination in a workshop, when anxieties typically run high, a minor typesetting error was discovered in a table of data in the test manual. The instructor commented that there were two or three other errors in the text that would be corrected in the next printing. One ENFP heatedly stated that he wanted the publisher to prepare a document listing all the typos in the text and to send it to him so he wouldn't have to buy a new text when the errors were corrected.

Focus on the Body When effective dominant Introverted Sensing types describe the nuances of their internal sensory experiences, one can marvel at the exquisite, evocative images that emerge. When an Extraverted

Intuitive type in the grip of inferior Introverted Sensing focuses on inner sensations and internal experiences, it often translates into exaggerated concern about physical "symptoms," whose diagnostic meaning is always dire and extreme.

In the grip of their inferior function, ENTPs and ENFPs frequently overinterpret real or imagined bodily sensations as indicative of illness. When they are in full command of their dominant and auxiliary functions, these types easily ignore or minimize messages from their bodies. So when they do focus on the body, it is done to the exclusion of everything else and with little experience of what is "normal" for them. A particular symptom can have only one cause, which must be life threatening or incurable: A pulled muscle is taken as a sign of heart disease; indigestion signifies an impending heart attack; and a headache is believed to be a brain tumor. It seems that when their Intuition isn't working, they react to messages from their bodies rigidly and absolutely.

An ENTP had been in a rare bad mood for several days but was unable to identify any cause. One morning while shaving, he noticed that when he turned his eyes to the left, the white in his right eye crinkled. He had never noticed that before and was terrified that something was terribly wrong with his eyes. Before making an appointment with an eye doctor, however, he decided to observe other people's eyes to determine just how bad his were. To his relief (and chagrin), he found that everyone's eyes moved the same way his did. He had simply never bothered to look at eyes—his own or other people's—at all closely before.

An ENFP fell and injured a small bone in her back, which she could feel as a bump. She asked a friend, who was a nurse, what the bump could be and was told that it was probably a cyst. She quickly translated the cyst into cancer and imagined herself on Medicaid dying alone in a squalid hospital ward. In fact, all that was necessary was a visit to a chiropractor to have the bone put back in place.

During a particularly stressful time, another ENFP woman insisted that her husband have an otherwise innocent-appearing wart removed because she feared it was malignant. An ENFP man reported that in times of great stress he becomes obsessed with illness. Once, when he had a routine liver function test, he became convinced he was dying of liver cancer before the test was even performed. Another ENFP told of owning a blood pressure cuff he rarely uses—except when he becomes very stressed, at which times he takes his blood pressure three times a day.

One ENTP described taking any fact and blowing it out of proportion—for example, imagining an illness in his child as a fatal disease. Others report having a low pain threshold, fearing the dentist, and reacting to stress with a number of somatic symptoms. In fact, though physical symptoms as an expression of stress are common across types, it may be possible that "somaticizing" is more prevalent among Extraverted Intuitive types. One ENTP had digestive problems for fifteen years. During a period of extreme stress, he developed a life-threatening bleeding ulcer. An ENFP and an ENTP discovered in a discussion that they both have medical conditions that force them to attend to their bodies—something they did not do prior to having the conditions. As a result, they more readily attend to their other physical needs as well.

There is an interesting contrast between the imagined negative outcomes of minor bodily symptoms reported by Extraverted Intuitive types and the catastrophizing that is an expression of the inferior Extraverted Intuition of Introverted Sensing types. Although there is some seeming similarity, the processes through which the two negative expressions occur are actually quite different. For Introverted Sensing types, the future is always somewhat suspect, so stress encourages them to imagine and anticipate a future filled with negative outcomes. Extraverted Intuitive types, in contrast, are typically optimistic and welcoming of future possibilities. But when they get stuck on a present fact or situation, they lose sight of the future, imagining it as an endless repetition of the negative situation that is occurring right now.

One way in which Extraverted Intuitive types may try to return to being themselves when chronically stressed is to vacillate between the extremes of frenetic Extraverted and Introverted Sensing. Because both extremes are likely to be exaggerated and undisciplined, little of substance is accomplished in either state. When they finally succumb to negative Introverted Sensing, it may take the form of moderate to severe depression and a sense of hopelessness about the future. One ENFP said, "I get into a downward spiral. One time I went into a stress-induced depression. I almost left my job and made it back through therapy."

Perhaps because ENTPs and ENFPs thrive on the threshold of chronic stress, they seem to have a high tolerance for situations that might prove debilitating for many other types. ENTPs in particular report very few sources of stress in their lives, and both types report a low incidence of heart disease and hypertension, ENTPs having the lowest incidence of all the types. This is in marked contrast to their opposite types, ISTJs and ISFJs.

Extraverted Intuitive types are likely to leave work situations in which conditions become intolerable, but usually not because they are overloaded or forced to work very hard. Rather, such conditions as working with incompetent people (especially for ENTPs) or being forced to adhere to unacceptable work values (especially for ENFPs) are likely to trigger quitting the noxious situation. Sometimes becoming ill or depressed and recognizing how different they have become can force these types to take action. Some of the flavor of what constitutes a noxious work setting is captured in this statement by an ENTP who said that stress was a very important factor in quitting her job: "I reacted by leaving an organization and becoming an independent consultant. I can select the work I want and the people I work with. I can arrange my own schedule. There are no stupid rules and regulations. I enjoy helping organizations function better, but I don't want to be part of one." She had earlier described the most stressful work demands of her previous job as "working with incompetent people, not having control of my own schedule and activities, and running up against a lot of stupid rules and regulations."

Lengthy Episodes in the Grip

The types of episodes described above are experienced by ENTPs and ENFPs as temporary states during which they are vulnerable to the three forms in which their inferior function is expressed. However, when Extraverted Intuitive types are chronically in the grip of inferior Introverted Sensing, inferior function behavior may become habitual. Little of their typical enthusiasm, open-minded acceptance of new ideas, and uncanny visioning of future trends will be seen. Instead, they will be irritable, critical of everyone around them, and obsessed with minutia. They are likely to find fault with everything and everyone, especially close family members and co-workers. If their obsessiveness involves a focus on imagined illness, they may be unable to shake their conviction that they are seriously ill, despite medical reassurances. Depression may result from this or simply as a consequence of their unnatural focus on negative realities in the present.

Chronic grip behavior may lead the individual and others to believe that he or she is typically irritable, impatient, and cranky, vacillating between withdrawal and frenetic activity. Since the process of becoming chronically in the grip is often gradual, even people who have known the person in a nonstressed state are likely not to notice what, in retrospect, will be recognized as a radical alteration of personality. The person will appear to be a rather exaggerated, poorly developed Introverted Sensing type.

However, there are also occasions when a lengthy time in the grip of inferior Introverted Sensing can stimulate new awareness and positive growth toward completion and individuation. Remember that Jung saw the inferior function as the doorway to the unconscious and an important part of the self-regulating capacity of our psyches.

Grip Experiences

The stories included in this section illustrate one or more forms of inferior Introverted Sensing as experienced by ENTPs or ENFPs. Notice how these grip experiences often include dominant Extraverted Intuition in an excessive, inappropriate degree. The wild but detailed imagination of these Extraverted Intuitive types adds to the believability of their experiences. There is also a characteristic drama revealed in relating the experiences.

"All Those Doctors Are Wrong!"

Theresa, an ENTP opera singer who had temporarily retired from singing to raise her children, was told by a physician that the kind of persistent ear problem she reported to him occasionally indicated a possible brain tumor. Though she was soon given a clean bill of health, she continued to obsess about her ear, interpreting every twinge and moment of dizziness as a signal that her condition had been misdiagnosed and she indeed was going to die of a tumor. She consulted other physicians, who found nothing seriously wrong but suggested, in light of her continuing concerns, that she consult a psychologist.

"In talking about my life situation," she explained, "I realized just how extremely different it was from before I had children. I was doing practically nothing to satisfy my artistic needs, except sometimes singing songs for my daughter's preschool class."

She was forced to realize that, although she very much enjoyed being with her children, she was perhaps overemphasizing her devotion to them to the exclusion of her own needs. In order to change her one-sided approach, Theresa arranged for more childcare, rented a small studio, and started giving singing lessons two mornings a week. Gradually, her obsession with her ear symptoms diminished and she felt more relaxed, less pressured, and generally more satisfied with her daily life.

An Unpleasant Experience Hanging Wallpaper

An ENFP woman contributed the following story:

> Having never before put up wallpaper, I attempted to wallpaper my bedroom walls with a pattern I later found out was difficult to match. This redecorating in my room was very important to me. With a preference for Extraversion, my surroundings certainly have an effect on my mood.
>
> It became paralyzing for me to decide how exactly to hang the paper because the pattern never seemed right. I agonized over this for hours on end, day and night, trying to make sure it was perfect. Already feeling chronically stressed by my lack of precision in both matching the pattern and cutting the paper to size, I became even more stressed when I realized I hadn't selected the proper wallpaper colors to match my paint. Everyone told me it looked great, but it didn't matter what they said; it lacked the detail and precision I wanted. As time and the stress went on, my negativity was insurmountable and my frustration, anger, and sense of hopelessness about my skills, abilities, and overall personhood were intolerable. How does this story end? I couldn't stand seeing my mistakes every night when I went to bed, so I rented a steamer and ripped it all down!
>
> Now, I think this whole mess was hilarious, and if I had been operating as my normal self, the room would have looked just fine (with a few wall hangings).

"Will I Have to Take Antidepressants for the Rest of My Life?"

Diane, a young mother of three children, had been seeing a psychotherapist for several months to help her deal with her reactions to a recent difficult divorce. She found herself questioning her competence as a wife and mother and felt rather shaky and inadequate in making decisions for herself and her children. She took the MBTI personality inventory early in therapy and verified ENFP as her type. She was gradually regaining her positive sense of herself, and both she and her therapist were quite satisfied with her progress.

One evening, she called her therapist in tears. "I was visiting with a friend this afternoon," she said. "We shared some wine, talked about our mutual friends, our children, and so on. I felt really calm and relaxed. As I was getting ready to leave, my friend said, 'You know, Diane, you seem really depressed.' I didn't feel depressed, and I was unaware that I was acting depressed. Do you think I'll have to take an antidepressant for the rest of my life?"

"No, I'm quite confident an antidepressant is not necessary," her therapist replied. "You haven't needed one before and don't need one now. But tell me something about your friend."

"Well," said Diane, "she's about my age and has two children and she's recently divorced."

"Oh?" said the therapist. "How is she doing with the divorce?"

"To tell you the truth," said Diane, "I think she's depressed."

In reviewing and discussing this incident, Diane recognized that her friend was projecting her own depression onto her. Diane was vulnerable to accepting her friend's judgment because she herself was distrustful of her own inner Feeling judgment. Her distrust was a consequence of her tendency to extravert her Feeling judgment rather than introvert it, as would be desirable for effective type development. Extraverts who extravert both of their preferred functions are often ready hosts for others' projections. So Diane "tunneled in" on her friend's statement, accepted it as true, and extended it over her entire future life span.

The experience was valuable for Diane because it made her aware of her readiness to fall into the grip of inferior Sensing. When in that state, she was quite prone to accepting others' projections. A primary focus of her subsequent psychotherapy was strengthening and affirming her inner Feeling judgment so that she would be less vulnerable to other people's inappropriate projections. She gradually became more trusting of her own inner judgment and less willing to rely on others' assessments of her.

"And I'll Have to Put the Animals to Sleep!"

Sarah, a divorced ENFP mother, had been working very hard, was under a lot of stress, and had just caught a cold. On coming home one evening, she found a letter from the Internal Revenue Service informing her that her income tax return would be audited. She described her response in the following way:

> I could feel myself physically sinking. Absorbed in this feeling, it suddenly became clear to me that I would have to sell my house in order to pay the additional taxes that would result from the audit. I then imagined the one-room apartment I would have to rent. Of course, the children would have to live with their dad, since I wouldn't have room for them. I kept feeling physically really awful.
>
> I thought about all the boxes I would have to collect to make the move to the apartment and imagined going from store to store to collect them. Then I realized that my corner cupboard, which I loved, would not fit in an apartment and I would have to sell it. I planned the garage sale at which I would have to sell all my extra things that wouldn't fit in the apartment.
>
> As dusk approached and the outside world became somewhat dark and gloomy, I felt overwhelmed with all the details I would have to attend to. It was then that I realized I would have to have our two dogs and three cats put to sleep. That felt really awful. I got to thinking about whether it would be less painful to take them to the vet one at a time or whether I should take them all at the same time.

About that time a friend, Elise, also an ENFP, dropped in on Sarah. Immediately noting Sarah's blank expression, she asked what was wrong. Sarah handed her the letter from the IRS and said dejectedly, "I'm going to have to sell the house."

To her credit, Elise did not laugh. She instinctively knew that Sarah could not recognize her premature conclusion and the absurdity of her reasoning. In the grip of the inferior function, there is no such thing as a sense of humor. Instead, Elise said, "Oh, that must feel really bad."

"Yes," said Sarah, bursting into tears, "and I'm going to have to put the animals to sleep!"

Again using good instincts, Elise did not argue with Sarah's remark, but invited her to go for a walk. As they walked, Sarah felt things loosening up, and she felt better by the time they returned home. Her friend left, promising to return the next day to help Sarah decide how to handle her audit.

In reflecting on the meaning and impact of this experience, Sarah acknowledged her chronic uneasiness about her record keeping and lack of attention to the everyday details of living. "I realized that perhaps I had been overdoing my laid-back approach to things and that maybe my quick descent into a negative state meant that my approach was too extreme," reasoned Sarah. She resolved to improve her record keeping and grew to feel more comfortable about this aspect of her life.

The next story highlights the long-term effects of stressful life events on an ENFP and enriches our understanding of childhood and adult responses to stress.

A Long Time to Be in the Grip

I was the third child of six. My early family life was relatively stable, with good relationships and values. However, after two years of an intense struggle with cancer that included many hospitalizations, my mother died. I was 9 years old. My 13-year-old sister, who was the eldest and also an ENFP, became obsessive about responsibilities, both household and scholastic. She had me making meals using the much-feared pressure cooker, scraping old wax off floors and rewaxing them, canning large quantities of fruit in the summer, and acting as a paper-hanger as she repapered parts of the house.

I escaped as quickly as possible from my family situation to tend our flock of sheep. I later became an obsessive caretaker.

In my thirties I burned out on elementary teaching and caregiving and spent five years even further in the grip in solitude, depression, and researching natural healing. I spent the next six years teaching and caregiving and almost burned out a second time. I finally discovered type, and it started me on the journey of correction, along with some counseling and much learning. I started to establish my identity and changed my career, which is still evolving, at 55, toward completion. My work has variety. I do career and personal counseling as well as team building in businesses, and I run seminars.

I have used type with my sister, and with other family members, too. We are reconnecting in ways that encourage completion of our lives—which feel twenty years behind schedule because we all coped with our early stress in different maladaptive ways. We've learned many important lessons from our lengthy grip experiences.

Return of Equilibrium

Extraverted Intuitive types seem to need time to reflect, fully experience themselves, and even "wallow" in their inferior state. ENFP men in particular report needing time alone. Meditation, which can be a useful way for all Extraverted types to attend to their Introverted functions, is particularly appealing to Extraverted Intuitive types in the grip of their inferior function.

As is the case for most types, Extraverted Intuitive types in the midst of a grip experience need others to back off and avoid patronizing them. It can be helpful if some of the overwhelming details are attended to, but attempts to assist by taking over and "solving the problem" for them are not appreciated. Talking to trusted friends helps, especially for ENTP and ENFP women, as long as the friends don't offer advice (or, if they do offer it, they don't expect it to be taken), make judgments, or try to talk them out of their negative state.

Movement out of the inferior function often is aided by a positive engagement of the Sensing function, especially in situations in which a neglect of behavior associated with Sensing has provoked an inferior function experience. Physical exercise, such as jogging, engaging in some quiet sensing, or visualizing a place of peace and silence can be helpful. ENFPs in particular mention exercise as helpful. For most Extraverted Intuitive types, attending to physical needs, such as sleeping a lot, eating good food, and getting massages, also accompanies the gradually diminishing effects of the inferior.

The role of the auxiliary function is apparent for ENTPs, who find it helpful to try to analyze what is happening, either alone or with a close friend who is able to accept the ENTP's emotion and help him or her sort out priorities. An ENTP said, "I make myself stop and really consider what it is that's worrying me—do a reality check of how I might achieve it. This stimulates me into positive actions to start dealing with the situation, rather than just worrying about it." Another ENTP suggested that others "talk to me as I am, combining the normal me and the anxious me."

For ENFPs, who may be communicating uncharacteristic coldness and indifference, what is needed from others is warmth, kindness, and approval. It is interesting to note that ENFP women in particular seem to call on their tertiary Thinking to help them, perhaps reflecting the value of being forced to develop Thinking in their work lives. One said, "I sort of talk myself out of it—often aloud, reasoning and feeling my way back to a more comfortable and productive position." And another said she needed "time out—to rationally evaluate the reality (the truth of the situation—not just as I see it.), assess things, and decide what I need to do."

A third ENFP woman described needing others to help "by applying logic to my irrational, exaggerated obsessions—bringing me back to earth."

Extraverted Intuitive types often respond to an inferior episode by resolving to pay more attention to details, especially the kind involved in their recent negative experience. They may also gain a new respect for their bodies and their physical limitations. They report being better able (at least for a while) to maintain a more balanced perspective regarding their often overly ambitious expectations of themselves. They may create a plan to attend to their bodies with such things as an exercise regimen, and to develop their inner judgment with such things as formal meditation or regular quiet time. They may also resolve to notice and deal more quickly with the overload that can signal an impending inferior function episode.

Expressions in Midlife

Ideally, midlife is accompanied by a positive, progressive integration of inferior Introverted Sensing and, along with it, tertiary Feeling or Thinking. For some ENTPs and ENFPs, however, this may not be the case.

When they have not satisfactorily accomplished their adult goals, Extraverted Intuitive types' demeanor and behavior may appear increasingly inappropriate. They may be seen as immature, "flaky," and irresponsible. Their way of dressing and choice of activities often overemphasize the youthfulness they no longer possess. They are not seen by others as aging gracefully.

Even if their personality is seemingly the same as it has always been, they may be rigid and inflexible in their insistence on an Extraverted Intuitive approach. A 50-year-old ENFP wore her teenage daughter's clothing, moved from one dissatisfying career to another, and avidly pursued each new intellectual fad that came along. A 55-year-old ENTP had married and divorced three women in ten years, with each wife younger than her predecessor.

Extraverted Intuitive types who are more ready to integrate inferior Sensing and tertiary Feeling or Thinking may find themselves struggling with the internal pull to develop their Introversion. They are so much a part of the external world and have found so much stimulation and enjoyment in it that there is almost a sense of loss as they find themselves paying more attention to internal things. One ENFP said:

> I realized that I was having internal conversations much more often than I did when I was younger. I didn't really want to—I like talking to other people—but after a while it felt less like I was cutting myself off from an external experience and more like there was some real energy in my internal dialogue.

Another ENFP described a difference in how she used her leisure time now that she was in her fifties. "I used to be completely oriented to inter-actions with others. Now I relax by being with a selected few individuals, reading (a variety of things), sewing, gardening, listening to music."

Extraverted Intuitive types can find surprising pleasure in accom-plishments related to their tertiary and inferior functions. ENTPs may gain great pleasure from the warmth, closeness, and satisfying harmony they find in relationships; ENFPs may pride themselves on newly devel-oped organizational skills and be especially pleased when others comment on their successful use of logical analysis in solving problems.

Movement from the tertiary to the inferior function may appear in the form of an increasing desire for and pleasure in being alone and quiet. There is greater enjoyment of solitary activities that require an apprecia-tion of one or more of the five senses. One ENFP in her fifties was vaca-tioning on an island on the East Coast. Each day while walking on the beach, she noticed a rock bed exposed by the outgoing tide. Each day she felt compelled to explore the bed. Finally, one day she sat down and found herself picking up and holding individual rocks—noting their texture, their subtle colors, the feel of them in her hands. "It was a very sensual experience," she later recalled. "It had great meaning internally and was deeply satisfying."

Sometimes spending a lengthy period in the grip of inferior Intro-verted Sensing can serve as an important stimulus to midlife development for Extraverted Intuitive types. The combination of the natural upheaval of midlife and the disruption and distress of a chronic grip experience may push an ENTP or ENFP into serious soul searching and reconsideration of long-standing goals, which may lead to significant changes in the way the second half of life is lived.

Knowledge from Grip Experiences

Even more than for other types, learning to recognize and avoid the stress and fatigue that may lead to a grip experience is a major learning experience for Extraverted Intuitive types. A group of ENTPs and ENFPs reported that they wanted to learn more about the transition between being too exaggerated in their natural preference and being in the grip. They explained that they are often in the grip or on the verge of it because of the prevalent stress in current work environments. In general, Extraverted Intuitive types are more willing to recognize the value of deadlines, focusing narrowly on a task, simplifying instead of complexifying their work lives, and completing undesirable tasks early to avoid stress.

ENTPs and ENFPs, especially those who are approaching midlife, also mention learning to enjoy time alone and the power of "holding back" in group situations. When stress either at work or at home is extreme and persists over time, Extraverted Intuitive types are likely to become ill, suffer from exhaustion, and eventually recognize the severity of their stress and the absence of joy in their lives. When this point is reached, they tend to act quickly and decisively, leaving the intolerable situation and finding a more hospitable arena.

Summary

In the grip of inferior Introverted Sensing, Extraverted Intuitive types tend to withdraw and become depressed, obsess about details, and become focused on their bodies. When they are obsessing about one or two inner facts, their dominant Extraverted Intuition may intrude in the form of a theory projecting the few facts into the distant future. Auxiliary Thinking or Feeling accompanies their return to equilibrium. ENTPs use logical analysis to do so, and ENFPs reconnect with their inner value structure and its relationship to their dominant Intuition.

As a result of important inferior function experiences, Extraverted Intuitive types acknowledge the limitations of their physical and mental energies, resolve to take better care of themselves, and integrate a greater appreciation for details, facts, structure, and careful planning. Table 17 provides an overview of the major features of their inferior function experience.

Table 17 Inferior Function of Extraverted Intuitive Types: ENTP and ENFP

Triggers for the Inferior Function	Forms of the Grip Experience
• Physical exhaustion	• Withdrawal and depression
• A focus on facts	• Obsessiveness
• Violation of values and principles	• Focus on the body

Ways of Returning to Equilibrium	New Knowledge
• Meditating	• Broadened perspective
• Attention to their physical needs by others	• Appreciation of the value of facts and details
• Support, not patronization	• Increased structure and planfulness

14

When Hidden Personalities Meet

THERE ARE MANY EXAMPLES of the puzzling and often distressing situations that can arise when a person is gripped by his or her inferior function. Not the least of these relate to their effects on other people and the way others respond to the person who is "in the grip."

One can respond to someone else's expression of the inferior function in a variety of ways, including judging him or her incompetent, unreliable, eccentric, unpredictable, crazy, and the like. But a common reaction to being with someone who is in the grip is to fall into the grip of one's own inferior function. Being in the grip can be catching! Even when this does not occur, dealing with others who are in the grip can be quite difficult, be they spouses, parents, children, siblings, bosses, colleagues, friends, or acquaintances.

This chapter provides examples of interactions between two activated inferiors functions in couples, parents and children, and people in work settings. It demonstrates how one person's inferior function can stimulate another's. Each section identifies some of the benefits of knowing about the characteristics of the inferior function when interacting with other people.

Many of the incidents and characterizations presented here are composites of actual situations and people. Some were dealt with in the context of psychotherapy and, as a result, represent only a brief and simplified description of an often complex relationship. Other examples were contributed by the people who experienced them or by people who observed others who appeared to be in the grip. In all cases, the stories may be taken as illustrative of the ways people interact when they are in the grip of their inferior functions. Bear in mind that these stories do not describe or explain everything that was relevant for the situation or the people involved and that, enlightening though it can be, the inferior function doesn't explain everything.

Couples

In Chapter 9, we saw an interaction between the inferior functions of Luis, an INTP (inferior Extraverted Feeling), and Judy, an ENFJ (inferior Introverted Thinking). For this couple, each partner's dominant function is the other's inferior. When both are tired, stressed, or otherwise vulnerable to their unconscious, they readily project or directly express their least-developed, unreliable side. In such a scenario, nothing can be resolved. Two "partial personalities" do the acting and projecting, leaving their more balanced selves confused, drained, and ineffectual.

In contrast, when both partners share the same dominant function, they also share the same inferior function. Therefore, when fatigue and stress levels are great, two "twin" immature personalities are likely to emerge and interact. In a variation on this theme, two people of the same type may express their inferior functions somewhat differently, which can have some interesting effects. This was the case for one ISTJ, who reported that when she is not herself, she is optimistic, daring, and adventurous, in contrast to her usual tendency to be pessimistic and worried. Her inferior Extraverted Intuition is expressed as impulsiveness. She said that her out-of-character state is usually provoked when her partner, who is also an ISTJ, is being particularly pessimistic and careful (inferior Extraverted Intuition as "catastrophizing").

Here are some other examples of what happens to couples when one or both partners are in the grip of their inferior functions. To help you follow the "action" of the stories, each begins with a listing of the key features of the inferior functions of both people involved in the interaction. Note that all three features of each person's inferior function are not necessarily revealed in any one incident.

"If You Love Me, You Won't Pick on Me!"

Edna, INFJ

Inferior Extraverted Sensing

Key Features of Inferior Function

- Obsessive focus on external data
- Overindulgence in sensual pleasures
- Adversarial attitude toward the outer world

Clark, INTP

Inferior Extraverted Feeling

Key Features of Inferior Function

- Logic emphasized to an extreme
- Hypersensitivity to relationships
- Emotionalism

Edna and Clark were the parents of four young children. They were devoted to their children and their professional lives, as well as to several time-consuming civic and recreational activities. Stress and fatigue were familiar companions in their lives.

In the grip of inferior Extraverted Sensing, Edna accused Clark of not helping her around the house or with their children. As she continued to obsess about Clark's lack of participation, she became convinced that he cared more for his work than he did for his family. She noticed that she was being short-tempered and impatient with the children. She felt overburdened and guilty in her conviction that she was alone as their parent. Her anger toward Clark mounted, and she became silent and withholding when she was not being actively critical of him.

Clark's inferior Extraverted Feeling interpreted Edna's criticism and withholding as a lack of appreciation and rejection of him as a husband and father. He said that being loved and appreciated by Edna was more important to him than anything else.

In discussing this repetitive cycle, both acknowledged feeling inadequate and guilty about how they performed as spouses and parents. They therefore readily projected doubts about themselves onto each other as faults and inadequacies. Both served as willing hosts for their mutual projections.

Over an extended period, they aired their innermost doubts and fears, which helped defuse their anger and resentment and remind them of their underlying positive feelings for each other. They agreed to try to stay more aware of their tendencies to resent each other, yet, knowing their history, they accepted the likelihood that this kind of conflict would happen again, even though they might be able to detect early warning signs more readily.

Letty and Rob at Their Worst

Letty, ESFJ

Inferior Introverted Thinking

Key Features of Inferior Function

- Excessive criticism
- Convoluted logic
- Compulsive search for truth

Rob, ISFJ

Inferior Extraverted Intuition

Key Features of Inferior Function

- Loss of control over facts and details
- Impulsiveness
- Catastrophizing

Letty and Rob were planning to get married. They were devoted to each other and very much in love. But because both were divorced and each had two nearly grown children, there were several complicated personal and business matters that needed to be settled, especially in Rob's case.

As the holidays approached, Letty noticed that Rob was procrastinating about taking care of some legal matters. She didn't say anything about this for several weeks. Then one evening when Rob called her to say that he wouldn't be coming over for the third night in a row because he was "too tired and stressed out," Letty lost control. She unleashed a barrage of angry recriminations, accusing Rob of being weak, ineffectual, and moody.

"You never keep your promises," she fumed. "If you're so wishy-washy about taking care of business matters, you must be just as ambivalent about our relationship! Maybe we should call the whole thing off!"

Rob was crushed by Letty's outburst. He later explained that he had been feeling rather down because the holiday season always brought forth both happy and sad memories of life with his ex-wife and their children. He became focused on the thought that since his first marriage had failed, perhaps the new one would, too. He imagined all the things that could go wrong in his relationship with Letty: The children would resent their stepparents, his business would fail and they wouldn't have enough money to do enjoyable things together, they would grow to hate each other, and so on.

As Rob's obsession with a negative future intensified, he was overwhelmed by the conviction that he would be unable to love Letty in the way she deserved. Perhaps the most sensible thing to do was to release her from her agreement to marry him so that she could be free to find a more worthy life partner.

In despair, he talked to Letty about his fears. At first she was shocked at his irrational response, but she later remembered that in other very stressful times Rob had overreacted and arrived at unwarranted conclusions. And when it was pointed out to her, she recognized her own hypercritical outburst as her usual reaction to feeling shut out of an important relationship. The couple was eventually better able to deal with the realities of their situation in a more rational and effective way.

THE "DOWNSIDE" OF COMPATIBILITY

Annette, ISTP

Inferior Extraverted Feeling

Beth, INTP

Inferior Extraverted Feeling

Key Features of Inferior Function

- Logic emphasized to an extreme
- Hypersensitivity to relationships
- Emotionalism

Annette and Beth had lived together for ten years and shared a close, satisfying relationship. They both worked very hard at their demanding careers and were frequently at their worst when they arrived home on workdays. Inadvertently, one or both would say the wrong thing, so that the other's feelings would get hurt. Their vulnerable condition often brought on tearful recriminations, the dredging up of a complete past history of insults and hurtful comments, and the like.

Though they very much liked being similar types, awareness of their shared vulnerabilities brought a mixed reaction. They were distressed to find that they were experts at hurting each other! In time, however, they were able to bypass the more minor insensitivities and wounds. Talking through major bouts with their shared inferior function after an episode occurred was helpful for each individually as well as for their relationship.

A CLASH OF THINKING AND FEELING

Ruth, ENFJ

Inferior Introverted Thinking

Key Features of Inferior Function

- Excessive criticism
- Convoluted logic
- Compulsive search for truth

Todd, ENTJ

Inferior Introverted Feeling

Key Features of Inferior Function

- Hypersensitivity to inner states
- Outbursts of emotion
- Fear of feeling

Ruth and Todd agreed that they very much loved, respected, and enjoyed being with each other. They also agreed that there was a repetitive pattern in their relationship that was very distressing to both of them.

Todd's work as an organizational consultant required him to travel several times a month, and he was often home only for a long weekend. Ruth's work as a physician was equally demanding, and although it did not require frequent travel, she often had to be available to her patients at a moment's notice. Their very busy lives allowed limited time for the two to be together, and they cherished that time. Why, then, did they spend most of their "together time" fighting—often replaying the same recriminations over and over again?

Ruth accused Todd of excluding her from decision making when he arranged his travel schedule and not consulting or informing her until after the fact. She felt he could arrange his schedule so he could be home more, and the fact that he didn't do so meant he really didn't want to be with her. Todd's habit of making unilateral decisions in favor of his work schedule also confirmed Ruth's conviction that he believed her career was less important than his and that he didn't really think she was good at her work, even though he "paid lip service" to her competence.

In response to Ruth's frequent barrages, Todd was overwhelmed with feelings of inadequacy. He insisted that he tried to arrange his schedule in the most logical, efficient fashion to maximize their time together. He felt that no matter how hard he tried, Ruth found reasons to criticize and belittle him. In response, he became angry and frustrated. Their heated and sometimes vicious arguments typically went on for two days prior to Todd's trips and for two days after he returned. As a result, they could count on only a few days of peace, tranquility, and pleasure in each other's company.

In one couples therapy session, Todd reported that Ruth frequently told him he was stupid. Ruth denied ever using the word stupid and was upset by Todd's statement. She assured him that she held his intellectual competence in the highest esteem. Todd was somewhat puzzled by Ruth's response. He explained that he had no doubt that Ruth considered him to be intelligent and competent in his work. He assumed that she believed him to be emotionally stupid and inadequate.

Todd's inferior Introverted Feeling made him sensitive about his relationship skills and his adequacy as a partner in an intimate relationship. He easily projected his own doubts and fears of his inadequacy onto

Ruth, interpreting her accusations as evidence of her negative judgment about him.

For her part, Ruth's inferior Introverted Thinking made her sensitive about her intellectual and work competence. She interpreted Todd's logical decision making and tendency not to share the reasoning behind his decisions as supporting her doubts and fears about her worthiness in her career. Each partner was highly sensitive about competence but operated with entirely different definitions of this concept. Different interpretations of "the same" word or concept are often at the heart of misunderstandings when people interact in highly charged circumstances.

Clarifying these issues in their sensitivities and projections onto each other proved quite helpful and energizing for Todd and Ruth. They became even more solidly committed to resolving similar misunderstandings and to eventually breaking their repetitive cycle of distressing arguments.

OPPOSITES IN LOVE

Roxanne, ENFP

Inferior Introverted Sensing

Key Features of Inferior Function

- Withdrawal and depression
- Obsessiveness
- Focus on the body

Ned, ISTJ

Inferior Extraverted Intuition

Key Features of Inferior Function

- Loss of control over facts and details
- Impulsiveness
- Catastrophizing

Roxanne and Ned had both been divorced from their respective ex-spouses for a number of years, and both acknowledged that their first marriages were mistakes of their youth and inexperience. Though both had

had several intimate relationships since their divorces, they agreed that their love for each other was different, total, with a passion neither had experienced before. They were devoted to their own and each other's adult children. Ned's children enjoyed warm, close relationships with Roxanne, and Roxanne's children admired and respected Ned. The families often spent time together, and all looked forward to their continued love and intimacy.

The couple sought help, however, because the intensity of their disagreements was increasing, the depression Roxanne had experienced several years before had returned, and Ned was increasingly negative, worried, and short-tempered.

The couple reported that Roxanne was spending more and more time developing her new interior design business, and although Ned fully supported her efforts, he was uneasy about her financial management of the business. He frequently encouraged her to be more systematic, and to adhere to a strict budget and a very conservative business plan. He could not see any realistic connection between the current financial facts of Roxanne's business and her enthusiasm and "blind" trust that everything would work out well in a few years.

Ned tried to counter his acknowledged lifelong tendency to worry about the future and anticipate the worst outcomes by focusing on his love for and devotion to Roxanne. He totally supported her in every way—but was unable to quell his anxieties about the future. "What makes it worse is that we spend less and less time together, " he said. "She is always working, and the warm family times with our children we both looked forward to are not happening."

Roxanne interpreted Ned's worry about the future and comments about wanting more time with her as extremely critical of her competence as a businesswoman, as an adult, as an intimate partner, and as a mother. "He thinks I'm stupid, that I just ignore facts and details and make decisions emotionally, on the spur of the moment. That's not the way it is. But I can't do things his way. That's not who I am. He says he loves me and supports me, but how could he when he has no faith in me and thinks I'm incompetent?"

Over time, Ned and Roxanne were able to recognize that each was hypersensitive in the areas of his or her inferior and tertiary functions. Roxanne readily projected her own uneasiness about her Sensing and Thinking competence onto Ned. His criticism of her in these areas thus felt like condemnations to her, and she could not appreciate that behind his uneasiness lay a sincere desire to help and support her. Ned was able to see that Roxanne's approach to life was very different from his, and that it was natural for her to trust in her Intuition about the future and in her Feeling judgment in making current decisions. While often scary and disconcerting, these were some of the qualities Ned admired and loved about her.

Both Ned and Roxanne became better able to express their fears, hopes, and sensitivities, and the frequency and intensity of misunderstandings diminished markedly. Although they were still unable to spend as much time together as both wanted, their enjoyment of that time was much greater and they looked forward to a continuing loving relationship.

Using Knowledge of the Inferior Function in Couple Relationships

Knowing "which buttons to push" often means knowing what to say or do to provoke an inferior function response in our loved ones. When people are familiar with the form of their own and others' inferior functions, they can use this knowledge either negatively or positively. Awareness of another person's vulnerabilities can give one power over that person, and awareness of our own vulnerabilities can tempt us to use them to excuse some of our own unpleasant behavior.

But the potential for enhancing the intimacy of a relationship far outweighs the negative possibilities that can accompany knowledge of the inferior function. When only one partner is in the grip, the other may be able to respond in a helpful way, thus encouraging the person to benefit from the experience. When both partners are "beside themselves," as in the above examples, the opportunity for new understanding comes only after both have emerged from their inferior state. It is then that discussion, review, and a new level of intimacy are likely to occur.

Knowing how the other person's inferior function is expressed can provide one with a helpful perspective. It can prevent the recipient of exaggerated, unfounded, hurtful statements from taking them as literal and enduring. We can stand back from the situation and observe it somewhat objectively and dispassionately. We can recognize the partial personality we are faced with as only somewhat representative of the person we usually experience. In the best of circumstances, this can help us avoid falling into the grip of our own inferior function in response to our partner's doing so.

Parents and Children

Parents and children can provoke each other's grip responses throughout the life of their relationship. People who know each other very well instinctively know what "buttons" will catapult each other into an inferior function response or some other equally unconscious personal complex.

"It's Not a Criticism; It's My opinion!"

Molly, ISTP

Inferior Extraverted Feeling

Key Features of Inferior Function

- Logic emphasized to an extreme
- Hypersensitivity to relationships
- Emotionalism

Bonnie, ENFP

Inferior Introverted Sensing

Key Features of Inferior Function

- Withdrawal and depression
- Obsessiveness
- Focus on the body

Molly and Bonnie were mother and daughter, ages 80 and 50, respectively. They had not lived in the same part of the country for more than thirty years. However, Molly and her husband, Bert, had visited their daughter several times a year before Bert's death, and Molly and the grandchildren had kept in touch by phone and spent holidays together as often as possible.

Mother and daughter maintained a cordial but somewhat distant and uncomfortable relationship. After Bert died and Molly's health began to deteriorate, Bonnie and Molly decided that it would be best for Molly to move across the country and rent an apartment near Bonnie's house.

The plan went forward and worked well for a while. Molly was able to maintain her independence but also had help and companionship readily available. Their rather distant relationship was unsatisfying for both of them, however. They both wanted to be closer emotionally now that they had the opportunity, so they sought help from a couples therapist.

Long-standing issues that were clearly related to their very different types emerged. Molly adored her daughter but tended to show her love by offering observations and suggestions about how Bonnie should raise her children, decorate her house, handle her finances, and so on.

"She's always criticizing me!" Bonnie complained.

"I'm not being critical," retorted Molly. "I'm just giving my opinion. You can take it or leave it."

Bonnie, for her part, very much wanted to share her own enthusiasm for meditation, alternative medicine, Yoga, dream workshops, and the like with her mother.

"You don't know what you're missing!" Bonnie said.

"I'm not interested; it's not for me," replied her mother.

Bonnie felt hurt, discounted, and angry. She obsessed about each remark her mother made, seeing the statements as verification of her mother's disapproval. After each such encounter she would avoid her mother. Molly interpreted Bonnie's staying away as confirmation that Bonnie did not care about her and her health difficulties. She was hurt and despaired for their relationship.

Expressing their mutual frustration as well as their intense love for each other enabled mother and daughter to let go of their need to fully understand each other in order to have a loving, intimate relationship. Bonnie was able to accept that much of what was important to her was "not for" her mother. Molly made an effort to say positive, appreciative things to Bonnie, and Bonnie responded by accepting her mother's compliments as genuine and loving.

"You Should Know Me Better than That!"

Mary, ISFJ

Inferior Extraverted Intuition

Key Features of Inferior Function

- Loss of control over facts and details
- Impulsiveness
- Catastrophizing

Sean, INTP

Inferior Extraverted Feeling

Key Features of Inferior Function

- Logic emphasized to an extreme
- Hypersensitivity to relationships
- Emotionalism

At 77, Mary was growing increasingly concerned about her health. She was nearly blind and suffered from arthritis and numerous other health problems. As a result, it was difficult for her to take care of her own affairs. She was advised to give power of attorney to her 50-year-old son, Sean. In discussing this with him, she commented that perhaps her lawyer should be a co-signer to the power of attorney. "That way you won't be able to take advantage of me," she told Sean.

Sean was silently furious at his mother's remark. Later, in talking to his wife about it, he said, "I felt annihilated by her comment. How could she think like that even for a minute? I don't have many intimate relationships, but I invest myself fully in the ones I do have. My mother and I have had a close relationship for fifty years. She should know me better than that!"

Sean continued to be distressed and despairing about his mother's comment for several days, but he gradually recognized that his mother was doing her typical "worst case analysis" in response to her increasing anxiety about her failing health. He was able to regain his equilibrium and forgive his mother without having to confront her and create more of a problem than the situation warranted.

For Mary's part, it was easy to interpret her hurtful remark as her inferior Extraverted Intuition taking over her perception. When she expressed her least-developed side to Sean, she in turn triggered his inferior Extraverted Feeling response. He felt hurt, demeaned, misunderstood, and unappreciated.

"The First Time You Wear It the Whole Thing Will Fall Apart"

Camille, ENFP

Inferior Introverted Sensing

Key Features of Inferior Function

- Withdrawal and depression

- Obsessiveness

- Focus on the body

Her Mother, ISTJ

Inferior Extraverted Intuition

Key Features of Inferior Function

- Loss of control over facts and details

- Impulsiveness

- Catastrophizing

Camille, in reflecting on her family life as a child and adolescent, contributed the following rather classic ISTJ-ENFP mother-daughter scenario:

> In thinking about my type and my mother's type, I believe that much of our interaction time during my teenage years was spent in our inferior functions. The pattern looked like this: I would be caught up in my Extraverted Intuition—this party or dance would be so wonderful! All my fantasies of popularity and social acceptance would come true, I would be beautiful and charming, people would compete for my atten-

tion. Then I would ask my mother if I could go to the event. She would immediately begin presenting all her negative fantasies—only riffraff would be there, no one from my crowd would go, I would use poor judgment and get into trouble, terrible things would happen.

I would then give her detail after detail: "Jane is going, Judy's mother said . . . , Susan gets to go, I wouldn't do this and that," etc. Finally, I would explode and go to my room to brood, recounting to myself every detail of my life, every word my mother and I had said, every instance of my mistreatment.

Here is a typical encounter: When I was 14, I had a vision of a skirt that would change my life—a pink, very full, gauzy skirt, perhaps worn with an off-the-shoulder peasant blouse. I could see myself looking very romantic. My mother, an accomplished seamstress, had done her best to teach me to sew. But I had to sew her kind of clothes—tailored, subtle plaids or checks, and always practical—and in her way—step-by-step, with careful attention to detail.

Using babysitting money, I went shopping, got the pattern for the skirt and yards of exactly the right gauzy pink material. I went home to begin my creation. But as I began laying out the material, pinning pattern pieces, getting ready to cut, I became possessed with the need to do it right. I pinned and repinned and repinned. My mother had never been as picky as I was being. Watching me, my mother began to pace and was soon saying, "The material will soon be worn out and unusable," "The first time you wear it the whole thing will fall apart," "The seams will pucker and you will never be able to . . ." She painted at least twenty different negative fantasies for me as, grim lipped, I perspired and pinned.

Camille said that this was just one of many similar mother–daughter encounters, which she and her mellowing ISTJ mother can now laugh about.

"He Doesn't Seem to Have Any Goals at All"

Paul, ENTJ

Inferior Introverted Feeling

Key Features of Inferior Function

- Hypersensitivity to inner states
- Outbursts of emotion
- Fear of feeling

Tom, ESFP

Inferior Introverted Intuition

Key Features of Inferior Function

- Internal confusion
- Inappropriate attribution of meaning
- Grandiose vision

Paul was concerned about his 17-year-old son, Tom, who was entering his senior year in high school. He confessed that their relationship had been difficult from the beginning, with Tom seeming to purposely defy every value and principle that was important to Paul. Nevertheless, Paul admired his son's popularity with his peers and his ease in social relationships.

He was somewhat more uneasy about Tom's ready pursuit of pleasure and rather frenetic level of physical activity. In early elementary school, Tom had been diagnosed as hyperactive and had been put on medication. The diagnosis was later found to be in error.

Paul was irritated by Tom's lackadaisical approach to school assignments, especially since his tested IQ was in the superior range. "I'm really worried about my son's lack of motivation and direction. He doesn't seem to have any goals at all!" Paul said.

Tom was quite clear about his preferences, which were nearly opposite those of his father. He acknowledged that the two of them rarely saw eye to eye: "He gets really uptight and upset about unimportant things, yells at me, and accuses me of not appreciating what I've got and everything he does for me. If I leave a smudge on my car when I polish it, he gets mad and tells me that if I'm this sloppy with my car, how will I ever succeed in life. It's really stupid!"

When particularly tired, Tom was unable to put his father's criticisms in perspective. He became overwhelmed with fears about his future and wondered if his father's view of him was true. "It's true I don't plan ahead much," admitted Tom. "Maybe there really is something missing in my character, like Dad seems to think." Tom then imagined all sorts of unpleasant, unavoidable failures that could occur if he continued on in his own way. But if he tried to emulate his very responsible and serious father, he envisioned a joyless, oppressive life. Either way, he felt doomed.

Paul's experience of his own inferior Introverted Feeling prevented him from appreciating all but the surface competencies of his son's type. His fears about his son's competence were way out of proportion, as was his conclusion that his son was not equipped for successful adulthood. He had a hard time envisioning and respecting Tom's talents and values.

Tom despaired of receiving his father's approval, but his rejection and derision of his father's concerns were more than a youthful desire for independence: The two approached life from very different perspectives. Paul readily descended into a raging, despairing state of inferior Introverted Feeling as he watched Tom's easygoing dominant Extraverted Sensing lifestyle. In his vulnerable position of inexperienced youth and with his basic respect for his father, Tom was vulnerable to his father's exaggerated emotional judgments, which emanated from his inferior Introverted Feeling.

"Promise Me You'll Tell Me if I Get to Be Like Him!"

Anna, ISTJ

Inferior Extraverted Intuition

Otis, ISTJ

Inferior Extraverted Intuition

Key Features of Inferior Function

- Loss of control over facts and details
- Impulsiveness
- Catastrophizing

Anna called her elderly father, Otis, to invite him for dinner at a local restaurant.

"I guess I'll come," he said. "But we'll have to go early so I don't get caught in traffic. And you know that place won't take reservations, and I don't want to sit around waiting all night. You don't know if they've changed the menu again, do you? Last time they didn't have my dessert, and I'd just as soon stay home if I can't get what I want when I go out. Money doesn't grow on trees, you know."

Anna groaned internally. "I'm paying for dinner, Dad. I was there a few nights ago and the menu is the same, so you can order your usual. I'll pick you up so you don't have to deal with traffic."

"No, no. Don't bother. It's too far out of your way and you'll waste gas. You've got to watch the pennies."

Anna was a highly paid engineer with a very secure future. "No, I don't have to watch my pennies, Dad. Why can't you just relax and have a good time? You always see the bad side of things."

"Well, you know, Anna, you should never take anything for granted," he advised. "You might have an okay job now, but what if the economy gets worse and they lay you off? By the way, do you have any savings? You know I only have my social security, so you won't be able to count on me to help you out."

"Dad, stop it!" shouted Anna into the phone. "You're always putting me down. Everyone else respects my work, but you think I'm going to be fired at any moment. You don't care anything about me. Nothing I do makes you happy. You're the most pessimistic, negative, irritating old man who ever lived, and I don't want to have dinner with you tonight or any night!"

Anna slammed down the phone and then called her best friend, Sally, and related the latest encounter with her father. "He just gets worse and worse. Soon we won't be able to talk to each other at all. And I think his memory is going. What if he gets to where he can't take care of himself and I have to take him in? I couldn't stand it. And what if he's right and I do lose my job? He'd really crow about that and say, 'Told you so, told you so,' like he always does when something bad happens."

Sally knew what to do in this situation, which came up regularly for Anna. She listened sympathetically, agreeing that Otis was being his usual crotchety self and recognizing how difficult it must be for Anna to deal with him.

"How about my joining you and your dad at the restaurant tonight? You know he's usually more sociable when I'm around."

"But I called it off," said Anna.

"Call it back on, then. You know he really loves to eat out, and he's probably sorry he upset you. He always is."

The three had a pleasant dinner together with little incident. Anna later observed to Sally that her father's negativity nearly always caused her to imagine the same kinds of unpleasant possibilities he came up with. She shuddered to think that she might get stuck like her father seemed to be, and made Sally promise to tell her immediately if she thought she was becoming like him.

Using Knowledge of the Inferior with Parents and Children

Anything that promotes understanding between parents and children of any age has to be an asset. Parents who understand psychological type have an objective way of accepting and appreciating differences between themselves and their children. Adolescent and adult children who understand typology have a valuable way of differentiating between parent-child issues and what may be "pseudo issues" attributable to type differences.

An understanding of the habitual out-of-character reactions of parents and children adds greatly to the value of psychological type knowledge. Family life can be stressful for many people, but it can also represent the comfort and security of ultimate acceptance. It is thus a safe place for people to be at their worst. Family members tend to be adept at identifying and handling each other's idiosyncrasies, but they often lack an accurate understanding and comfortable acceptance of their own and each other's foibles. Recognizing the influence of the inferior function can objectify such aberrations and enable family members to view extreme behavior within the context of normal personality.

At Work

In light of the different types' very different work energizers and stressors as well as the prevalence of continuous stress at work, it should come as no surprise that the workplace frequently bears witness to incidents in which people's inferior functions emerge and interact. This can be more devastating than in intimate relationships, where one can usually trust that love and the strength of the bond will mitigate any negative effects of the episode. At work, we are held to higher standards of behavior and there is less tolerance for people's chronic and even temporary aberrations.

There is a good deal of information about each type's responses to work stress in the preceding eight chapters, and a number of stories about work-stimulated grip experiences. There was Eleanor, the INTP CPA, and Jenny, the ESTJ manager. Eleanor did not know much about typology when her grip experience occurred. When she discovered that it could be well explained as an inferior function episode, she was relieved. In contrast, when Jenny had her grip experience, she was knowledgeable about all aspects of typology. Nevertheless, she was vulnerable to the stress that pushed her into her inferior function. Many people have become aware of inferior function responses as a reaction to stress, especially in the past ten years. As a result, it is not uncommon for people in many organizations to identify their own and others' atypical behavior as being in the grip.

Many people report that knowing the form of their own and their co-workers' inferior functions can minimize their effects, enable people who are in the grip to regain their equilibrium more rapidly, encourage understanding and compassion in the workplace, and even prevent unpleasant and unproductive confrontations from occurring at work. The following example illustrates this point. The stories in this section illustrate the potential consequences of interactions between two activated inferior functions at work.

FRANK AND ZEKE

Frank, ENFP

Inferior Introverted Sensing

Key Features of Inferior Function

- Withdrawal and depression
- Obsessiveness
- Focus on the body

Zeke, ESTP

Inferior Introverted Intuition

Key Features of Inferior Function

- Internal confusion
- Inappropriate attribution of meaning
- Grandiose vision

Frank, a police sergeant in the criminal division, was having difficulty in his relationship with Zeke, a legal adviser he worked with. Zeke persistently questioned and criticized Frank's communication style and competence in a demeaning, combative manner. Frank was in great distress during an eight-month period during which Zeke verbally attacked him on a daily basis.

As a result, Frank's generally positive self-image of competence and ability to communicate effectively changed to extreme self-doubt. He felt especially distrusting of his intuition, which had always been his most reliable guide in his work. He found himself obsessing about every memo he wrote, questioning his interrogation methods, and making minute revisions to his case reports.

It was in this context that an important but difficult and complicated case came up that required Frank and Zeke to work closely together. As the case dragged on, Frank observed Zeke coming up with all kinds of doomsday predictions about the case based on improbable, inappropriate theories. Zeke imagined bizarre legal and medical ramifications, despite the fact that these matters were far outside his area of expertise.

Frank, who knew about the manifestations of the inferior function, guessed that the stress of the case might well account for Zeke's aberrant behavior. He was concerned, however, that if Zeke continued talking in this strange manner, the case might be jeopardized. He therefore made every effort to appease Zeke and prevent him from bringing even worse repercussions into the situation.

Frank also realized that sooner or later he and Zeke would have to confront each other and that, with his negative experiences with Zeke and his ongoing diminished self-confidence, he could easily slip into the grip of his own inferior function. He knew what would happen to him if he did: He would become upset, argumentative, hostile, and confrontational. He would lash out at everyone around him, make off-the-wall accusations, and obsess about his own and everyone else's inattention to facts. Frank knew that "losing it" would not serve him or his department well.

Being aware and prepared for this probability circumvented a likely inferior function episode for Frank. By anticipating things, he was able to distance himself and deal with the situation in a quiet, objective, and reasonable manner.

Knowing When to Stop

Patsy, ENFP
Inferior Introverted Sensing

Key Features of Inferior Function

- Withdrawal and depression
- Obsessiveness
- Focus on the body

Ginny, INTP
Inferior Extraverted Feeling

Key Features of Inferior Function

- Logic emphasized to an extreme
- Hypersensitivity to relationships
- Emotionalism

Patsy and Ginny are business partners. By mutual agreement, Ginny takes care of all the finances of the business—making deposits to the right accounts, balancing the accounts, paying the bills on time, figuring the taxes, filling out forms, and so on. Although the business is doing very well, the cash flow is uneven, and staying current on all bills requires some real maneuvering at times.

Ginny has learned that it works best if she just takes care of all this without discussing it with Patsy. For Patsy, there is no good time for financial discussions. Talking about it first thing in the morning "spoils what was going to be a nice day." Talking about it last thing in the day means "I'll be awake all night." It doesn't seem to matter if it's positive information or negative information that's at issue—just talking about money is painful for her. And specifics seem to be taken out of context. A statement by Ginny that "We're a little overextended right now, so let's be careful just to purchase things we really need" may lead to phone calls from Patsy saying, "I'm at the office supply and I just bought a box of paper clips for $1.99, but now I'm feeling guilty. I think we have a bunch of papers in our files with clips on them that we could take off and reuse. Should I return this box?"

Patsy prefers not to know very much about the finances of their business. She says, "Just tell me, do we have money?" The desired answer is yes or no, with no other information. Most of the time, Patsy and Ginny deal with the financial issues pretty well, but there is one pattern they have noticed that gets both of them dangerously close to being beside themselves. Here is how it typically goes.

Patsy wants to go on a trip or buy something, and Ginny has to tell her to hold back because their finances are tight.

Ginny: "We have only $1,000 in the bank, and we can't expect to receive the check from X for another couple of weeks, and the American Express bill that's due next week is for $950."

Patsy: "Why is that bill so high; we didn't charge anything, did we?"

Ginny: "It's for your plane tickets for those two business talks you did out of town last month."

Patsy: "But we were reimbursed for those last month. Where are the reimbursement checks? Why don't we save the reimbursement checks to pay the bills when they come due?"

Ginny: "It would be nice if we could put all the reimbursement checks into a savings account and draw the money out when we get the bills. Unfortunately, we needed those checks to pay the rent on the first of the month because we hadn't received the check from the state government. It wouldn't make sense to be late on the rent, get a penalty, and damage our credit rating while we're holding on to $800 in checks. The money comes in and then goes out. That's the logic of it."

After many repetitions of this scenario, Patsy and Ginny have learned to end their conversations when they get to this point. In the past, however, as these discussions went on, Patsy would become more and more insistent that the crux of the problem was Ginny's mishandling of reimbursement checks. Ginny would eventually become hurt and tearful and accuse Patsy of not appreciating how hard she worked to keep their finances in order. And the cycle would go on and on. Their understanding of their own and each other's response to the stress associated with finances has enabled them to inhibit their inferior functions before they get past the point of no return.

The INFP Psychotherapy Supervisor

Carol, ESFJ

Inferior Introverted Thinking

Key Features of Inferior Function

- Excessive criticism
- Convoluted logic
- Compulsive search for truth

Andrew, INFP

Inferior Extraverted Thinking

Key Features of Inferior Function

- Judgments of incompetence
- Aggressive criticism
- Precipitous action

Carol, a family therapist in a mental health center, was pleased to discover that her unit's new supervisor, Andrew, was an INFP. Carol values her friendships with INFPs and is particularly appreciative of the therapeutic insights of her INFP colleagues. She therefore grew increasingly puzzled and distressed when early encounters with Andrew frequently became destructive and hostile.

In performing his job as supervisor, Andrew appeared obsessively concerned with record keeping and client confidentiality, and he was meticulous about following established cautionary procedures. His primary focus was on the prevention of possible lawsuits against the mental health facility. Consequently, when a client even hinted at suicide, homicide, or any other severe acting-out behavior, Andrew insisted on pages of documentation on all interactions, treatment plans, and so on.

Whenever Carol approached Andrew for therapeutic advice, Andrew invariably inquired only about the accuracy of the records and whether Carol had said or done anything "dangerous." This response from Andrew made Carol doubt her own value as a therapist and question what Andrew expected of her. When Carol was not overwhelmed by her concerns about her therapeutic skills, she felt frustrated, angry, and shortchanged by

Andrew. Any attempt on Carol's part to establish harmony, seek out Andrew's knowledge as a therapist, or provide some commonsense evaluation of a situation was met with increased criticism and negativity from Andrew.

Andrew seemed to be chronically in the grip of inferior Extraverted Thinking. His self-doubt about his competence to do his job and the pressure of being responsible for a number of therapists and many clients were apparently overwhelming for him. His response overemphasized minute details that might "trip him up" and inevitably might lead to the discovery of his incompetence and a dreaded lawsuit for failure to treat some client appropriately.

Carol's feelings about this continuing situation varied from sympathy for Andrew's obvious unhappiness to irritation about and resentment of Andrew's failure to give his best to his staff members. The continuing situation was distressing for everyone involved.

"Are These People Really Adults?"

Felice, ISFP

Inferior Extraverted Thinking

Key Features of Inferior Function

- Judgments of incompetence
- Aggressive criticism
- Precipitous action

Glen, INTJ

Inferior Extraverted Sensing

Key Features of Inferior Function

- Obsessive focus on external data
- Overindulgence in sensual pleasures
- Adversarial attitude toward the outer world

Felice had been the administrator of a large church for more than fifteen years. She was good at her job, which was broad and complex. She managed church membership, religious school operations, space rentals for weddings and other events, and volunteers. In short, she stayed on top of everything. Her accounting methods were not terribly systematic, but after twenty years, she knew everything so well that, even with unorthodox record keeping, church finances were always in order and the church was consistently solvent.

Felice was directly responsible to the church's minister, Glen. Glen was thankful that Felice took care of all the financial data and handled the day-to-day affairs of the church in a manner that pleased the congregation and freed him from having to get involved in areas he didn't enjoy.

Felice and Glen got along fine most of the time. But Felice confessed to her son that sometimes Glen was completely unreasonable, usually when he had to present church affairs at a finance meeting of church officers. The day before such meetings, he would fly into a frenzy and demand detailed, specific financial information about every aspect of the church's activities.

"Just get it off the computer!" he would demand. "That's what you have it for!" Glen did not know how to operate a computer, but he had great respect for its capabilities. Felice had never been able to convince him that a person can't simply get something out of a computer that hasn't been put in. He believed all you had to do was push some button and whatever you needed would magically appear.

Felice believed that to be an effective administrator, she had to accommodate Glen's wishes. But she couldn't do this because what he wanted often could not be produced. She had never confronted him about this, for, in her mind, it would not be proper.

Glen heaped more and more verbal abuse on Felice as she failed to provide the desired financial figures. So, in her distress, frustration, and resentment, she turned into a tyrant, taking it out on everyone in the church—employees, volunteers, parishioners, delivery people, and so on. She became rigid, dictatorial, and withholding.

One spring, the church school had requested and received approval for a sum for a summer picnic for seventy-five children. Two days before the picnic, the teacher went to Felice to get the check. Little did the teacher know that the day before, Glen had (erroneously) decided that the church was in debt and told Felice there was no money for anything.

Felice angrily told the teacher that there was no money at all and she would have to cancel the picnic. There was nothing anyone could do about it, she said, and if the teacher had any complaints, she should go to the minister. The angry teacher then berated the minister, who got angry at Felice, who in turn took it out on her staff, who became puzzled, hurt, and demoralized.

"Everyone is at their worst," said a longtime church volunteer, "especially Glen and Felice. It's as if they both turn into eight-year-olds, and immature ones at that!"

Using Knowledge of the Inferior in the Workplace

People demonstrate their best and worst selves at work. We show our competence in areas in which we are skilled and experienced and in which we are appreciated by co-workers and rewarded by employers for our performance. But the stress that is chronic in most work situations can thwart our best efforts and elicit our own and others' least effective sides. Understanding the forms of different inferior functions can provide the potential for understanding, predicting, and explaining out-of-character behavior at work.

Power relationships in the workplace add a particularly potent, often destructive dimension to expressions of the inferior function. An employee who is often beside himself may be fired for being unreliable; a co-worker may get a reputation for being impossible to work with based on a few people's experiencing her while she was in the grip; and a supervisor's out-of-character behavior may just be viewed as "something you have to watch out for and fear."

Characterizing people and judging them on the basis of their most aberrant behavior is wasteful and often unwarranted. It is here that knowledge of the inferior function can prove particularly beneficial in discouraging negative judgments about people that are based on their occasional aberrant behavior. Extreme out-of-character reactions to the stresses of the workplace can be viewed in the context of the consistency of personality rather than its unpredictability. This can provide the rationality necessary to distinguish between true unreliability, poor performance, and faulty leadership and intermittent episodes of the inferior function.

People who recognize their own and others' inferior functions at work report that they are better able to keep things in perspective for themselves and others. This can have a positive effect on productivity and employee satisfaction, which in turn may reduce some of the stresses of the workplace. And when someone is chronically in the grip at work due to long-term, unrelenting stress, eventually becoming aware of this can be vital information that encourages taking action to modify stress or leave a stressful situation.

Conclusion

The "grip" experiences described in this chapter are but a few of the many ways in which personal and professional interactions can trigger an inferior function. Remember, however, that even though activation of the inferior function may contribute to an exaggerated reaction on someone's part, the content involved should not be ignored. Important truths often emerge when a usually reticent person relinquishes social inhibitions, or when a normally cheerful and confident individual reveals his or her innermost doubts and fears.

15

In and Out of the Grip

THIS CHAPTER INCLUDES DISCUSSIONS of some remaining issues related to the inferior function experience, some intriguing areas for further exploration, and some recommendations for applying the inferior function concept in everyday life. The following areas will be discussed:

- Living life in your inferior function
- The role of the inferior function in job burnout
- Questions about the role of the auxiliary function
- Maturity and the grip
- Trivializing the inferior function
- Overusing the concept of the inferior function
- The value of opposites

Living Life in Your Inferior Function

Life circumstances sometimes require a person to operate in his or her inferior function for extended periods. Some individuals develop excellent skills in their fourth function and also put their dominant function to innovative use. However, when in a vulnerable state, they can easily slip into a full-blown inferior function experience.

When life circumstances force people to operate out of their fourth, least-preferred, function rather than their dominant function, we might expect to see exaggerated, perhaps inappropriate, demonstrations of the function involved. When a way of being does not come naturally, there is a tendency to work hard to achieve success in using it. Sometimes a person who seems to be a caricature of his or her type, whose type qualities are extreme, is really the opposite or near opposite type—perhaps trying too hard to do it well.

This was the case for Joe, the director of training in a large corporation. Known within the company as a hard-nosed, rigid, often punitive person who insisted that rules be followed meticulously, he was particularly callous when personal problems arose for employees, such as marital difficulties or sick children. He insisted that, as adults, people must learn to separate their work lives from their personal lives.

Several people familiar with type were convinced that Joe was an ESTJ with a marked inability to use his tertiary Intuition and inferior Feeling functions in an adaptive way. When a consultant administered the MBTI personality inventory to senior members of the firm, they were amazed to discover that Joe had verified his reported type as INFP. Later discussions with Joe revealed that his role model was his very effective predecessor, Bill—a mature ESTJ.

It is not uncommon for the demands of a career to force development and frequent use of our least-preferred processes. If the demands are not excessive, this is not necessarily problematic. Whether serious problems develop depends on a variety of factors, such as satisfying avocations, good income, family life, and friends. Limited opportunity to fully develop or satisfy one's personality preferences is but one of the disappointments people are likely to experience during their lives. Sad as this may be, though, it is heartening to see the innovative ways in which some people manage to exercise and validate their type.

There are also some general societal pressures that encourage people to live out of their inferior functions. For example, men with a preference for Feeling may get a message that their style is unacceptable because it is not "masculine," and they may therefore develop an exaggeratedly critical Thinking approach, coming across as excessively "macho," or even crass and abusive toward women.

Men with a preference for Thinking who are in "Feeling" professions may show a seemingly artificial overconcern for people. An ENTJ minister recalled that during his six months in a pastoral counseling training program, he focused on his and his client's emotions, even though he felt uncomfortable, condescending, and phony about doing so. He saw himself as emotionally and intellectually incompetent in comparison to other ministers, who appeared comfortable in their roles as counselors.

Women in our society must also deal with the pressures of cultural expectations. Women who prefer Thinking may be seen by others and may see themselves as lacking in those feminine qualities that society considers essential to being an acceptable woman. In response, they may overcompensate with an exaggerated focus on fulfilling family expectations, helping others, and demonstrating "feminine" interests. This may be especially true for women with a Thinking preference who include the traditional roles of wife and mother in their lives. Their style of dress may tend toward lace and pastel colors, and they may feign ineptitude about such traditionally "masculine" things as mechanical devices and finances.

Women with a Feeling preference who choose traditionally male dominated careers may also find themselves operating out of their inferior functionss because a Thinking approach is often touted as the path to career success. Like male Feeling types, they may develop exaggerated Thinking characteristics—an abrasive, critical manner, very tailored clothing, and a harsh approach to expressions of emotion and Feeling concerns. For example, an INFP senior lawyer was viewed by new associates as unrelenting in her criticism of their work, and lacking any softness or social graces.

Additional examples of some of the above situations can be found in N. L. Quenk, 1989, and A. T. Quenk and N. L. Quenk, 1982.

The Role of the Inferior Function in Job Burnout

There is ample evidence that the preconditions for the inferior function experience are often present in the workplace and can force people to spend an extended period in the grip of their inferior function. But the influence of the inferior function may also be evident when people work out of their preferred functions in their jobs. In fact, job burnout symptoms can be interpreted to be the result of (or at least influenced by) overuse or one-sided use of one's personality type. The characteristics of job burnout in different types reveal a predictable pattern consistent with inferior function attributes.

The definitive work in this area was done by Anna-Maria Garden (1985, 1988). Garden's initial research questioned the generalizability of research conclusions about burnout because the subject samples used in such research were drawn primarily from the human services professions—groups generally overrepresented with Feeling types. Garden noted that a major reported effect of job burnout is negative, hostile, and "depersonalized" reactions to people—responses quite opposite those that are typical of people-oriented Feeling types.

Garden's research (1988) explored the relationship between personality type preferences (specifically Sensing, Intuition, Thinking, and Feeling) and the ways people experienced and expressed job burnout. She found a similar reversion or reversal for each of the four functions—that is, there was a "loss of the attributes typically expected of that type." She identified the "type" of burnout for each of the four preferences she examined as follows:

- For Feeling types, a loss in (or lower level of) the inclination to care for others

- For Thinking types, a loss in achievement orientation or ambitiousness

- For Sensing types, a loss in groundedness

- For Intuitive types, a loss of enthusiasm and originality (p. 13)

Further, Garden (1988) found that "in some instances, an increase in the characteristics associated with one's opposite was apparent. Thinking types, for example, showed higher levels of concern for others and Sensing types showed an increase in the level of boredom" (p. 14).

More recent research on burnout (Myers, et al., 1998), which used the *Maslach Burnout Inventory* (Maslach, 1996) in relation to the sixteen types, supported Garden's results and provided more specific information about the forms of burnout each type experiences. For a summary of results for each type, see Myers, et al., 1998, and N. L. Quenk, 2000a.

The qualities of burnout identified by Garden's innovative and careful research show at least some of the major characteristics described in this book. Perhaps a consideration of such burnout evidence, in conjunction with knowledge of the inferior function of each type, can lead to increased understanding of the burnout phenomenon and more effective approaches to intervention.

Questions About the Role of the Auxiliary Function

Does a well-developed auxiliary function "protect" a person from readily falling into the grip of the inferior function or speed the return of equilibrium once a person is in the grip? If the inferior function sometimes is activated simply as a response to an extreme state, and not for some self-regulating purpose, are "less-developed" people more vulnerable than people who are "well developed"? For example, are ENFPs who extravert their auxiliary Feeling as well as their dominant Intuition more vulnerable to their inferior function than ENFPs who more adaptively introvert their auxiliary Feeling? There is some anecdotal evidence to suggest this (N. L. Quenk, 1985b).

Can one actively try to engage the auxiliary function as a way to end the grip experience and thus shorten it—or, once constellated, does the inferior function have to play out fully and completely before it dissipates naturally?

Some people report an interesting effect if their business or life partner's dominant function is the same as their own auxiliary function. In this circumstance, one partner is likely to say or do "the right thing" to help the other when he or she is in the grip. Thus, an ESTJ (dominant Extraverted Thinking, auxiliary Introverted Sensing) might mention the logical consequences of the fact an INTJ (dominant Introverted Intuition, auxiliary Extraverted Thinking) is stuck on, or an ISFP (dominant Introverted Feeling, auxiliary Extraverted Sensing) might offer quiet reassurance and emotional support to his ESFP (dominant Extraverted Sensing, auxiliary Introverted Feeling) partner. If this is generally true, it provides further evidence for the role of the auxiliary function in the restoration of psychological balance.

Maturity and the Grip

People of all types report that the frequency and intensity of their grip experiences tend to decrease with age, notwithstanding the often startling episodes characteristic of the middle years. Even without specific knowledge of psychological type theory or understanding of the adaptive nature of inferior function experiences, people tend to become familiar with and often benefit from these experiences.

Sometimes "familiarity breeds contempt," however, and a mature person learns to ignore and reject these kinds of experiences. If this becomes habitual, they may miss out on important developmental information. For others, repetition of the form of the inferior can encourage development of a repertoire of helpful responses. These may include stopping what they are doing, taking time to attend to neglected sides of themselves, and reflecting on some aspect of their lives. When this occurs, the psyche may receive the stimulation necessary to permit the person to proceed in his or her personal growth and development.

Trivializing the Inferior Function

Often when we name an experience, we run the risk of minimizing and trivializing it. Then when we experience it we say, "Ah, yes. I know what this is. It's nothing but my midlife crisis" (or my grief process, or my empty nest syndrome, or my inferior function). We may then disregard the experience and miss out on an important opportunity to develop our awareness of ourselves and our lives.

If Jung is correct about the role of the inferior function in the self-regulation of the psyche, then it would be an error to treat it in a dismissive, trivial manner. We might rather approach encounters with our least-developed side with the utmost respect, neither avoiding it nor attempting to forcibly overcome it.

Overusing the Concept of the Inferior Function

Have you ever had the experience of learning a new word and then seeing and hearing it everywhere? Once our awareness is heightened, we begin to notice words or other things we didn't see before. Often when we learn a new concept we try to apply it everywhere and feel compelled to try to explain everything with it. Done judiciously, this is a good way to become familiar with a new idea as well as recognize its limitations. People who are newly introduced to typology often stretch the limits of the theory by insisting that virtually everything is related to one's type.

It is well to remember, therefore, that typology, including the inferior function, is only one way, albeit one very rich and intriguing way, of understanding individual differences. There are many other useful explanatory systems. It is probably a testimony to the incredible complexity of human beings that no one personality theory proves entirely adequate to the task of explaining us.

It has been wisely said that "If the only tool you have is a hammer, you'll treat everything as if it is a nail." Avoiding that pitfall will encourage our best use of Jung's personality theory and his concept of the inferior function.

The Value of Opposites

An opposite by definition requires opposition. Thus, the inferior and dominant functions need each other and are reflections of each other. When we consider those things we despise, we can assume that their opposites are what we very much value; by considering what we value, we implicitly identify the things we despise. Awareness of both sides is equally important.

For those of us who characteristically emphasize the positive, recognizing the negative side of things can be distressing, but it can also stimulate valuable insights into ourselves and others. Those who most naturally focus on the negative and objectionable things around them can find in this perspective a way to appreciate the positive and satisfying counterparts that can moderate this limited view.

At the end of Chapter 1 there is a description of what you could expect from this book—its nonpathological approach and its focus on the valuable limitations of consciousness. Ideally, you have come away from your reading with a richer awareness of those unconscious, inferior parts of yourself that embody your own wisdom.

APPENDIX A

DESCRIPTIONS OF THE SIXTEEN

PERSONALITY TYPES

ESTJ
Extraverted Thinking with Sensing

ESTJ people use their thinking to run as much of the world as may be theirs to run. They like to organize projects and then act to get things done. Reliance on thinking makes them logical, analytical, objectively critical, and not likely to be convinced by anything but reasoning. They tend to focus on the job, not the people behind the job.

They like to organize facts, situations, and operations related to a project, and make a systematic effort to reach their objectives on schedule. They have little patience with confusion or inefficiency, and can be tough when the situation calls for toughness.

They think conduct should be ruled by logic, and govern their own behavior accordingly. They live by a definite set of rules that embody their basic judgments about the world. Any change in their ways requires a deliberate change in their rules.

They are more interested in seeing present realities than future possibilities. This makes them matter-of-fact, practical, realistic, and concerned with the here-and-now. They use past experience to help them solve problems and want to be sure that ideas, plans, and decisions are based on solid fact.

They like jobs where the results of their work are immediate, visible, and tangible. They have a natural bent for business, industry, production, and construction. They enjoy administration, where they can set goals, make decisions, and give the necessary orders. Getting things done is their strong suit.

Source: Myers, I. B. (1987). *Introduction to Type®* (4th ed.). Palo Alto, CA: CPP, Inc. Reprinted with permission.

Like the other decisive types, ESTJs run the risk of deciding too quickly before they have fully examined the situation. They need to stop and listen to the other person's viewpoint, especially with people who are not in a position to talk back. This is seldom easy for them, but *if* they do not take time to understand, they may judge too quickly, without enough facts or enough regard for what other people think or feel.

ESTJs *may* need to work at taking feeling values into account. They may rely so much on their logical approach that they overlook feeling values—what they care about and what other people care about. If feeling values are ignored too much, they may build up pressure and find expression in inappropriate ways. Although ESTJs are naturally good at seeing what is illogical and inconsistent, they may need to develop the art of appreciation. One positive way to exercise their feeling is to appreciate other people's merits and ideas. ESTJs who make it a rule to mention what they like, not merely what needs correcting, find the results worthwhile both in their work and in their private lives.

ENTJ
Extraverted Thinking with Intuition

ENTJ people use their thinking to run as much of the world as may be theirs to run. They enjoy executive action and long-range planning. Reliance on thinking makes them logical, analytical, objectively critical, and not likely to be convinced by anything but reasoning. They tend to focus on the ideas, not the person behind the ideas.

They like to think ahead, organize plans, situations, and operations related to a project, and make a systematic effort to reach their objectives on schedule. They have little patience with confusion or inefficiency, and can be tough when the situation calls for toughness.

They think conduct should be ruled by logic, and govern their own behavior accordingly. They live by a definite set of rules that embody their basic judgments about the world. Any change in their ways requires a deliberate change in their rules.

They are mainly interested in seeing the possibilities beyond what is present, obvious, or known. Intuition heightens their intellectual interest, curiosity for new ideas, tolerance for theory, and taste for complex problems.

ENTJs are seldom content in jobs that make no demand upon their intuition. They are stimulated by problems and are often found in executive jobs where they can find and implement new solutions. Because their interest is in the big picture, they may overlook the importance of certain details. Since ENTJs tend to team up with like-minded intuitives who may also underestimate the realities of a situation, they usually need a person around with good common sense to bring up overlooked facts and take care of important details.

Like the other decisive types, ENTJs run the risk of deciding too quickly before they have fully examined the situation. They need to stop and listen to the other person's viewpoint, especially with people who are not in a position to talk back. This is seldom easy for them, but *if* they do not take time to understand, they may judge too quickly, without enough facts or enough regard for what other people think or feel.

ENTJs *may* need to work at taking feeling values into account. Relying so much on their logical approach, they may overlook feeling values—what they care about and what other people care about. If feeling values are ignored too much, they may build up pressure and find expression in inappropriate ways. Although ENTJs are naturally good at seeing what is illogical and inconsistent, they may need to develop the art of appreciation. One positive way to exercise their feeling is through appreciation of other people's merits and ideas. ENTJs who learn to make it a rule to mention what they like, not merely what needs correcting, find the results worthwhile both in their work and in their private lives.

ISTP
Introverted Thinking with Sensing

People with ISTP preferences use their thinking to look for the principles underlying the sensory information that comes into awareness. As a result, they are logical, analytical, and objectively critical. They are not likely to be convinced by anything but reasoning based on solid facts.

While they like to organize facts and data, they prefer not to organize situations or people unless they must for the sake of their work. They can be intensely but quietly curious. Socially they may be rather shy except with their best friends. They sometimes become so absorbed with one of their interests that they can ignore or lose track of external circumstances.

ISTPs are somewhat quiet and reserved, although they can be quite talkative on a subject where they can apply their great storehouse of information. In everyday activities they are adaptable, except when one of their ruling principles is violated, at which point they stop adapting. They are good with their hands, and like sports and the outdoors, or anything that provides a wealth of information for their senses.

If ISTPs have developed their powers of observing the world around them, they will have a firm grasp on the realities of any situation, and show a great capacity for the important and unique facts of a situation. They are interested in how and why things work and are likely to be good at applied science, mechanics, or engineering. ISTPs who do not have technical or mechanical interests often use their talents to bring order out of unorganized facts. This ability can find expression in law, economics, marketing, sales, securities, or statistics.

ISTPs *may* rely so much on the logical approach of thinking that they overlook what other people care about and what they themselves care about. They may decide that something is not important, just because it isn't logical to care about it. If ISTPs always let their thinking suppress their feeling values, their feeling may build up pressure and find expression in inappropriate ways. Although good at analyzing what is wrong, ISTPs sometimes find it hard to express appreciation. But if they try, they will find it helpful on the job as well as in personal relationships.

ISTP people are in some danger of putting off decisions or of failing to follow through. One of their outstanding traits is economy of effort. This trait is an asset if they judge accurately how much effort is needed; then they do what the situation requires without fuss or lost motion. *If* they cannot judge accurately, or if they just don't bother, then nothing of importance gets done.

INTP
Introverted Thinking with Intuition

People with INTP preferences use their thinking to find the principles underlying whatever ideas come into their awareness. They rely on thinking to develop these principles and to anticipate consequences. As a result, they are logical, analytical, and objectively critical. They are likely to focus more on the ideas than the person behind the ideas.

They organize ideas and knowledge rather than situations or people, unless they must for the sake of their work. In the field of ideas they are intensely curious. Socially, they tend to have a small circle of close friends, and like being with others who enjoy discussing ideas. They can become so absorbed with an idea that they can ignore or lose track of external circumstances.

INTPs are somewhat quiet and reserved, although they can be quite talkative on a subject to which they have given a lot of thought. They are quite adaptable so long as their ruling principles are not violated, at which point they stop adapting. Their main interest lies in seeing possibilities beyond what is present, obvious, or known. They are quick to understand and their intuition heightens their insight, ingenuity, and intellectual curiosity.

Depending on their interests, INTPs are good at pure science, research, mathematics, or engineering; they may become scholars, teachers, or abstract thinkers in fields such as economics, philosophy, or psychology. They are more interested in the challenge of reaching solutions to problems than of seeing the solutions put to practical use.

Unless INTPs develop their perception, they are in danger of gaining too little knowledge and experience of the world. Then their thinking is done in a vacuum and nothing will come of their ideas. Lack of contact with the external world may also lead to problems in making themselves understood. They want to state the exact truth, but often make it so complicated that not everyone can follow them. If they can learn to simplify their arguments, their ideas will be more widely understood and accepted.

INTPs *may* rely so much on logical thinking that they overlook what other people care about and what they themselves care about. They may decide that something is not important, just because it isn't logical to care about it. *If* INTPs always let their logic suppress their feeling values, their feeling may build up pressure until it is expressed in inappropriate ways.

Although they excel at analyzing what is wrong with an idea, it is harder for INTPs to express appreciation. But if they try, they will find it helpful on the job as well as in personal relationships.

ESFJ
Extraverted Feeling with Sensing

People with ESFJ preferences radiate sympathy and fellowship. They concern themselves chiefly with the people around them and place a high value on harmonious human contacts. They are friendly, tactful, and sympathetic. They are persevering, conscientious, orderly even in small matters, and inclined to expect others to be the same. They are particularly warmed by approval and sensitive to indifference. Much of their pleasure and satisfaction comes from the warmth of feeling of people around them. ESFJs tend to concentrate on the admirable qualities of other people and are loyal to respected persons, institutions, or causes, sometimes to the point of idealizing whatever they admire.

They have the gift of finding value in other people's opinions. Even when these opinions are in conflict, they have faith that harmony can somehow be achieved and they often manage to bring it about. To achieve harmony, they are ready to agree with other's opinions within reasonable limits. They need to be careful, however, that they don't concentrate so much on the viewpoints of others that they lose sight of their own.

They are mainly interested in the realities perceived by their five senses, so they become practical, realistic, and down-to-earth. They take great interest in the unique differences in each experience. ESFJs appreciate and enjoy their possessions. They enjoy variety but can adapt well to routine.

ESFJs are at their best in jobs that deal with people and in situations where cooperation can be brought about through good will. They are found in jobs such as teaching, preaching, and selling. Their compassion and awareness of physical conditions often attracts them to health professions, where they can provide warmth, comfort, and patient caring. They are less likely to be happy in work demanding mastery of abstract ideas or impersonal analysis. They think best when talking with people, and enjoy communicating. They have to make a special effort to be brief and businesslike and not let sociability slow them down on the job.

They like to base their plans and decisions upon known facts and on their personal values. While liking to have matters decided or settled, they do not necessarily want to make all the decisions themselves. They run some risk of jumping to conclusions before they understand a situation. If they have not taken time to gain first-hand knowledge about a person or situation, their actions may not have the helpful results they intended. For example, ESFJs beginning a new project or job may do things they assume should be done, instead of taking the time to find out what is really wanted or needed. They have many definite "shoulds" and "should nots," and may express these freely.

ESFJs find it especially hard to admit the truth about problems with people or things they care about. If they fail to face disagreeable facts, or refuse to look at criticism that hurts, they will try to ignore their problems instead of searching for solutions.

ENFJ
Extraverted Feeling with Intuition

People with ENFJ preferences radiate sympathy and fellowship. They concern themselves chiefly with the people around them and place a high value on harmonious human contacts. They are friendly, tactful, and sympathetic. They are persevering, conscientious, and orderly even in small matters, and inclined to expect others to be the same. ENFJs are particularly warmed by approval and are sensitive to indifference. Much of their pleasure and satisfaction comes from the warmth of feeling of people around them. ENFJs tend to concentrate on the admirable qualities of other people and are loyal to respected persons, institutions, or causes, sometimes to the point of idealizing whatever they admire.

They have the gift of being able to see value in other people's opinions. Even when opinions are in conflict, they have faith that harmony can somehow be achieved, and they often manage to bring it about. To bring harmony, they are ready to agree with others' opinions within reasonable limits. They need to be careful, however, not to concentrate so much on the viewpoints of others that they lose sight of their own.

They are mainly interested in seeing the possibilities beyond what is present, obvious, or known. Intuition heightens their insight, vision, and curiosity for new ideas. They tend to be interested in books and moderately tolerant of theory. They are likely to have a gift of expression but may use it in speaking to audiences rather than in writing. They think best when talking with people.

They are at their best in jobs that deal with people, and in situations that require building cooperation. ENFJs are found in jobs such as teaching, preaching, counseling, and selling. They may be less happy in work demanding factual accuracy, such as accounting, unless they can find personal meaning in their work. They have to make a special effort to be brief and businesslike and not let sociability slow them down on the job.

They base their decisions on their personal values. While they like to have matters decided or settled, they do not necessarily want to make all the decisions themselves. ENFJs run some risk of jumping to conclusions before they understand a situation. If they have not taken time to gain first-hand knowledge about a person or situation, their actions may not have the helpful results they intended. For example, ENFJs beginning a new project or job may do things they assume should be done, instead of taking the time to find out what is really wanted or needed. They have many definite "shoulds" and "should nots," and may express these freely.

ENFJs find it especially hard to admit the truth about problems with people or things they care about. If they fail to face disagreeable facts, or refuse to look at criticism that hurts, they will ignore their problems instead of searching for solutions.

ISFP
Introverted Feeling with Sensing

People with ISFP preferences have a great deal of warmth, but may not show it until they know a person well. They keep their warm side inside, like a fur-lined coat. When they care, they care deeply, but are more likely to show their feeling by deeds rather than words. They are very faithful to duties and obligations related to things or people they care about.

They take a very personal approach to life, judging everything by their inner ideals and personal values. They stick to their values with passionate conviction, but can be influenced by someone they care deeply about. Although their inner loyalties and ideals govern their lives, ISFPs find these hard to talk about. Their deepest feelings are seldom expressed; their inner tenderness is masked by a quiet reserve.

In everyday activities they are tolerant, open-minded, flexible, and adaptable. If one of their inner loyalties is threatened, though, they will not give an inch. They usually enjoy the present moment, and do not like to spoil it by rushing to get things done. They have little wish to impress or dominate. The people they prize the most are those who take the time to understand their values and the goals they are working toward.

They are interested mainly in the realities brought to them by their senses, both inner and outer. They are apt to enjoy fields where taste, discrimination, and a sense of beauty and proportion are important. Many ISFPs have a special love of nature and a sympathy with animals. They often excel in craftsmanship, and the work of their hands is usually more eloquent than their words.

They are twice as good when working at a job they believe in, since their feeling adds energy to their efforts. They see the needs of the moment and try to meet them. They want their work to contribute to something that matters to them—human understanding, happiness, or health. They want to have a purpose beyond their paycheck, no matter how big the check. They are perfectionists whenever they deeply care about something, and are particularly suited for work that requires both devotion and a large measure of adaptability.

The problem for *some* ISFPs is that they may feel such a contrast between their inner ideals and their actual accomplishments that they may burden themselves with a sense of inadequacy. This can be true even when they are being as effective as others. They take for granted anything they do well and are the most modest of all the types, tending to underrate and understate themselves.

It is important for them to find practical ways to express their ideals; otherwise they will keep dreaming of the impossible and accomplish very little. If they find no actions to express their ideals, they can become too sensitive and vulnerable, with dwindling confidence in life and in themselves. Actually, they have much to give and need only to find the spot where they are needed.

INFP
Introverted Feeling with Intuition

People with INFP preferences have a great deal of warmth, but may not show it until they know a person well. They keep their warm side inside, like a fur-lined coat. They are very faithful to duties and obligations related to ideas or people they care about. They take a very personal approach to life, judging everything by their inner ideals and personal values.

They stick to their ideals with passionate conviction. Although their inner loyalties and ideals govern their lives, they find these hard to talk about. Their deepest feelings are seldom expressed; their inner tenderness is masked by a quiet reserve.

In everyday matters they are tolerant, open-minded, understanding, flexible, and adaptable. But if their inner loyalties are threatened, they will not give an inch. Except for their work's sake, INFPs have little wish to impress or dominate. The people they prize the most are those who take the time to understand their values and the goals they are working toward.

Their main interest lies in seeing the possibilities beyond what is present, obvious, or known. They are twice as good when working at a job they believe in, since their feeling puts added energy behind their efforts. They want their work to contribute to something that matters to them—human understanding, happiness, or health. They want to have a purpose beyond their paycheck, no matter how big the check. They are perfectionists whenever they care deeply about something.

INFPs are curious about new ideas and tend to have insight and long-range vision. Many are interested in books and language and are likely to have a gift of expression; with talent they may be excellent writers. They can be ingenious and persuasive on the subject of their enthusiasms, which are quiet but deep-rooted. They are often attracted to counseling, teaching, literature, art, science, or psychology.

The problem for *some* INFPs is that they may feel such a contrast between their ideals and their actual accomplishments that they burden themselves with a sense of inadequacy. This can happen even when, objectively, they are being as effective as others. It is important for them to use their intuition to find ways to express their ideals; otherwise they will keep dreaming of the impossible and accomplish very little. If they find no channel for expressing their ideals, INFPs may become overly sensitive and vulnerable, with dwindling confidence in life and in themselves.

ESTP
Extraverted Sensing with Thinking

People with ESTP preferences are friendly, adaptable realists. They rely on what they see, hear, and know first-hand. They good-naturedly accept and use the facts around them. They look for a satisfying solution instead of trying to impose any "shoulds" or "musts" of their own. They are sure a satisfying solution will turn up once they have grasped all the facts.

They solve problems by being adaptable, and often can get others to adapt, too. People generally like them well enough to consider any compromise they suggest. They are unprejudiced, open-minded, and tolerant of most everyone—including themselves. They take things as they are and thus may be very good at easing a tense situation and pulling conflicting factions together.

They are actively curious about objects, scenery, activities, food, people, or anything new presented to their senses. Their expert abilities in using their senses may show in: (a) a continuous ability to see the need of the moment and turn easily to meet it, (b) the ability to absorb, apply and remember great numbers of facts, (c) an artistic taste and judgment, or (d) the handling of tools and materials.

With their focus on the current situation and realistic acceptance of what exists, they can be gifted problem solvers. Because they are not necessarily bound by a need to follow standard procedures or preferred methods, they are often able to see ways of achieving a goal by "using" the existing rules, systems, or circumstances in new ways, rather than allowing them to be roadblocks.

They make their decisions by using the logical analysis of thinking rather than the more personal values of feeling. Their thinking enables them to crack down when the situation calls for toughness, and also helps them grasp underlying principles. They learn more from first-hand experience than from study or reading, and are more effective in actual situations than on written tests. Abstract ideas and theories are not likely to be trusted by ESTPs until they have been tested in experience. They may have to work harder than other types to achieve in school, but can do so when they see the relevance.

ESTPs do best in careers needing realism, action, and adaptability. Examples are engineering, police work, credit investigation, marketing, health technologies, construction, production, recreation, food services, and many kinds of troubleshooting.

ESTPs are strong in the art of living. They get a lot of fun out of life, which makes them good company. They enjoy their material possessions and take the time to acquire them. They find much enjoyment in good food, clothes, music, and art. They enjoy physical exercise and sports, and usually are good at these.

How effective they are depends on how much judgment they acquire. They may need to develop their feeling so that they can use their values to provide standards for their behavior, and direction and purpose in their lives. *If* their judgment is not developed enough to give them any character or stick-to-it-iveness, they are in danger of adapting mainly to their own love of a good time.

ESFP
Extraverted Sensing with Feeling

ESFP people are friendly, adaptable realists. They rely on what they can see, hear, and know first-hand. They good-naturedly accept and use the facts around them, whatever these are. They look for a satisfying solution instead of trying to impose any "should" or "must" of their own. They are sure that a solution will turn up once they have grasped all of the facts.

They solve problems by being adaptable, and often can get others to adapt, too. People generally like them well enough to consider any compromise they suggest. They are unprejudiced, open-minded, and tolerant of most everyone—including themselves. They take things as they are and thus may be very good at easing a tense situation and pulling conflicting factions together.

With their focus on the current situation and realistic acceptance of what exists, they can be gifted problem solvers. Because they are not necessarily bound by a need to follow standard procedures or preferred methods, they are often able to see ways of achieving a goal by "using" the existing rules, systems, or circumstances in new ways, rather than allowing them to be roadblocks.

They are actively curious about people, activities, food, objects, scenery, or anything new presented to their senses. Their expert abilities in using their senses may show in: (a) a continuous ability to see the need of the moment and turn easily to meet it, (b) the skillful handling of people and conflicts, (c) the ability to absorb, apply, and remember great numbers of facts, or (d) an artistic taste and judgment.

They make their decisions by using the personal values of feeling rather than the logical analysis of thinking. Their feeling makes them tactful, sympathetic, interested in people, and especially good at handling human contacts. They may be too easy in matters of discipline. They learn far more from first-hand experience than from books, and do better in actual situations than on written tests. Abstract ideas and theories are not likely to be trusted by ESFPs until they have been tested in experience. They may have to work harder than other types to achieve in school, but can do so when they see the relevance.

ESFPs do best in careers needing realism, action, and adaptability. Examples are health services, sales, design, transportation, entertainment, secretarial or office work, food services, supervising work groups, machine operation, and many kinds of troubleshooting.

ESFPs are strong in the art of living. They get a lot of fun out of life, which makes them good company. They enjoy their material possessions and take the time to acquire and care for them. They find much enjoyment in good food, clothes, music, and art. They enjoy physical exercise and sports and usually are good at these.

How effective they are depends on how much judgment they acquire. They may need to develop their feeling so that they can use their values to provide standards for their behavior, and direction and purpose in their lives. If their judgment is not developed enough to give them any character or stick-to-it-iveness, they are in danger of adapting mainly to their own love of a good time.

ISTJ
Introverted Sensing with Thinking

People with ISTJ preferences are extremely dependable and have a complete, realistic, and practical respect for the facts. They absorb, remember, and use any number of facts and are careful about their accuracy. When they see that something needs to be done, they accept the responsibility, often beyond the call of duty. They like everything clearly stated.

Their private reactions, which seldom show in their faces, are often vivid and intense. Even when dealing with a crisis they look calm and composed. Not until you know them very well do you discover that behind their outer calm they are viewing the situation from an intensely individual angle. When ISTJs are "on duty" and dealing with the world, however, their behavior is sound and sensible.

ISTJs are thorough, painstaking, systematic, hard-working, and careful with particulars and procedures. Their perseverance tends to stabilize everything with which they are connected. They do not enter into things impulsively, but once committed, they are very hard to distract or discourage.

ISTJs often choose careers where their talents for organization and accuracy are rewarded. Examples are accounting, civil engineering, law, production, construction, health careers, and office work. They often move into supervisory and management roles.

If they are in charge of something, their practical judgment and valuing of procedure makes them consistent and conservative, assembling the necessary facts to support their evaluations and decisions. They look for solutions to present problems in the successes of the past. With time they become masters of even the smallest elements of their work, but don't give themselves any special credit for this knowledge.

They *may* encounter problems if they expect everyone to be as logical and analytical as they are. They then run the danger of inappropriately passing judgment on others or overriding less forceful people. A useful rule is to use their thinking to make decisions about inanimate objects or their own behavior, and to use their perception to understand others. If they use their senses to see what really matters to others, so that it becomes a fact to be respected, they may go to generous lengths to help.

Another problem may arise *if* the ISTJ's thinking remains undeveloped. They may retreat, becoming absorbed with their inner reactions to sense-impressions, with nothing of value being produced. They may also tend to be somewhat suspicious of imagination and intuition, and not take it seriously enough.

ISFJ
Introverted Sensing with Feeling

People with ISFJ preferences are extremely dependable and devotedly accept responsibilities beyond the call of duty. They have a complete, realistic, and practical respect for the facts. When they see from the facts that something needs to be done, they pause to think about it. If they decide that action will be helpful, they accept the responsibility. They can remember and use any number of facts, but want them all accurate. They like everything clearly stated.

Their private reactions are often vivid and intense, and sometimes quite unpredictable to others. These private reactions seldom show in their faces, and even when dealing with a crisis, they can look calm and composed. Not until you know them very well do you discover that behind their outer calm they are looking at things from an intensely individual angle, often a delightfully humorous one. When ISFJs are "on duty" and dealing with the world, however, their behavior is sound and sensible.

ISFJs are thorough, painstaking, hard-working, and patient with particulars and procedures. They can and will do the "little" things that need to be done to carry a project to completion. Their perseverance tends to stabilize everything with which they are connected. They do not enter into things impulsively, but once in, they are very hard to distract or discourage. They do not quit unless experience convinces them they are wrong.

ISFJs often choose careers where they can combine their careful observation and their caring for people, as in the health professions. Other fields attractive to ISFJs are teaching, office work, and occupations that provide services or personal care. ISFJs show their feeling preference in their contacts with the world. They are kind, sympathetic, tactful, and genuinely concerned; traits that make them very supportive to persons in need.

Because of their concern for accuracy and organization, ISTJs often move into supervisory roles. If they are in charge of something, their practical judgment and appreciation of what works make them conservative and consistent. They take care to collect the facts necessary to support their evaluations and decisions. As they gain experience, they compare the present problem to past situations.

For an ISFJ, problems may arise if their judgment is not developed. If their feeling preference remains undeveloped, they will not be effective in dealing with the world. They may instead retreat, becoming silently absorbed in their inner reactions to sense-impressions. Then nothing of value is likely to come out. Another potential problem is that they tend to be somewhat suspicious of imagination and intuition and not take it seriously enough.

ENTP
Extraverted Intuition with Thinking

People with ENTP preferences are ingenious innovators who always see new possibilities and new ways of doing things. They have a lot of imagination and initiative for starting projects and a lot of impulsive energy for carrying them out. They are sure of the worth of their inspirations and tireless with the problems involved. They are stimulated by difficulties and most ingenious in solving them. They enjoy feeling competent in a variety of areas and value this in others as well.

They are extremely perceptive about the attitudes of other people, and can use this knowledge to win support for their projects. They aim to understand rather than to judge people.

Their energy comes from a succession of new interests and their world is full of possible projects. They may be interested in so many different things that they have difficulty focusing. Their thinking can then help them select projects by supplying some analysis and constructive criticism of their inspirations, and thus add depth to the insights supplied by their intuition. Their use of thinking also makes ENTPs rather objective in their approach to their current project and to the people in their lives.

ENTPs are not likely to stay in any occupation that does not provide many new challenges. With talent, they can be inventors, scientists, journalists, troubleshooters, marketers, promoters, computer analysts, or almost anything that it interests them to be.

A difficulty for people with ENTP preferences is that they hate uninspired routine and find it remarkably hard to apply themselves to sometimes necessary detail unconnected with any major interest. Worse yet, they may get bored with their own projects as soon as the major problems have been solved or the initial challenge has been met. They need to learn to follow through, but are happiest and most effective in jobs that permit one project after another, with somebody else taking over as soon as the situation is well in hand.

Because ENTPs are always being drawn to the exciting challenges of new possibilities, it is essential that they develop their judgment. *If* their judgment is undeveloped, they may commit themselves to ill-chosen projects, fail to finish anything, and squander their inspirations on uncompleted tasks.

ENFP
Extraverted Intuition with Feeling

People with ENFP preferences are enthusiastic innovators, always seeing new possibilities and new ways of doing things. They have a lot of imagination and initiative for starting projects, and a lot of impulsive energy for carrying them out. They are stimulated by difficulties and are most ingenious in solving them. ENFPs can get so interested in their newest project that they have time for little else. Their energy comes from a succession of new enthusiasms and their world is full of possible projects. Their enthusiasm gets other people interested too.

They see so many possible projects that they sometimes have difficulty picking those with the greatest potential. Their feeling can be useful at this point to help select projects by weighing the values of each. Their feeling judgment can also add depth to the insights supplied by their intuition.

The ENFP's feeling preference shows in a concern for people. They are skillful in handling people and often have remarkable insight into the possibilities and development of others. They are extremely perceptive about the attitudes of others, aiming to understand rather than judge people. They are much drawn to counseling, and can be inspired and inspiring teachers, particularly where they have freedom to innovate. With talent, they can succeed in almost any field that captures their interest— art, journalism, science, advertising, sales, the ministry, or writing, for example.

A difficulty for ENFPs is that they hate uninspired routine and find it remarkably hard to apply themselves to the sometimes necessary detail unconnected with any major interest. Worse yet, they may get bored with their own projects as soon as the main problems have been solved or the initial challenge has been met. They may need to learn to follow through and finish what they have begun, but are happiest and most effective in jobs that permit one project after another, with somebody else taking over as soon as the situation is well in hand.

Because ENFPs are always being drawn to the exciting challenges of new possibilities, it is essential that they develop their feeling judgment. If their judgment is undeveloped, they may commit themselves to ill-chosen projects, fail to finish anything, and squander their inspirations by not completing their tasks.

INTJ
Introverted Intuition with Thinking

People with INTJ preferences are relentless innovators in thought as well as action. They trust their intuitive insights into the true relationships and meanings of things, regardless of established authority or popularly accepted beliefs. Their faith in their inner vision can move mountains. Problems only stimulate them—the impossible takes a little longer, but not much. They are the most independent of all the types, sometimes to the point of being stubborn. They place a high value on competence—their own and others'.

Being sure of the worth of their inspirations, INTJs want to see them worked out in practice, applied and accepted by the rest of the world; they are willing to spend any time and effort to that end. They have determination, perseverance, and will drive others almost as hard as they drive themselves. Although their preference is for intuition, they can, when necessary, focus on the details of a project to realize their vision.

INTJs often value and use confidently their intuitive insights in fields such as science, engineering, invention, politics, or philosophy. The boldness of their intuition may be of immense value in any field, and should not be smothered in a routine job.

Some problems *may* arise from the INTJ's single-minded concentration on goals. They may see the end so clearly that they fail to look for other things which might conflict with the goal. Therefore they need to actively seek the viewpoints of others.

INTJs may neglect their feeling to the point of ignoring other people's values and feelings. If they do, they may be surprised by the bitterness of their opposition. An INTJ's own feeling has to be reckoned with also, for if too much suppressed, it may build up pressure and find expression in inappropriate ways. Their feeling needs to be used constructively, such as through appreciation of other people. Given their talent for analysis, appreciation may be hard for them, but they will find it helpful on the job as well as in personal relationships.

To be effective, INTJs must develop their thinking to supply needed judgment. *If* their judgment is undeveloped, they will be unable to criticize their own inner vision, and will not listen to the opinions of others. They will therefore be unable to shape their inspirations into effective action.

INFJ
Introverted Intuition with Feeling

People with INFJ preferences are great innovators in the field of ideas. They trust their intuitive insights into the true relationships and meanings of things, regardless of established authority or popularly accepted beliefs. Problems only stimulate them—the impossible takes a little longer, but not much.

They are independent and individualistic, being governed by inspirations that come through intuition. These inspirations seem so valid and important that they sometimes have trouble understanding why everyone does not accept them. Their inner independence is often not conspicuous because INFJs value harmony and fellowship; they work to persuade others to approve of and cooperate with their purposes. They can be great leaders when they devote themselves to carrying out a sound inspiration, attracting followers by their enthusiasm and faith. They lead by winning (rather than demanding) acceptance of their ideas.

They are most content in work that satisfies both their intuition and their feeling. The possibilities that interest them most concern people. Teaching particularly appeals to them, whether in higher education, or through the arts or ministry. Their intuition provides insight into the deeper meanings of the subject and they take great satisfaction in aiding the development of individual students.

When their interests lie in technical fields, INFJs may be outstanding in science, or research and development. Intuition suggests new approaches to problems and feeling generates enthusiasm that sparks their energies. Intuition powered by feeling may be of immense value in any field if not smothered in a routine job.

Some problems *may* result from the INFJ's single-minded devotion to inspirations. They may see the goal so clearly that they fail to look for other things that might conflict with the goal. It is also important that their feeling is developed, since this will supply necessary judgment. *If* their judgment is undeveloped, they will be unable to evaluate their own inner vision and will not listen to feedback from others. Instead of shaping their inspirations into effective action, they may merely try to regulate everything (small matters as well as great ones) according to their own ideas, so that little is accomplished.

APPENDIX B

SELECTED QUOTATIONS FROM

JUNG ON HIS TYPOLOGY

Differentiation of Functions

Whatever we persistently exclude from conscious training and adaptation necessarily remains in an untrained, undeveloped, infantile, or archaic condition, ranging from partial to complete unconsciousness. Hence, besides the motives of consciousness and reason, unconscious influences of a primitive character are always normally present in ample measure and disturb the intentions of consciousness. For it is by no means to be assumed that all those forms of activity latent in the psyche, which are suppressed or neglected by the individual, are thereby robbed of their specific energy. For instance, if a man relied wholly on the data of vision, this would not mean that he would cease to hear. (1960, p. 124)

So long as a function is still so fused with one or more of the other functions—thinking with feeling, feeling with sensation, etc.—that it is unable to operate on its own, it is . . . not differentiated, not separated from the whole as a special part and existing by itself. Undifferentiated thinking is incapable of thinking apart from other functions; it is continually mixed up with sensations and fantasies. . . . To the extent that a function is largely or wholly unconscious, it is also undifferentiated; it is not only fused together in its parts but also merged with the functions. . . . Without differentiation direction is impossible, since the direction of a function towards a goal depends on the elimination of anything irrelevant. Fusion with the irrelevant precludes direction; only a differentiated function is *capable* of being directed. (1976a, pp. 424, 425)

Now experience shows that there is only *one* consciously directed function of adaptation. If, for example, I have a thinking orientation I cannot at the same time orient myself by feeling, because thinking and feeling are two quite different functions. In fact, I must carefully exclude feeling if I am to satisfy the logical laws of thinking. . . . I withdraw as much libido as possible from the feeling process, with the result that this function becomes relatively unconscious. Experience shows again, that the orientation is largely habitual; accordingly the other unsuitable functions, so far as they are incompatible with the prevailing attitude, are relatively unconscious, and hence, unused, untrained and undifferentiated. (1960, p. 35)

I do not believe it is humanly possible to differentiate all four functions alike, otherwise we would be perfect like God, and that surely will not happen. There will always be a flaw in the crystal. We can never reach perfection. Moreover, if we could differentiate the four functions equally we should only make them into consciously disposable functions. Then we would lose the most precious connection with the unconscious through the inferior function, which is invariably the weakest; only through our feebleness and incapacity are we linked up with the unconscious, with the lower world of the instincts and with our fellow beings. Our virtues only enable us to be independent. There we do not need anybody, there we are kings; but in our inferiority we are linked up with mankind as well as with the world of our instincts. It would not even be an advantage to have all the functions perfect, because such a condition would amount to complete aloofness. I have no perfection craze. My principle is: for heaven's sake do not be perfect, but by all means try to be complete—whatever that means. (1976b, p. 97)

Experience has shown that it is practically impossible, owing to adverse circumstances in general, for anyone to develop all his psychological functions simultaneously. . . . As a consequence of this one-sided development, one or more functions are necessarily retarded. These functions may properly be called inferior in a psychological but not pathological sense, since they are in no way morbid but merely backward as compared with the favoured function. (1976a, p. 450)

We know that three of the four functions of consciousness can become differentiated, i.e., conscious, while the other remains connected with the matrix, the unconscious, and is known as the "inferior" function. It is the Achilles' heel of even the most heroic consciousness. . . . (1959, p. 237)

It is an empirical fact that only *one* function becomes more or less suc-cessfully differentiated, which on that account is known as the superior or main function, and together with extraversion or introversion constitutes the type of conscious attitude. This function has associated with it one or two partially differentiated auxiliary functions which hardly ever attain the same degree of differentiation as the main function, that is, the same degree of applicability by the will. Accordingly they possess a higher degree of spontaneity than the main function, which displays a large mea-sure of reliability and is amenable to our intentions. (1959, p. 238)

Just as adaptation to the environment may fail because of the one-sidedness of the adapted function, so adaptation to the inner world may fail because of the one-sidedness of the function in question. (1960, p. 36)

Primitive Consciousness

You know all our *raisonnement* is done in a way by the primitive but only in his unconscious, because his functions are not yet developed out of his unconscious, so it manifests, of course, in the form of a revelation. It is as if a voice told them in the night what should be done. (1976c, p. 26)

There are individuals whose thinking and feeling are on the same level, both being of equal motive power for consciousness. But in these cases there is also no question of a differentiated type, but merely of relatively undeveloped thinking and feeling. The uniformly conscious or uniformly unconscious state of the functions is, therefore, the mark of a primitive mentality. (1976a, p. 406)

Characteristics of the Inferior

The inferior function is practically identical with the dark side of human personality. The darkness which clings to every personality is the door into the unconscious and the gateway to dreams, from which those two twi-light figures, the shadow and the anima, step into our nightly visions or, remaining invisible, take possession of our ego-consciousness. A man who is possessed by his own shadow is always standing in his own light and falling into his own traps. (1959, p. 123)

The fourth function is contaminated by the unconscious and, on being made conscious, drags the whole of the unconscious with it. We must then come to terms with the unconscious and try to bring about a synthesis of opposites. (1953, p. 146)

[The inferior function] may be either unconscious or conscious, but in both cases it is autonomous and obsessive and not influenceable by the will. It has all the "all-or-none" character of an instinct. Although emancipation from the instinct brings a differentiation and enhancement of consciousness, it can only come about at the expense of the unconscious function, so that the conscious orientation lacks that element which the inferior function could have supplied. Thus it often happens that people who have an amazing range of consciousness know less about themselves than the veriest infant, and all because the fourth would not come—it remained down below or up above in the unconscious realm. (1969, p. 166)

[The inferior function] is also found in psychology as the opposition between the functions of consciousness, three of which are fairly differentiated, while the fourth, undifferentiated, "inferior" function is undomesticated, unadapted, uncontrolled, and primitive. Because of its contamination with the collective unconscious, it possesses archaic and mystical qualities, and is the complete opposite of the most differentiated function. . . . (1969, p. 121)

As a rule, the inferior function does not possess the qualities of a conscious differentiated function. The conscious differentiated function can as a rule be handled by intention and by the will. If you are a real thinker, you can direct your thinking by your will, you can control your thoughts. . . . But the feeling type can never do that because he cannot get rid of his thought. The thought possesses him, or rather he is possessed by his thought. Thought has a fascination for him, therefore he is afraid of it. The intellectual type is afraid of being caught by feeling because his feeling has an archaic quality, and there he is like an archaic man—he is the helpless victim of his emotions. (1976b, pp. 19, 20)

Positive as well as negative occurrences can constellate the inferior coun-
ter-function. When this happens, sensitiveness appears. Sensitiveness is a
sure sign of the presence of inferiority. This provides the psychological
basis for discord and misunderstanding, not only as between two people,
but also in ourselves. The essence of the inferior function is autonomy: it
is independent, it attacks, it fascinates and so spins us about that we are no
longer masters of ourselves and can no longer rightly distinguish between
ourselves and others. (1966, p. 58)

Value of the Inferior

And it is a fact that it has the strongest tendency to be infantile, banal,
primitive, and archaic. Anybody who has a high opinion of himself will do
well to guard against letting it make a fool of him. On the other hand,
deeper insight will show that the primitive and archaic qualities of the
inferior function conceal all sorts of significant relationships and symbol-
ical meanings. . . . (1969, p. 165)

The "other" in us always seems alien and unacceptable; but if we let ourselves be aggrieved the feeling sinks in, and we are the richer for this little bit of self-knowledge. (1970a, p. 486)

And yet it is necessary for the development of character that we should
allow the other side, the inferior function, to find expression. We cannot
in the long run allow one part of our personality to be cared for symbi-
otically by another; for the moment when we might have need of the
other function may come at any time and find us unprepared. . . . And the
consequences may be bad: the extravert loses his indispensable relation
to the object, and the introvert loses his to the subject. Conversely, it is
equally indispensable for the introvert to arrive at some form of action not
constantly bedevilled by doubts and hesitations, and for the extravert to
reflect upon himself, yet without endangering his relationships. (1966,
p. 58)

We know from experience that the inferior function always compensates,
complements, and balances the "superior" function. . . . The inferior function is the one of which least conscious use is made. This is the reason for

its undifferentiated quality, but also for its freshness and vitality. It is not at the disposal of the conscious mind, and even after long use it never loses its autonomy and spontaneity, or only to a very limited degree. Its role is therefore mostly that of a *deus ex machina*. It depends not on the ego but on the self. Hence it hits consciousness unexpectedly, like lightning, and occasionally with devastating consequences. It thrusts the ego aside and makes room for a supraordinate factor, the totality of a person, which consists of conscious and unconscious and consequently extends far beyond the ego. (1959, p. 303)

The "inferior" function, however, just because of its unconsciousness, has the great advantage of being contaminated with the collective unconscious and can thus restore the vital connection with the latter. (1959, p. 332)

Extraversion and Introversion

Strictly speaking, there are no introverts and extraverts pure and simple, but only introverted and extraverted function-types, such as thinking types, sensation types, etc. There are thus at least eight clearly distinguishable types. (1976a, p. 523)

When we come to analyze the personality, we find that the extravert makes a niche for himself in the world of relationships at the cost of unconsciousness (of himself as subject); while the introvert, in realizing his personality, commits the grossest mistakes in the social sphere and blunders about in the most absurd way. These two very typical attitudes are enough to show—quite apart from the types of physiological temperament described by Kretschmer—how little one can fit human beings and their neuroses into the strait jacket of a single theory. (1954, p. 118)

We can therefore formulate the occurrence as follows: in the introvert the influence of the object produces an inferior extraversion, while in the extravert an inferior introversion takes the place of his social attitude. And we come back to the proposition from which we started: "The value of the one is the negation of value for the other." (1966, p. 58)

Sensation (Sensing)

But the sensation type remains with things. He remains in a given reality. To him a thing is true when it is real. Consider what it means to an intuitive when something is real. It is just the wrong thing; it should not be, something else should be. But when a sensation type does not have a given reality—four walls in which to be—he is sick. (1976b, p. 19)

The specifically compulsive character of the neurotic symptoms is the unconscious counterpart of the easy-going character of the pure sensation type, who, from the standpoint of rational judgment, accepts indiscriminately everything that happens. . . . This coercion overtakes the sensation type from the unconscious, in the form of compulsion. . . . If he should become neurotic, it is much harder to treat him by rational means because the functions which the analyst must turn to are in a relatively undifferentiated state. (1976a, p. 365)

Intuition

The intuitive is always bothered by the reality of things; he fails from the standpoint of realities; he is always out for the possibilities of life. He is the man who plants a field and before the crop is ripe is off again to a new field. . . . Give the intuitive four walls in which to be, and the only thing is how to get out of it, because to him a given situation is a prison which must be undone in the shortest time so that he can be off to new possibilities. (1976b, p. 19)

Thinking

If you know that *thinking* is highly differentiated, then feeling is undifferentiated. What does that mean? Does it mean these people have no feelings? No, on the contrary. They say, "I have very strong feelings. I am full of emotion and temperament." These people are under the sway of their emotions, they are caught by their emotions, they are overcome by their emotions at times. If, for instance, you study the private lives of professors it is a very interesting study. If you want to be fully informed as to how the intellectual behaves at home, ask his wife and she will be able to tell you a story! (1976b, p. 18)

In the pursuit of his ideas [the introverted thinker] is generally stubborn, headstrong and quite unamenable to influence. His suggestibility to personal influences is in strange contrast to this. He has only to be convinced of a person's seeming innocuousness to lay himself open to the most undesirable elements. . . . His style is cluttered with all sorts of adjuncts, accessories, qualifications, retractions, saving clauses, doubts, etc., which all come from his scrupulosity. (1976a, p. 385)

The feeling of the introverted thinking type is extraverted. He has the same kind of strong, loyal and warm feeling described as typical for the extraverted thinking type, but with the difference that the feeling of the introverted thinking type flows toward definite objects. (1976b, pp. 18, 19)

The more the feelings are repressed, the more deleterious is their secret influence on thinking that is otherwise beyond reproach. . . . The self assertion of the personality is transferred to the formula. Truth is no longer allowed to speak for itself; it is identified with the subject and treated like a sensitive darling whom an evil-minded critic has wronged. (1976a, p. 350)

Because of the highly impersonal character of the conscious attitude, the unconscious feelings [of the introverted thinker] are extremely personal and oversensitive, giving rise to secret prejudices—a readiness, for instance, to misconstrue any opposition to his formula as personal ill-will, or a constant tendency to make negative assumptions about other people in order to invalidate their arguments in advance—in defense, naturally, of his own touchiness. His unconscious sensitivity makes him sharp in tone, acrimonious, aggressive. Insinuations multiply. His feelings have a sultry and resentful character—always a mark of the inferior function. (1976a, p. 350)

I have frequently observed how an analyst, confronted with a terrific thinking type, for instance, will do his utmost to develop the feeling function directly out of the unconscious. Such an attempt is foredoomed to failure, because it involves too great a violation of the conscious standpoint. Should the violation nevertheless be successful, a really compulsive dependence of the patient on the analyst ensues, a transference that can only be brutally terminated, because, having been left without a standpoint, the patient has made the standpoint the analyst. . . . In order to cushion the impact of the unconscious, an irrational type needs a stronger development of the rational auxiliary function present in consciousness (and vice versa). (1976a, p. 407)

Feeling

Disappointment [is] the strongest incentive to differentiation of feeling . . . [it] can supply the impulse either for a more or less brutal outburst of affect or for a modification and adjustment of feeling, and hence for its higher development. This culminates in wisdom if feeling is supplemented by reflection and rational insight. Wisdom is never violent: where wisdom reigns there is no conflict between thinking and feeling. (1970b, p. 334)

It is true that feelings, if they have an emotional character, are accompanied by physiological effects; but there are definitely feelings which do not change the physiological condition. These feelings are very mental, they are not of an emotional nature. That is the distinction I make. Inasmuch as feeling is a function of values, you will readily understand that this is not a physiological condition. It can be something as abstract as abstract thinking. You would not expect abstract thinking to be a physiological condition. Abstract thinking is what the term denotes. Differentiated thinking is rational; and so feeling can be rational in spite of the fact that many people mix up the terminology. (1976b, p. 30)

If you have a value which is overwhelmingly strong for you it will become an emotion at a certain point, namely, when it reaches such an intensity as to cause a physiological enervation. (1976b, p. 26)

The reverse is true of the feeling type. The feeling type, if he is natural, never allows himself to be disturbed by thinking; but when he gets sophisticated and somewhat neurotic he is disturbed by thoughts. Then thinking appears in a compulsory way, he cannot get away from certain thoughts.

He is a very nice chap, but he has extraordinary convictions and ideas, and his thinking is of the inferior kind. He is caught by this thinking, entangled in certain thoughts. . . . On the other hand, an intellectual, when caught by his feelings, says, "I feel just like that," and there is no argument against it. Only when he is thoroughly boiled in his emotion will he come out of it. He cannot be reasoned out of his feeling, and he would be a very incomplete man if he could. (1976b, pp. 18, 19)

She begins consciously to feel "what other people think." Naturally, other people are thinking all sorts of mean things, scheming evil, contriving plots. . . . (1976a, p. 391)

The Shadow

The individuation process is invariably started off by the patient's becoming conscious of the shadow, a personality component usually with a negative sign. This "inferior" personality is made up of everything that will not fit in with, and adapt to, the laws and regulations of conscious life. It is compounded of "disobedience" and is therefore rejected not on moral grounds only, but also for reasons of expediency. Closer investigation shows that there is at least one function in it which ought to collaborate in orienting consciousness. Or rather, this function does collaborate, not for the benefit of conscious, purposive intentions, but in the interests of unconscious tendencies pursuing a different goal. It is this fourth, "inferior" function which acts autonomously towards consciousness and cannot be harnessed to the latter's intentions. It lurks behind every neurotic dissociation and can only be annexed to consciousness if the corresponding unconscious contents are made conscious at the same time. . . (1969, pp. 197, 198)

But the shadow is merely somewhat inferior, primitive, unadapted, and awkward; not wholly bad. It even contains childish or primitive qualities which would in a way vitalize and embellish human existence, but—convention forbids! (1969, p. 78)

The personal unconscious is the shadow and the inferior function. (1970b, p. 199)

General Comments on Typology

So, too, there are four aspects of psychological orientation, beyond which nothing fundamental remains to be said. In order to orient ourselves, we must have a function which ascertains that something is there (sensation); a second function which establishes *what* it is (thinking); a third function which states whether it suits us or not (feeling); and a fourth function which indicates where it came from and where it is going (intuition). When this has been done there is nothing more to say. Schopenhauer proves that the "Principle of Sufficient Reason" has a fourfold root. This is so because the fourfold aspect is the minimum requirement for a complete judgment. . . . (1969, p. 167)

One always has to answer people in their main function, otherwise no contact is established. (1976b, p. 140)

A typology is therefore designed, first and foremost, as an aid to a psychological critique of knowledge . . . the valuable thing here is the critical attempt to prevent oneself from taking one's own prejudices as the criterion of normality. Unfortunately, this happens only too easily; for instance, extraversion is "normal," but introversion is pathological auto-eroticism. (1970a, p. 471)

The reader should understand that these four criteria are just so many viewpoints among others, such as will-power, temperament, imagination, memory, morality, religiousness, etc. There is nothing dogmatic about them, nor do they claim to be the ultimate truth about psychology; but their basic nature recommends them as suitable principles of classification. Classification has little value if it does not provide a means of orientation and a practical terminology. I find classification into types particularly helpful when I am called upon to explain parents to children or husbands to wives, and vice versa. It is also useful in understanding one's own prejudices. (1976b, p. 219)

Other Comments

As a rule, the unconscious compensation does not run counter to consciousness, but is rather a balancing or supplementing of the conscious orientation. (1976a, p. 419)

A psychological theory, if it is to be more than a technical makeshift, must base itself on the theory of opposition; for without this it could only reestablish a neurotically unbalanced psyche. There is no balance, no system of self-regulation, without opposition. The psyche is just such a self-regulating system. (1966, p. 61)

I told you that unconscious things are very *relative*. When I am unconscious of a certain thing I am only relatively unconscious of it; in some respects I may know it. The contents of the personal unconscious are perfectly conscious in certain respects, but you do not know them under a *particular aspect or at a particular time.* (1976b, p. 57)

Neurotic phenomena are nothing but exaggerations of normal processes. (1959, p. 139).

To have overwhelming emotions is not in itself pathological, it is merely undesirable. We need not invent such a word as pathological for an undesirable thing, because there are other undesirable things in the world which are not pathological, for instance, tax collectors. (1976b, p. 24)

Notes

Chapter 1

1. Words in the text that appear in boldface type are defined in the glossary at the back of this book.

2. For additional introductory material about psychological type theory, readers are referred to Myers, 1995, 1998; Hirsh & Kummerow, 1989; Myers et al., 1998; and other general introductory works.

3. Other personality theories must also explain out-of-character behavior. The most prevalent alternative theories, those based on personality traits, typically must add new traits or combinations of traits to account for these behaviors. One advantage of Jung's system lies in its parsimony; that is, it requires relatively few elements to explain a broad range of phenomena. For a detailed comparison of trait and type theories, see N. L. Quenk, 1993, 2000a.

4. This table is an adaptation of an exercise developed by Nancy Barger for MBTI training workshops.

5. This contrasts with Freud's causal, reductive approach, which reduces behavior to its initial causes, most notably childhood traumatic events associated with sexual and aggressive instincts. The psychological repression (removal from consciousness) of such events causes neurotic symptoms. Freud saw only moderate opportunity for personality changes during adulthood.

6. See for example, Allen & Brock, 2000; Barger & Kirby, 1995; Hirsh & Kise, 1996; Kummerow, Barger, & Kirby, 1997; and N. L. Quenk, 2000a.

Chapter 2

7. The distinctive features of consciousness are permanence, regularity, and duration. The conscious sphere operates on probabilities, and a conscious approach is flexible and can respond to contingencies; the unconscious has an all-or-none character. As a result, the variables of permanence, the regularity of predicting such things as cause and effect, and a sense of the extension of time into the past, present,

and future are absent. The unconscious thus approaches life rigidly and responds in a fixed and automatic manner regardless of changing circumstances (A. Quenk, personal communication, 1992).

8. Readers unfamiliar with Myers' descriptions of the sixteen types will find an early version of them in Appendix A. See also Myers et al., 1998.

Chapter 3

9. Jung, though he did not deal explicitly with the attitude of either the auxiliary or the tertiary function, would probably have agreed with Myers. He sometimes described the "auxiliary functions" or the "inferior functions" as having an opposite attitudinal "cast." Harold Grant (1983) proposed a more "balanced" approach, with the tertiary function taking the attitude opposite that of the auxiliary function—that is, the same attitude as the dominant function. A third hypothesis I have proposed is that, given the somewhat borderline status of the tertiary function, it may take either attitude, depending on circumstances or other idiosyncratic factors. During the last year of her life, Isabel Myers reconsidered her earlier approach, suggesting that perhaps the tertiary function, because it was not under a great deal of pressure, could take either attitude at different times (Katharine Myers, personal communication, 1992). Recent research by Mitchell (1992a) provides empirical support for this hypothesis.

Glossary

Adaptation In Jungian psychology, "relating to, coming to terms with, and balancing internal and external factors. . . . A vital aspect of individuation" (Samuels, Shorter, & Plaut, 1986).

Archetypes Common human experiences and patterns of response to experiences such as birth, death, mother, father, hero, child, marriage, and so on. These themes link us to each other and to our ancestors, providing the vital connection to our past, present, and future as individuals and as a species.

Collective unconscious The nonpersonal, objective layer of the unconscious that is the repository of the **archetypes**. Its sphere is larger than that of the **personal unconscious.**

Compensation In Jungian psychology, the self-regulatory mechanism whereby the psyche regains the balance it has lost as a result of one-sidedness. It involves the "equal and opposite" discharge of unconscious psychic energy, which compensates a one-sided conscious approach.

Complex In Jungian psychology, "a collection of images and ideas, clustered round a core derived from one or more archetypes, and characterized by a common emotional tone. When they come into play [become "constellated"], complexes contribute to behaviour and are marked by affect whether a person is conscious of them or not" (Samuels et al., 1986).

Consciousness In Jungian psychology, the opposite of unconsciousness. Consciousness is characterized by a person's ability to control and direct psychological contents and to maintain full awareness of them and their effects.

Constellation The clustering or grouping together of elements so that they emerge as an activated, unified whole. In Jung's theory, constellated mental contents usually cohere around a central core, often an archetypal image. Psychic elements such as complexes and the inferior function are constellated, or come into play, when certain conditions are present.

Differentiated function Sensing, Intuition, Thinking, or Feeling that is separate and exists by itself—that is, it is not intermingled with one or more of the other functions and therefore can operate independently.

Differentiation For Jung, "the development of differences, the separation of parts from the whole" (1976a, p. 424). According to Jung, psychological type functions must be differentiated into opposites in order for them to be used effectively by people. Without such differentiation, separate, distinct, opposite mental processes are absent.

Individuation In Jungian psychology, a process whereby a person becomes a complete individual, unique and distinct from other individuals and any group (collective). The process is lifelong and involves the gradual integration of unconscious elements (such as psychological type functions) into consciousness. Somewhat similar to the concept of self-actualization described by A. H. Maslow (1954).

Inferior function The function opposite to the dominant function, also called the *fourth function* or *least-preferred function.* The inferior function is assumed to be the most unconscious, least differentiated, and least capable of conscious development. It can be a source of both difficulties and positive personality development.

Midlife A highly individual and therefore indeterminate period of time extending from mature adulthood through the beginning of old age. For Jung, it is characterized by a shift of psychological focus from issues of personal and career identity to concerns with psychological completion through integration of previously neglected aspects of one's personality.

Personal unconscious In Jungian psychology, the repository of an individual's repressed mental contents and personal information that has not yet become salient. These contents are largely subsumed within the **shadow,** the route to which is through the **inferior function.** The personal layer of the unconscious is in contrast to the objective, nonpersonal **collective unconscious**.

Projection In Jungian psychology, a mechanism whereby a person's unconscious, unacknowledged psychological features are attributed to another person or other relevant object outside him- or herself. Typically, the person or object being projected upon has at least some of the quality being projected. For Jung, unconscious material, such as is associated with the inferior function, appears in projected form.

Prospective approach Jung's focus on the purposes of behavior and symptoms, in contrast to Freud's causal, **reductive approach.** For Jung, the goal or end point of human development is individuation or psychological completeness.

Psyche "The totality of all psychic processes, conscious as well as unconscious" (Jung, 1976a, p. 463). Included in Jung's encompassing term are all structures of **consciousness,** including the **differentiated** psychological type functions, as well as all structures of the personal unconscious (including the inferior function) and the collective unconscious.

Reductive approach Jung's characterization of Freud's causal explanation of psychological symptoms, which reduces behavioral and psychological manifestations to their initial causes, often childhood traumas associated with sexual and aggressive instincts.

Self-regulating psyche The ability of the psyche to regain its balance or equilibrium through the process of **compensation.** The psyche is thus designed both
to correct itself when it is "out of balance" and to progress toward completion
or **individuation.**

Shadow In Jungian psychology, the negative, unacceptable part of the psyche, characteristically a major portion of the **personal unconscious.** It is the repository of all those things a person does not wish to acknowledge about him- or
herself. It often provides the content expressed when the inferior function has
been constellated.

Trait A human characteristic assumed to be distributed normally; that is, the majority (68 percent) of people have an "average" amount of the trait, with fewer
people characterized by the extremes. Examples of traits are height, weight,
intelligence, dominance, sociability, and assertiveness. Traits are universal, and
people vary only in the amount of the trait they possess. Most personality theories are based on a trait approach.

Type (personality type) One of sixteen descriptive categories identified by the
MBTI personality inventory composed of enduring preferences for one of each
of four pairs of opposite mental processes (Extraversion versus Introversion,
Sensing versus Intuition, Thinking versus Feeling, and Judging versus Perceiving). The particular combination of the four preferences, along with their
dynamic interplay, yields a unique category, which cannot be fully defined or
adequately described by merely adding up its four component parts.

Type development (See Differentiation and Differentiated function.)

Unconscious In Jungian psychology, the opposite of conscious. The term identifies contents or material that is outside the person's awareness and has the character of an instinct in that its manifestations are automatic and not under a person's control. Jung includes two spheres in his concept of the unconscious, the
personal unconscious and the **collective unconscious.**

References

Allen, J., & Brock, S. A. (2000). *Health care communication using personality type: Patients are different!* Philadelphia, PA: Taylor and Francis.

Barger, N. J., & Kirby, K. (1995). *The challenge of change in organizations. Helping employees thrive in the new frontier.* Mountain View, CA: Davies-Black.

Druckman, D., & Bjork, R. A. (Eds.). (1991). *In the mind's eye: Enhancing human performance.* Washington, DC: National Academy Press.

Freud, S. (1933). *The interpretation of dreams.* New York: Basic Books.

Garden, A.-M. (1985). Burnout: The effect of Jungian type. *Journal of Psychological Type, 10,* 3–10.

Garden, A.-M. (1988). Jungian type, occupation and burnout: An elaboration of an earlier study. *Journal of Psychological Type, 14,* 2–14.

Grant, H. (1983). *From image to likeness.* New York: Paulist Press.

Hirsh, S. K., & Kise, J. A. G. (1996). *Work it out: Clues for solving people problems at work.* Mountain View, CA: Davies-Black.

Hirsh, S. K., & Kummerow, J. (1989). *Lifetypes.* New York: Warner Books.

Hugo, V. (1988). *Wisdom of the ages.* DOS 2.0 or greater. MCR Agency Inc.

Jung, C. G. (1953). Psychology and alchemy. In R. F. C. Hull (Trans.), *Collected works* (Vol. 12). Princeton, NJ: Princeton University Press.

Jung, C. G. (1954). The practice of psychotherapy. In R. F. C. Hull (Trans.), *Collected works* (Vol. 16). Princeton, NJ: Princeton University Press.

Jung, C. G. (1959). The archetypes and the collective unconscious. In R. F. C. Hull (Trans.), *Collected works* (Vol. 9i). Princeton, NJ: Princeton University Press.

Jung, C. G. (1960). The structure and dynamics of the psyche. In R. F. C. Hull (Trans.), *Collected works* (Vol. 8). Princeton, NJ: Princeton University Press.

Jung, C. G. (1966). Two essays on analytical psychology. In R. F. C. Hull (Trans.), *Collected works* (Vol. 7). Princeton, NJ: Princeton University Press.

Jung, C. G. (1969). Psychology and religion: West and east. In R. F. C. Hull (Trans.), *Collected works* (Vol. 11). Princeton, NJ: Princeton University Press.

Jung, C. G. (1970a). Civilization in transition. In R. F. C. Hull (Trans.), *Collected works* (Vol. 10). Princeton, NJ: Princeton University Press.

Jung, C. G. (1970b). Mysterium coniunctionis. In R. F. C. Hull (Trans.), *Collected works* (Vol. 14). Princeton, NJ: Princeton University Press.

Jung, C. G. (1976a). Psychological types. In R. F. C. Hull (Trans.), *Collected works* (Vol. 6). Princeton, NJ: Princeton University Press.

Jung, C. G. (1976b). The symbolic life. In R. F. C. Hull (Trans.), *Collected works* (Vol. 18). Princeton, NJ: Princeton University Press.

Jung, C. G. (1976c). *The visions seminars*. New York: Spring Publications.

Kummerow, J. M., Barger, N. J., & Kirby, L. K. (1997). *Worktypes*. New York: Warner Books.

Kummerow, J. M., & Quenk, N. L. (1992). *Interpretive guide for the MBTI expanded analysis report*. Mountain View, CA: CPP, Inc.

Maslach, C., Jackson, S. E., & Leiter, M. P. (1996). *Maslach Burnout Inventory manual* (3rd ed.). Mountain View, CA: CPP, Inc.

Maslow, A. H. (1954). *Motivation and personality*. New York: Harper.

McCrea, R. R., & Costa, P. T. (1989). Reinterpreting the Myers-Briggs Type Indicator from the perspective of the Five-Factor Model of Personality. *Journal of Personality, 57*, 17–40.

Mitchell, W. D. (1992a). Unpublished research.

Mitchell, W. D. (1992b). Reconsidering a classic typology and its measurement. Unpublished manuscript.

Myers, I. B. (1987). *Introduction to type®* (4th ed.). Mountain View, CA: CPP, Inc.

Myers, I. B. (1995). *Gifts differing: Understanding personality type*. Mountain View, CA: Davies-Black. (Original work published 1980)

Myers, I. B., McCaulley, M. H., Quenk, N. L., & Hammer, A. L. (1998). *MBTI manual: A guide to the development and use of the Myers-Briggs Type Indicator* (3rd ed.). Mountain View, CA: CPP, Inc.

Quenk, A. T. (1985). *Psychological types and psychotherapy*. Gainesville, FL: Center for Applications of Psychological Type.

Quenk, A. T., & Quenk, N. L. (1982). The use of psychological typology in analysis. In M. Stein (Ed.), *Jungian analysis*. LaSalle, IL: Open Court.

Quenk, N. L. (1982). The inferior function and the shadow in Jungian psychology. *MBTI News, 4*.

Quenk, N. L. (1984). The dynamics of type development. *MBTI News, 7*, 1–2.

Quenk, N. L. (1985a). Conflicts in function development. *MBTI News, 7*, 1–2.

Quenk, N. L. (1985b). Directionality of the auxiliary function. *MBTI News, 8*, 27–29.

Quenk, N. L. (1989). Jung's theory of psychological types and the self-contained patient. In E. M. Stern (Ed.), *Psychotherapy and the self-contained patient*. New York: Haworth Press.

Quenk, N. L. (1993a). *Beside ourselves: Our hidden personality in everyday life*. Mountain View, CA: Davies-Black.

Quenk, N. L. (1993b). Personality types or personality traits: What difference does it make? *Bulletin of Psychological Type, 16*.

Quenk, N. L. (2000a). *Essentials of the Myers-Briggs Type Indicator assessment*. New York: Wiley.

Quenk, N. L. (2000b). *In the grip: Understanding type, stress, and the inferior function* (2nd ed.). Mountain View, CA: CPP, Inc.

Samuels, A., Shorter, B., & Plaut, F. (1986). *A critical dictionary of Jungian analysis*. London: Routledge & Kegan Paul.

Spoto, A. (1989). *Jung's typology in perspective*. Boston: Sigo Press.

Thorne, A., & Gough, H. (1991). *Portraits of type: An MBTI research compendium*. Mountain View, CA: CPP, Inc.

Von Franz, M. L. (1971). The inferior function. In M. L. Von Franz & J. Hillman, *Jung's typology*. New York: Spring Publications,

Wheelwright, J. B., Wheelwright, J. H., and Buehler, H. A. (1964). *Jungian type survey: The Gray-Wheelwright Test* (16th rev.). San Francisco: Society of Jungian Analysts of Northern California.

Index

adaptation, 5–6, 13, 26
archetypes, 10
auxiliary function: description of, 30–31;
     differentiation of, 51; of ENFJ, 156,
     166; of ENTJ, 81; of ENTP, 258; of
     ESTJ, 81; of INFP, 99; of INTJ, 208;
     Intuition, 123, 156; of ISFP, 116; of
     ISTP, 141; role of, 57, 295

behavior: changes in, 1–2; completion-
     directed goal of, 9
Briggs, Katharine, 2

collective unconscious, 10
compensation: description of, 6–8;
     inferior function's role, 52–53
consciousness: description of, 10; differ-
     entiation of functions, 51; lowering
     of, 46; modern, 24–25; primitive, 321
couple relationships: description of, 264;
     Extraverted Feeling inferior and
     Extraverted Feeling inferior,
     267–268; Extraverted Sensing
     inferior and Extraverted Feeling
     inferior, 264–265; inferior function
     knowledge used in, 272–273;
     Introverted Sensing inferior and
     Extraverted Intuition inferior,
     270–272; Introverted Thinking
     inferior and Extraverted Intuition
     inferior, 266–267; Introverted
     Thinking inferior and Introverted
     Feeling inferior, 268–270
cultural expectations, 293

differentiation: within a function or
     attitude, 21; definition of, 20; of
     opposites in a pair, 20–21, 24
dominant function: definition of, 29–30,
     35; Extraverted Feeling, 123, 129,
     146; Extraverted Intuition, 38, 215,
     221, 238; Extraverted Sensing, 170,
     192, 198; Extraverted Thinking,
     74, 99, 105; features of, 63–64;
     Introverted Feeling, 81, 98;
     Introverted Intuition, 38, 171,
     176, 178, 190; Introverted Sensing,
     214, 239, 245; Introverted Thinking,
     122, 131, 147, 152; judging versus
     perceiving function as, 36–37; in
     less-preferred attitude, 39–41;
     one-sided use of, 47; at work, 64
dreams, 10, 13

ENFJ: auxiliary function of, 156, 166;
     characteristics of, 39, 146, 305–306;
     convoluted logic in, 154–155; criti-
     cism, excessiveness in, 153–154;
     description of, 305–306; dynamics
     of, 145; ENTJ and, 268–270; equi-
     librium return, 163–164; grip
     experiences of, 156–163, 165–166;
     hobbies of, 149; inferior function
     eruptions and forms of, 149–156,
     167; interests of, 149; midlife
     expressions, 164–165; projections
     of inferior function by, 148–149;
     provocations for, 150; sensitivities
     of, 148–149; stressors for, 150–151;